A Century Remembered

Reminiscences of everyday life in the Eastwood area

edited by Michael Bennett

Eastwood Historical Society
2000

First published in 2000 by the Eastwood Historical
Society, 18 Park Crescent, Eastwood, Nottingham,
NG16 3DU.

© Eastwood Historical Society
All Rights Reserved. No part of this publication may
be reproduced, stored in a retrieval system, or
transmitted in any form or by any means, electronic,
mechanical, photocopying, recording or otherwise,
without the prior permission of the publishers.

Originated by History into Print, The Local History
Press Ltd, 3 Devonshire Promenade, Lenton,
Nottingham. NG7 2DS.
Printed by The Russell Press, Nottingham.
Design and layout by Two Faces Design,
80 Watling Street, Towcester, Northants NN12 6BS

ISBN 0 9517209 2 9

Previous publications :
Around Old Eastwood (1991)
Eastwood : More Recollections (1993)

Opinions expressed in this book are those of the
contributors and do not necessarily reflect those of the
Eastwood Historical Society. Every effort has been
made to verify facts and to obtain permission to use
copyright material, but apologies are offered to anyone
whose rights have been inadvertently infringed.

The Society welcomes comments concerning this
publication, offers of further reminiscences and the
loan of photographs for copying. Correspondence
should be addressed to:

Eastwood Historical Society (Reminiscences)
c/o Eastwood Library
Wellington Place
Nottingham Road
Eastwood
NOTTINGHAM
NG16 3GB

Contents

		Page Number
Acknowledgements		4
Introduction		5
1.	Home Sweet Home	7
2.	The Happiest Days Of Your Life?	23
3.	Our Working Lives	43
4.	Six Days Shalt Thou Labour	57
5.	Hard Times	69
6.	For King, Queen and Country	81
7.	Wartime Life On The Home Front	93
8.	Shops and Businesses	119
9.	Getting Around	145
10.	Leisure Time	157
11.	High Days and Holidays	209
12.	A Miscellany Of Memories	225

Acknowledgements

The Eastwood Historical Society wishes to thank the following for help in compiling this book:

Ivy Attenborough, Constance Barrett, Mary Bend, Keith Brindley, Jean Brinsley, Mick Brown, Stella Burrows, Don Chambers, Margaret Chambers, Karen Clarke, Rt. Hon. Kenneth Clarke QC, MP, Christine Cook, Evelyn Draper, Jean Duckworth, Paddy Farrell, Enid Goodband, Sybil Griffin, Bill Gregory, George Hardy, Eileen Harvey, Roger Harvey, Fay Hickinbotham, Derek Hickinbotham, Eddie Hicking, Hilda Hill, Maurice Holmes, Susan Jackson, Leila Keam, Rose Keech, Jean Kirkham, Vera Kirkham, Doreen Lockett, Pat Lord, Kenneth Lord, David Machin, Ken Marsland, Vera Musgrove, Melba Nicholson, James Noon, Graham Parker, Mick Parkes, Bernard Pass, Pat Potter, Noel Pratt, David Price, Doris Reeve, Carl Richards, Betty Richardson, David Richmond, Fred Skillington, Florence Smith, Winifred Stoakes, James Whitehead, Mavis Williamson and John Wright for contributing their reminiscences.

The families of the late Percy Cross, Alice Geeson, Edward Painter, Kenneth Poynter, Patricia Purdy, Lily Rose, John Gregory Simpson, Lily Whittamore and Nellie Wilson for allowing their reminiscences to be published.

The above contributors and Peggy Bestwick, Maureen Budden, Pauline Burrows, Enid Doona, John Henshaw, Harry Higton, Iris Hobson, Elizabeth Hose, Ian Johnson, Margaret Moseley, Margaret Neville, Leslie Parkes, Don Rowley, Maurice Smith, Rolfe Stenson and Peggy Webb for the loan of photographs and documents. Unfortunately there is insufficient space to print all the photographs which have been loaned but it is hoped to include them in a future publication.

Joan Bray, Peter Jordan, Dave Sawyer, Maree Smith, the staff of Eastwood Library, *The Eastwood & Kimberley Advertiser*, Susan Griffiths and Barbara Hornby of the Local History Press, Brian Smith of B & A Photographics, and the committee members of the Society for assistance in the preparation of the book.

The reminiscences of Alice Geeson and of Kenneth Poynter were originally published in the *Worksop Guardian* and the *Journal of the D.H.Lawrence Society* respectively and are reproduced with permission.

 The Society gratefully acknowledges the grants from the Millennium Festival Awards For All programme and from the Eastwood Phoenix Project Community Chest which have helped towards the costs of publication

Introduction

When I retired from the library service in 1998 the Eastwood Historical Society asked if I would consider the compilation of a third book of photographs. I agreed but suggested that, with the approach of the year 2000, it would be appropriate to mark the turning of a century and millennium with a more ambitious publication, and so the idea for this book was born.

A Century Remembered is not a chronological history of events. The area is fortunate in having a local weekly newspaper *The Eastwood & Kimberley Advertiser* which has been recording those events since before the end of the 19th century and is continuing to do so into the 21st, and a complete file on microfilm is available at Eastwood Library. *A Century Remembered* does of course include major events, but the aim is to present them in the context of the everyday lives of ordinary people. All those countless small details of life which individually may seem very mundane, collectively make up a fascinating picture of a community which has seen many social and economic changes since 1900.

No doubt there will be criticism that there is nothing about this, that or the other subject. The simple response is that no-one chose to write about it! I began the project by approaching some thirty people who I felt would respond enthusiastically, as indeed they did, and many of them got others involved. I am grateful to them all. Every potential contributor was given a long 'catch-all' list of possible subjects for reminiscence. With a few exceptions, I deliberately did not suggest subjects to individuals as I wanted people to have the freedom to choose the memories which were important to them.

For the purposes of this book the boundaries of the Eastwood area are defined as Eastwood, Brinsley, Underwood, Moorgreen, Watnall, Newthorpe and Giltbrook. For convenience the contents are divided into twelve broad subject groups, but many of the reminiscences and photographs could equally appropriately have been included in another chapter.

There is no commentary, but dates of birth are shown in order to put the memories in context.

I first saw Eastwood on a cold and foggy November day in 1967. The cold outside was quickly dispelled by the warmth of the welcome of the people of Eastwood and the surrounding area, and for me one of the things which comes out of these reminiscences is a sense of that warmth of a caring community both in good times and bad.

I hope that the book causes some discussion and friendly argument, but I would be especially pleased if it prompts more memories to be recorded and photographs preserved for future generations. May you enjoy reading *A Century Remembered* as much as I have enjoyed compiling it.

Michael Bennett

A Note About Money

The UK's currency was decimalised in February 1971. As most of the reminiscences in this book relate to events prior to 1971, all prices are expressed in 'old' money. To avoid the constant repetition in the text of decimal equivalents, for the benefit of younger readers and as a reminder to older readers the following guide to pre-decimal currency may be useful.

There were 20 shillings (s) to the pound (£) and 12 pence (d) to the shilling, written e.g. £2 12s. 6d. (2 pounds, 12 shillings and 6 pence). An amount of less than one pound was written e.g. 10/6 (10 shillings and 6 pence).

Decimal equivalents
2.4 'old' pennies (d) = 1 'new' penny (p)
1 shilling = 5p   2 shillings = 10p
5 shillings = 25p   10 shillings = 50p

Frequent reference is made to the old half-crown coin, worth two shillings and sixpence (the equivalent of 12.5p), the sixpence (2.5p), the ha'penny (half an 'old' penny) and farthing (a quarter of a penny).

Chapter One

*'I remember,
I remember the house
where I was born ...'*

Home Sweet Home

We lived behind our shop at the corner of Dovecote Road and Nottingham Road at Hill Top. The shop premises took up most of the space, leaving us with no parlour or front room, just a 15 foot square living room and a scullery scarcely big enough to hold our wash tub, mangle and copper. There was a cellar filled with coal which was shot through the pavement grating. The cellar steps had to be our pantry; most of our food was unprotected and always covered with coal dust. There was no sink or tap in the house, and we had to fetch the water from the one standpipe in the yard.

The corner of Nottingham Road and Dovecote Road in the 1930s. Percy (Jack) Cross whose reminiscences appear throughout the book was born at the shop in 1906, although by the time of this photograph it was run by David Smart. Note the fields and allotments on the right where Charles Avenue is now. The tall building on Dovecote Road is the Christians Meeting House/Church of Christ.

However, we all grew up in those conditions accepting them as normal. In fact we considered ourselves rather better off than many folk, for didn't we have gaslight and not the dim paraffin lamp and candlelight which many Hill Top residents put up with? Upstairs were three small bedrooms, with whitewashed walls and bare floorboards much stained with spillings from the pots kept for night use. The beds abounded with bugs and fleas, which again we accepted as normal. Mother's bedroom however was 'special,' graced with wallpaper and a strip of lino, for it had to be our sick-bay when illness struck. The pangs of childbirth were suffered there, and as a death chamber the last rites were murmured in it.

Outside we shared a dirt yard with four neighbouring families, and there were frequent rows over washing-line 'rights.' On the far side stood a row of five closets and a communal ash-tip. That yard served as the playground and miniature football pitch for about 15 yelling kids.

*Percy (Jack) Cross
born 1906*

I was born, the daughter of a miner, in a terraced house on Frances Street, Brinsley only ten minutes walk away from the modern bungalow where I now live. It was a street of terraced and some detached working-class houses built at the turn of the century on an unadopted road. They had two or three bedrooms with a parlour, living room and in some cases a scullery which housed the sink with its solitary cold water tap and the copper. The house was heated by a single coal fire in the living room. Coal was always plentiful as it formed part of the miner's wage. The fire also heated water from the boiler which was situated by the fireplace.

Vera Musgrove
born 1918

The sitting room of my Grandma's home was a picture of Victorian opulence. The heavy mahogany dining chairs were ranged round the big square table which was draped with a maroon chenille cloth edged with heavy fringing, in which I often secretly threaded my fingers. There were plush easy chairs echoing the colour scheme of maroon and blue in the carpet square. The mantelpiece was dominated by a pair of china spaniels, black and white, with lustrous appealing eyes. These were much admired, but I was only allowed to look, not touch!

Hung above the fireplace was a huge gilt-framed family group with Grandma, Grandad, Uncle John and my pretty teenage Mum all dressed in their best. Grandad was seated, proudly wearing his gold watch chain from which was suspended a piece of shiny black coal in its gold setting that I loved to stroke. Grandma was standing close to him, stately in shiny black satin. Uncle John, just a boy then, wore his best black suit but my Mum outshone them all in a high-necked blouse with frills and tucks which she had made herself. At that time she was an apprentice dressmaker who eventually became highly skilled and made all my dresses.

Doris Reeve (née Whittamore)
born 1921

A Century Remembered

I was born in a neat little terraced house, 145 Nottingham Road, in one of the two rows of miners' cottages also known as Walkers Row, after the colliery owners. In a good position on the main road, with a nice front garden as well as a vegetable garden at the back, they were quite sought after by the miners at Moorgreen Colliery. My father John (always known as Jack) went back to work at the pit after service in the First World War, three years of which were spent as a prisoner of war in Germany, and as a result of which his health suffered badly.

The house was lit by gas, and the cooking was done on a blackleaded range in the living kitchen and on a gas ring. Gas lighting meant a stock of mantles had to be kept for their continual replacement. There was no bathroom of course, and water for bathing in the tin bath was heated in the boiler at one side of the range. There was also a copper for boiling clothes in the wash house next to the back door. Life must have been hard for my mother, especially with Dad coming home dirty from the pit, but we seemed to have a good standard of living and were well dressed.

Leila Gregory with her aunt Kitty and, in the doorway, mother Becky at 145 Nottingham Road (Walkers Row) in 1931.

Leila Keam (née Gregory Simpson)
born 1930

We lived at 23 Nottingham Road behind and above my father's shop (Brittain's). Upstairs there were six bedrooms on two storeys and a big lounge; the dining room, kitchen and scullery were downstairs behind the shop. I remember that we had a maid, as did many of the shopkeepers. Because of the shop we had gas lighting, which was unusual then. They were upright mantles at first, but later we had the incandescent clusters which gave out a wonderful light in comparison with the old ones. Most small houses were lit by candles or paraffin lamps. At spring-cleaning time we used to take up all the carpets and put them over a long line in the garden. Then we hit each side with a flat beater to make the dust 'pother' out.

Winifred Stoakes (née Brittain)
born 1909

I was born at the Eastwood Hall Lodge where my father was the tenant, and I lived there for 30 years. When my father left school he was apprentice gardener and later head gardener at Newthorpe Grange; in the 1950s and '60s he was head gardener at Eastwood Hall. As well as maintaining the grounds he had a walled garden with a greenhouse growing flowers and vegetables. These were sold on Fridays to employees at the Hall (at that time the No.5 Area HQ of the National Coal Board) – a very busy day!

David Richmond
born 1938

I was born into a typical miner's household in Princes Street. My father worked at the colliery as a 'butty' (contractor). I remember him coming home one day and, after paying out his men's wages, saying to my mother, 'Well Nan, that's my best week's money for you yet — six pounds.' In those days £6 was a fair sum of money and would have seen the family well. At least I never remember us going hungry. We were not rich or well-to-do but we were a proud family and careful with what we had.

The house we lived in had a small square back yard with the toilet, or closet as we always called it, just opposite the back door, and the ash-pit beyond. Our house contained the usual four main rooms. Downstairs there was the kitchen/living room area and the front parlour, whilst upstairs were the two bedrooms. Beneath the stairs was a pantry, and the stairs themselves led off directly from the front

A Century Remembered

Communal washing lines in the 'squares' behind Princes Street (on the left), where Kenneth Poynter was born in 1904. Bounded by Victoria, Scargill, Albert, Wellington and Princes Streets, the 213 houses — known as The Buildings — were built between 1854 and 1860 by the colliery company for its employees.

parlour. The kitchen had a blackleaded fireplace consisting of a central fire-grate with an oven on one side and a boiler on the other. Here the family meals were prepared, and great pride was taken by each household in maintaining this unit, so much so that one household was ever in competition with its neighbour to see who could produce and keep the best shine.

In front of the fireplace stood the fender, a low rectangular unit which marked the boundary of the hearth. In the latter stood the fire-tongs and the poker and also the rake for clearing out the dead ashes. Beyond the fender was a large pegged rug about two yards long by one yard wide, this being the only floor covering. The remainder of the floor consisted of red or blue quarry tiles on which stood the kitchen table and dining chairs. Above the fireplace was the mantelpiece on which were displayed various ornaments and the family clock.

The wall adjacent to that containing the fireplace had in it the kitchen window, and this in turn faced out onto the back yard. Beneath the kitchen window, on the left inside, was the sink with only a cold water supply in those days. Against the wall opposite the fireplace stood the dresser, a kind of sideboard which held, amongst other things, the family linen in order to keep it aired. It was in this room that most of our daily life was spent.

The front parlour on the other hand was of a different order of things. This room was more 'sacred,' being reserved for use on Sundays or when guests arrived. The floor was covered with linoleum and on it stood two leather armchairs and a couch. On one side was a small open iron fire-grate, and opposite was a chiffonier on which were displayed the family ornaments and of course the inevitable aspidistra!

*Kenneth Poynter
born 1904*

Our terraced house was a typical miner's dwelling, with the downstairs rooms called the scullery, kitchen, pantry and parlour, and an outside lavatory. The cold floors were openly displayed with red quarry brick tiles or covered with lino and pegged rugs (you could always see last year's discarded jumper staring up in its new role!) The coal fire blazed smokily from our black-leaded range.

Jean Duckworth (née Leverton)
born 1941

I was born in Castle Street in a well maintained 'two-up, two-down' house, with a wash house at the bottom of the garden. I remember my father bringing home his miner's wages, three sovereigns. For sixpence he could buy a pint of beer, a packet of Woodbines and a box of matches. Our rent was 3/6d a week. The rent collector wore a black bowler hat and carried a Gladstone bag. Other regular payments were one old penny a week for the doctor's expenses and sixpence for the Christmas Club.

Florence Smith (née Cross)
born 1918

Bridge Terrace was aptly named. A railway bridge between Langley Mill and Newthorpe stations had to be crossed to get there, and another bridge over the Nottingham Canal led into the fields beyond. This hump-back canal bridge of red brick marked our boundary and as children we crossed it only if accompanied by older brothers and sisters. I wondered if a hobgoblin lived under it! The canal was known to us as Top Cut and the Erewash Canal just below was of course Bottom Cut. Bridge Terrace was built over a flat space between the road and Top Cut. The inverted T-shaped terrace comprised thirty or so houses with no water laid on. There was one cold tap in the centre where all the people gathered for a good gossip. The toilets were primitive 'ash-holes.'

Bridge Terrace.

The houses were well built and roomy and in any other decade might well have been modernised. The front room downstairs was the parlour with the best furniture covered over with sheets. In the lace-curtained window was a large aspidistra on a stand. We were rarely allowed in that room. Gas lighting kept the cold air away. Even when the gas street lighting was superseded by electricity the gas lamps in the houses were never replaced, and the gas man still called to empty the meters. He tipped the pennies onto the table and separated the dud and foreign coins from the others! The rest were put into £1 piles and then rolled up in brown paper, the ends neatly sealed. The agreed rebate was handed over to a grateful tenant and the bulk locked into a Gladstone money bag.

Unbeknown to us the Council was building some new houses to rent at Mill Road and nearly all the Terrace families were moved into luxurious accommodation – running hot and cold water, individual toilets and bathrooms. WOW! We moved in 1937 or '38 but this paradise was not to last long for the war came along and our lives were changed once again.

Fred Skillington
born 1931

Friday night was Bath Night ..

Friday night was bath night, which meant removing the battered tin bath from the outside wall and placing it in front of the fire. The hot water was ladled from the boiler which always sported bits of floating rust, and afterwards cold water was re-ladled to refuel the system. When bathtime was over, the bath was carried outside, emptied, cleaned and stored.

Jean Duckworth

In my mind's eye I can see our baths even now. They were hung on pegs just outside the back door, a small one for me with white enamel inside, and a long tin one for my parents. As a child I had a bath every night, but the adults' bath night, usually Friday, was a ritual — all done after I had gone to bed. I expect they both used the same water, one after the other, because they would surely never fill it twice. The boiling of the water, then the filling and emptying of the tub, was a huge job. When I was twelve we moved from Nottingham Road to Percy Street. It was not a new house and it did not have any form of central heating but it did have a bathroom.

Winifred Stoakes

'Sandy' makes use of Jean Brinsley's old tin bath!

Homewards treks the miner in all his dirt and dust,
Tin bath stands on the hearth so get a wash he must.
Coal fire burning brightly in the blackleaded grate,
Water in the boiler for he's in such a state.
No pithead baths for Dad for these came too late
The miners took their muck home; this really was their fate.
Long since these days have gone, we've lovely bathrooms now,
The 'good old days' are over, ne'er to return we vow.

Vera Musgrove

A single cold tap in the yard served five homes, all without inside water. We kept two buckets in the house, one for drinking water (two cats and a dog also freely drank from it) and the other for domestic use. Our crowded living room housed, when the family was fully fledged, 14 children and our two parents — 16 bodies in all! Dad and four of my brothers, all colliers, had to bath each night with no privacy, a performance which took from 5 o'clock until 8.30 with the fire, boiler and the scullery copper going full blast all the time. There was no letting-up on Saturday nights either, because we kids had to have our pre-Sunday swill in second and third-hand water. A row of cleaned boots and a chair laden with clean pairs of drawers, chemises and pinnies signified that 'tomorrow was Sunday.' We boys never had underwear or nightwear.

Members of the Skillington family — Hilda (here aged 9), Evelyn (13) and Fred (16) — have all written reminiscences for this book. They are pictured with younger brother Brian (7) at home on Mill Road in 1947.

All that business every night in that one small room with all the other necessary daily activities — the washing-up of pots and pans on the kitchen table (there was no sink); ironing, mending, cooking; sweat-soaked pit clothes hanging everywhere to dry for the morning; a crying baby or babies to comfort, feed or nappy change. And every few minutes the shop bell would ring to interrupt those chores. My poor mother! Not only did she slog along like a patient donkey to the point of exhaustion by day, but her night's rest had to be interrupted at 5 a.m. to wake the collier lads for work.

Percy Cross

Setting Up Home

When first married we lived in one of four houses among eight pensioners and to me at 21 they seemed ancient! However we were very happy together and they taught me a lot. Four gardens adjoined our long one so I saw a lot of those neighbours. Miss Buxton, who had managed a shoe shop, always heard me pull the mangle out and she would say, 'Could you just put this sheet in your tub?' She would then walk round and show me how it must be well rinsed in the deep sink. Mrs Walker, a railwayman's widow, was friendly and interesting. She was also very kind when I needed to stay in bed for three weeks. Miss Haywood in the third bungalow had been in 'good' service and we could hear her scolding herself for dropping crumbs. She used a deep voice for the reprimand and a child-like voice for the apologies. Next was Mrs Chaplin. I cleaned her bungalow on Fridays for two shillings and did her laundry for which she paid a penny each for towel and tea-cloth, a penny ha'penny for vest and bloomers, and twopence for a sheet. She came to the window to see if the sheets were looped onto the line instead of lying lengthways. I also had lessons on the correct way of putting the clothes through the mangle if any of the buttons were broken!

Alice Geeson (née Worley)
born 1912

My husband Wilfred and I moved into Addison Villas in 1931 when the rent was seven shillings a week. There was hot and cold running water and a bathroom. The kitchen floor was quarry tiles on which I used Red Cardinal polish.

Sybil Griffin (née Bolton)
born 1905

I got married in 1928. In consideration of setting up a home we went to view some new property, three-bedroomed detached houses being erected just below Newthorpe Common. However the builder wanted the prohibitive price of £600 each for them, far beyond my means then. The repayments were ten shillings a week, and on my wage of just over £3 a week we simply could not afford to speculate. Instead we went to live with my wife's widowed mother. By staying there we were able to help out a little in the running of the house.

Kenneth Poynter

When we were married in 1942 my husband Cyril was in a reserved occupation, being a signalman on the railways, and we lived with my mother. Later we lodged in a house on Barber Street, but eventually we needed more room so we applied for and got one of the brand new 'prefabs' on Halls Lane, Newthorpe Common. We were one of the first families in. It was lovely; we had good neighbours and were quite happy there. However, there were only two bedrooms and the family was growing up. In 1948 we moved into a new three-bedroomed council house on William Avenue, built on where allotments and the fields used for the Wakes fairs had been. There were outbuildings and grass at the front and back, and the rent was 15/9d a week. In 1965 we got a mortgage (just under £3 a month) to buy our own house on Nottingham Road.

Mary Bend (née Smith)
born 1918

From Ash-pits to Water Closets

Up the garden was the earth closet. A wooden seat stretched from one side to the other with two holes, a small one for the children and a larger one for adults. Next to it was the ashpit where the ashes from the coal fire were placed. Periodically council men came and cleared the whole lot out, and what a horrible job that was!

Vera Musgrove

Before water closets were installed the toilet was at the end of the garden, which was about 80 feet long. Around midnight the night soil men would arrive on a horse and cart to empty the buckets. All windows would be shut even at the height of summer. Usually there were no locks on the toilet door, so you would sing to let anyone know it was occupied. It is said that quite a lot of singers started their career in this way!

Ken Marsland
born 1924

Delivered to your Door ...

My great-grandmother Marian Elizabeth was born into the Annable family in 1884 on Engine Lane. There was a rather large clan of the Annables living on the lane at that time, including her mother Kate, her uncle Charlie, uncle John, his wife Mary and her cousins Frederick, Frank, Kate Emma, Elizabeth, Jonathan and possibly her grandfather Jobe Annable. The identity of Marian's father is not known but her marriage certificate includes the name of Smalley in brackets before her surname Annable.

The family occupied three houses on Engine Lane from where the children went to Beauvale School. They held many occupations, with John senior being a joiner who sold ladders which he made. Charlie used to deliver milk by horse and cart and often Marian would help him on his round, ladling out the milk. She was a small woman, only 4ft 8ins high. In 1916 she married Arthur, the son of Frank and Maude Parker who ran a bespoke tailor's shop on Queen Street (as Queens Road was then called), Eastwood. The Annables and Parkers became involved in mining, and I think the Annable family were shaft sinkers and moved to the Mansfield area early in the century.

Graham Parker

Coal was delivered, a ton at a time. As it was just dropped in front of the house it had to be wheelbarrowed in. When we lived on Percy Street a man called Cliff used to come and do it for us. He charged a shilling but my mother always gave him twice that. A ton would last several weeks. We always tried to get Lodge Colliery (Newthorpe) 'sit-back' coal because it would burn down to nothing, leaving no clinker. When we lived at the shop on Nottingham Road the coal was dropped straight into the cellar because of course it could not be left on the main road.

Our milk was delivered from the farm every morning by Mr Neville. On his open cart were two large churns. He would pour the milk from them into a bucket which he brought to our door and then, using one of two scoops — a pint or a half-pint — would fill our jug. Talk about hygiene!

Before the days of refrigerators we kept our food in the larder, which if the house was well planned was on the north side, the coolest. I remember our first refrigerator, in the early 1930s, and I especially recall the wonderfully cold milk, a lovely sensation. We acquired that fridge in an unusual way. My mother and I used to go to whist drives in Nottingham, and one day a woman was talking about her refrigerator. We told her it sounded marvellous, and she said, 'Of course they are in short supply; you can't get them at all.' Just as we were leaving she said to my mother, 'If I sent you something would you pay for it?' to which mother replied, 'Of course, what is it?' The woman said, 'I am not going to tell you, but it will be delivered, cash on delivery.' When this enormous thing came it was packed in a sort of fabric case, and only when that was removed did we realise that it was an

Marian Annable delivering milk from the churn in Eastwood, c.1907

electric refrigerator. They were quite rare in houses at that time. Those in shops were mostly gas and very noisy. When we switched ours on it didn't make a sound and we thought it wasn't working, but next day it was cold.

Winifred Stoakes

There were no refrigerators or freezers, and perishable food such as butter, bacon, meat and milk were put on a large flat stone called a thrall.

Ken Marsland

Monday was always Washday

In the yard was a small wash house containing a wooden mangle and a brick copper heated by a coal fire. It was in this building that the weekly ritual of the family's wash was performed. On Monday mornings the square at the back of our house on Princes Street was festooned with dozens of clothes lines as the miners' wives did their weekly washing, and woe betide you if you were out playing and your ball caught any of the clothes on the line!

Kenneth Poynter

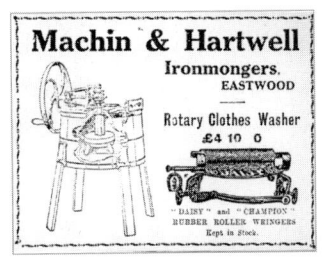

1925 advertisement for the latest technology to ease the housewife's washday burden

Preparation for washday began on Sunday night when the fire was laid underneath the copper. The maid was up at 6 o'clock on Monday morning to light the fire which heated the water for boiling the clothes. When washed they were taken out and mangled, then 'ponched' all in a big tub. It was a terrific day. If it was raining everything had to be dried on a clothes horse around the fire. Washday had to be Monday regardless of the weather and the clothes dried because Tuesday was ironing day!

Ironing was a real chore when I was young. The only way to heat the original irons was to stand them on a special rack over the open fire. To check if they were hot enough you had to spit on the plate; if the spittle rolled off they were ready! Then you rubbed on some beeswax to make the iron go smoothly over the clothes. You always had two irons on the go, one in use while the other was warming on the fire, and you kept changing them over. We used these until well after the First World War, and I remember using the first gas iron before the coming of the electric ones.

Winifred Stoakes

The sound of washday that I remember is the rhythmic thump thump of the 'ponch' in the tub. This tub was usually an empty dubbing barrel from the local colliery which had been turned upside-down over a fire to get all the dubbing out then scalded with boiling water from the copper in the scullery. This same boiler would be used for various purposes — for bath water, for boiling the ham at Christmas and boiling the Christmas puddings months before the event.

Ken Marsland

Louisa Morley doing her weekly wash in the yard of her house on the 'Top Fronts' of The Breach, now Garden Road, c. 1954

We cooked on an open fire, with an oven at one side and a boiler on the other. If you were lucky there was a tap at the bottom to run off the hot water; if not you had to ladle it out. I remember my mother getting her first gas cooker and she thought it was marvellous. It was a small black thing with an oven and two rings, and she boasted that no longer would she have to light a fire in the summer. The kitchen used to get unbearably hot.

Winifred Stoakes

Feeding the Family and Keeping Warm

The only hot water was ladled from the boiler next to the coal fire. This fire was never allowed to go out; a large lump of coal, known as the raker, was put on at bedtime and would be kept alight until the next morning when it was broken up to form the base of the new day's fire. The man of the house would carefully select the rakers and put them aside for this job. Woe betide the wife who accidentally used a raker for just 'mending' the fire!

Mavis Williamson (née Purdy)
born 1922

In winter the oven shelf would be wrapped in a cloth and used as a bed warmer. Friday was usually the day when the fire grate and gas stove were blackleaded and polished until you could see your face in them.

Ken Marsland

Ready to tackle washday are (left to right) Eliza Carlin, Elsie Carlin and a neighbour on Lynncroft in 1942

We had no bathroom so I would either wash in my bedroom with cold water or go down to the kitchen sink for a hot water wash. The bedrooms were freezing in winter — you could see your breath. There was a fire only in the kitchen, the dining room and the lounge (which we called a drawing room then). It was the maid's job to clean out the three grates and make the fires in the morning. The first bit of extra heating we had was a paraffin lamp, an Aladdin, which was portable. We thought it was wonderful to be able to take it into the bedroom. However, it was awful when it went wrong. I remember coming home one day when the lamp had been left on and everything was festooned in black!

Winifred Stoakes

I sat looking at the fireplace and gas fire the other evening and remembered the day when my mother said, 'I'll show you how to make a good fire ...'

We had come to live at Eastwood after spending several years abroad and the children were feeling the cold. We had only the open fire to heat the living room and dining room. One Sunday my mother came up. We had the settee pulled up to the fire to keep warm and she said, 'Come out of the way — I'll show you how to make a good fire,' and before long we had a glowing fire right up the chimney back.

On the following Monday come late afternoon and with the children due home from school, I followed the instructions given and before long had a good fire going. Going so well in fact that I had the chimney on fire and had to send for the fire brigade. I had to pull the carpet back and tried to carry the burning coals outside to put on the garden. The firemen duly arrived and put the fire out, leaving a trail of muddy boots and soot everywhere. My children coming round the corner from school thought it was really exciting to see a fire engine in the road — that was until they found it was outside their home! But worse was to come when as he was leaving a fireman said, 'Don't light the fire for at least two days in case the brickwork in the chimney cracks.'

When my mother came the next weekend her first words were, 'I think you'd better get a gas fire.' And that is how I came to be looking at the fireplace and gas fire …

Jean Brinsley (née Painter)
born 1937

Nine-year old Jean Painter in 1946 doing her Sunday morning chore of shelling peas

Chapter Two *The Happiest Days of your Life?*

When I was five I went to the British School behind the Congregational Church on Albert Street. My first teacher was Miss Lizzie Watts. In the next year or so we were sent to the Church Schools (on Church Walk) while the British School was altered for the boys and the Devonshire Drive Schools were built for the girls and infants. We thought Devonshire Drive was marvellous. We started to learn other subjects as well as the three Rs and we had small plots of garden. I was very proud of mine. Our work included cooking and cleaning lessons but I did not like the blackleading.

Lily Rose
born 1902

Devonshire Drive Infant and Junior School

I was never very fond of school, wherever I went, but I suppose they were happy times really. I remember my teachers at Devonshire Drive — Miss Birkin (later Mrs Hawkins), Miss Banton, and I was very fond of Miss Burton who had very poorly feet and walked badly. I should think that there were about forty children in each class, boys and girls together. I remember in Miss Banton's class sitting next to a boy from New Eastwood. We were being taught English and he said, 'Miss, is a verb a doing word?' I've never forgotten that.

Devonshire Drive School 1914–15.

At the age of 11 I went to the Heanor Grammar School. My mother had promised that I should go there like my brother and sister. It was a bit of a struggle as it was a fee-paying school in those days. We used to stand at Skelton's (at the corner of Church Street) to wait for the bus. One day there was a dreadful accident there when people on the pavement were killed by an army convoy lorry which went out of control.

Constance Barrett
born 1924

My schooldays were special to me. My favourite subjects — English, history and geography — were considered important in those days. A retentive memory and a thirst for general knowledge made learning easy for me. Devonshire Drive School which I attended was on two floors, like many built in Nottinghamshire around that period. The six classrooms on the ground floor housed the infants of both sexes. Afterwards, at the age of nine we girls occupied the upper floor and the boys were transferred. We were upgraded by our ability rather than age, so I only used four of the classrooms. At 11 years old I was in Standard 7 where I stayed for three years, full of frustration and longing for more education. I didn't even sit the grammar school entrance exam. There was no point, with further education having to be paid for.

The classes housed fifty or more pupils with whom the teachers coped well. Discipline was good; we had learned that lesson at home. Our mentors must have been exceptionally clever because they each taught every subject. A typical day's lessons would be scripture, mental arithmetic, geography, then — after playtime — arithmetic until 12 noon. Then we all went home for an hour and a half. Afternoon would resume with English, history, and perhaps nature study, painting or sewing.

If my favourite subject was English, then my least liked was painting or drawing, indeed anything appertaining to handiwork. Sewing didn't come into it until my 12th year, and what a nightmare that was! Until then I had avoided that chore, giving my left-handedness as a reason. Miss Meakin however would have none of that. 'Left-handed or not,' she said, 'you will learn to sew,' and she promptly gave me some pieces of unbleached calico which would eventually be a nightdress. The material was hard, and try as I might the seams which should have been flat stuck up like a sore thumb. Eventually though, the garment was finished, with the scalloped neckline in buttonhole stitch and the embroidered butterfly in lazy daisy stitch and French knots — the best part of it. If I thought making the thing was bad, worse was to come. We were sent home one lunchtime with the

A Century Remembered

*Devonshire Drive School 4th year pupils 1949.
Back row (l to r): Mr Sprittlehouse (Headmaster), Peter Faby, John Brown, Barry Kirkland, Michael Bradley, Billy Peach, Ralph Goodwin, Jeffrey Yates, Richard Machin, Harold Chambers, Mr Pearson (teacher).
3rd row: Shirley Pearson, Patricia Bagguley, Jean Quigley, Jean Rogers, Pat Williamson, Marion Rowland, Brenda Hallam, Hilary Blagg, Madeline Wakefield, Nova Booth, Marion Naylor, Betty Gibson.
2nd row: Ann Hankin, Kathleen Whelan, Maureen Vickers, Winnie Worrall, Margaret Linley, Elsie Martin, Jean Trueblood, Pat Biggs, Joan Bingham, Pat Brown, Janis Carter, Beryl Topps.
Front row: Edgar Buckley, Barry Woodcock, David Richmond, Lenny Ross, Eric Hart, Alan Gascoyne.*

garments and with a request to bring the payment that afternoon. Pride forbade that I tell teacher about our financial situation, and when I kept pestering my mother while she was speaking with a neighbour, she — also not caring to admit she hadn't the money — smacked me for the first and only time in my life.

*Alice Geeson
born 1912*

I started at Devonshire Drive School in 1910 and left when I was 13 to help my mother, who did not enjoy good health, to run the family home.

*Sybil Griffin
born 1905*

I went first to Devonshire Drive Infant School, where Miss Beddowes was the headmistress and Miss Banton was one of the teachers. There were 30 to 40 children in the class, seated at double desks, boys and girls together. We had to sit next to someone we liked. I remember that one of the first things we did every day was our 'times tables,' a ritual that stood my generation in good stead in later life. I moved on to the Junior School, and then at the age of 12 went to Heanor Grammar School.

*Winifred Stoakes
born 1909*

My early schooldays were spent at Devonshire Drive where the headmaster was Mr J Sprittlehouse. I remember Mrs Battersby and Miss Bonsall teaching me. It being wartime, we always had to have our gas masks with us and we had regular

Page 25

practices with them. I played the triangle in the school band, and our star piece was Chopin's *Polonaise*.

David Richmond
born 1938

When I started school in 1955 the Infant teachers were Miss Chadwick, Mrs Godber, Mrs Renwick and Mrs Smith, and the Headmistress was Miss Vosper. In Mrs Renwick's class we were in a separate building across the playground. We used to sit around the fire in there for story time. All the toilets were outside, one set for the infants and one set for the juniors. There was a dividing line in the playground where juniors were not allowed to cross into the infants' playground.

The Headmaster at the Junior School was Mr Sprittlehouse, and the teachers were Miss Musgrove, Miss Battersby and Mr Pearson. There were separate entrances for boys and girls. We had to line up every morning, dinnertime and playtime before going back into school. We had to stand up straight, an arm's length from the next person, in straight lines and be quiet before we were allowed into school.

Every Christmas Mr Sprittlehouse conducted a carol service which always ended with his favourite carol *Ding Dong Merrily On High*. We were taught to write in pencil, but when we reached a good standard we were allowed to write in ink. In our last year at school the pen was wooden with a nib which we dipped into the ink-well set into the desk.

I was Head Girl at the Junior School. There were also several prefects, and we all wore badges and at lunch time had to sit at the head of the tables in order to help the younger children. In the final year we sat the 11+ exam. Those who passed went to the Grammar School; those who didn't went on to the Secondary Modern School.

Karen Clarke (née Rowland)
born 1950

Bagthorpe and Underwood Schools

I went into a classroom,
I sat upon a chair,
A door closed behind me,
My mother wasn't there.
I yelled and screamed in protest,
This really wasn't fun,
How could she go and leave me?
My schooldays had begun.

I will never forget my first day at school. I was suddenly propelled into a classroom I had never seen before with a group of children and their teacher, not knowing a soul. However, comforted by the kindly grey-haired lady who proved to be my teacher, Mrs Hind, I settled down and had four very happy years at Bagthorpe Infant School. The school was organised into four classes. Mrs Hind had the reception class of 5 to 6 year-olds; Miss Cross the first class (6 to 7); Miss Gill Standard 1 (7 to 8); and Miss Wells Standard 2 (the 8 to 9 year-olds). The Headmistress ran the school and also taught Standard 2. Female teachers were almost always single; women had to give up teaching on marriage. Occasionally a widow was brought in by special arrangement.

The first class and Standard 1 shared a large room divided by a curtain which was drawn back so that the whole school could have Assembly together. I remember this very well because on the day I cried I was hauled out and placed on the front line of Standard 2 by the Headmistress. At some point a pile of hymn books was placed in my tiny hands. Apparently I was supposed to pass them one by one down the line until everybody had a book. No-one explained this to me and eventually I dropped the whole pile of books on the floor. Exasperated, Miss Hamilton came across and smacked me hard on the back of both hands. I was never smacked at home and the shock was awful. I did not dare to cry again and never told my mother, but the feeling of injustice stayed with me for a long time.

The teacher I remember most is Miss Gill. When I was seven I caught measles and had to stay in bed. To my great surprise a fire appeared in the bedroom grate and the room was draped in frills and valances which I had never seen before. All this because the doctor was expected! Then at tea-time a classmate knocked on our door and brought me a message from Miss Gill. When I opened it it said 'this is for Vera' and there was a lovely shiny threepenny bit. It was the greatest treasure because I only got a ha'penny on a Friday and a penny from Grandma for Sunday.

To a lesser degree I remember Miss Wells, my teacher in Standard 2. There must have been a bereavement in her family because she always wore a black dress. I kept wishing my teacher would wear a pretty dress but after six months she wore it again remodelled for another six months. People wore black for a whole year when someone close had died.

Classrooms were equipped with either tables and chairs or desks seating four children arranged to face the teacher who had a blackboard and easel. They graduated in height according to our age and in Standards 1 and 2 they had ink pots as we went from pencil to pen and ink. This classroom arrangement meant the teacher could keep an eye on everybody and haul a disruptive pupil to the front row. How difficult it has become for the present day teacher or even me who retired from Devonshire Drive School over 20 years ago to keep an eye on children scattered in various work areas in the well-equipped classrooms of today.

Most of my teachers had come up on the old pupil-teacher system, staying on in a school (when their contemporaries left at 14) to develop their teaching skills with the help of the head teacher and staff. At about 18 they would get a teaching post and be known as uncertificated teachers, or they could decide to go to a teacher training college for two years, paying the fees themselves, and become a certificated teacher. Thus there were two salary scales. When you think of the academic requirements needed today you realise how far we have moved, but that is not to say there were no dedicated teachers in my time of course and lots of us owe a great deal to them.

Teaching was formal. We were taught as a class and moved up as a class each year. It was all talk and chalk

— it was a school where children marched in reciting tables, building up words on the blackboard, spelling learned from the blackboard, copy-writing to learn the correct formation of letters; and best of all were the poems learned by heart, some of which I still remember learning by rote all the way.

The school day was in two parts, the morning from 9 until 12 and the afternoon from 1.15 to 3.45. I went home to a hot meal cooked by my mother who was always there. One day I had the brilliant idea of staying at school for dinner-time. My mother packed some egg sandwiches, and my brother and I stayed at school. It was an experiment I never repeated for it was the longest day I ever spent in the infant school. Home time could not come quickly enough, so with the advent of school dinners during my teaching career I always felt very sympathetic to the young five-year old who was suddenly plunged into what must appear to him a very long school day.

The school toilets were situated across the playground and I was introduced to the water lavatory for the first time. I wouldn't use it at all at first as I was terrified of falling down the hole and being flushed away. The old wooden seat at home was far more secure! The caretaker was Mr Green who lived in a house situated on the edge of the playground. He made lovely coal fires in two of the classrooms and kept all the pipes warm. We could sit there in the wintertime and dry our gloves. In the Upper Standard for the price of a ha'penny we could buy a hot drink of Horlicks at morning playtime, long before the days of school milk.

Bagthorpe Infant School did not cater for 9 to 10 year-olds. At the age of 9 we had to leave Bagthorpe and go up to Underwood before coming back to the Upper Standard, and it was a very daunting experience at Underwood because a Miss Shaw taught me. It was a most unprofitable year as Miss Shaw got through numerous canes trying to keep an extremely unruly class in order. They were rough at Underwood compared with Bagthorpe! In the Upper Standard I can remember learning that lovely longhand writing which loops, thin up-stroke and thick down-stroke, and we had to do this copy-writing every day until we had got

A Century Remembered

a reasonable hand.

My favourite teacher in the junior school was 'Tuffy' Naylor. I think he was called Tuffy because his parents kept a toffee shop. He took the music lessons, and I can remember there was a teacher on the staff called Rosie and I don't know whether it was by accident or design but he taught us a song which began 'Once a boy a rosebud saw, a rosebud in the heather, rosy rosy rosy bud, rosebud in the heather.' Rosie lived not far from me, and when we were within a safe distance we used to chant this after her. Another chant I can remember was 'Our teacher's a funny 'un, with a face like a Spanish onion, with a bum like a squashed tomato and legs like two props !'

It was at Bagthorpe that I eventually won a scholarship and went on to a school outside the village. At the age of eleven therefore I said goodbye to a lot of my friends because they stayed on at school and left at fourteen, many of them going to work in the mines and factories. I went to Sutton. I could have taken a junior scholarship but I didn't — I don't know why — and instead I took what was called an Intending Teachers Scholarship and from then on I concentrated on teaching.

Vera Musgrove
born 1918

I n the mid-thirties when we had to go to school we attended the local Council School at New Eastwood. This building made of wood and corrugated iron was known affectionately as the 'Tin Tack.' It was a good school and we had good teachers.

Fred Skillington
born 1931

New Eastwood School

New Eastwood Council School 1912.

A Century Remembered

Beauvale Schools

The clarion call of the school bell summoned me to Beauvale School (Mr Wibberley was the ringer in my day). There was little truancy; a fierce Attendance Officer checked the registers and visited the homes of absent pupils with stern warnings when needed. Other regular school visits were made by doctors and nurses when all the children were weighed and tested for heart, sight and hearing. How many of us dreaded the fortnightly searches for head-lice, when badly infected boys and girls had their hair cropped and heads soaked with paraffin. I did not escape this humiliation, but my most frequent trouble was ringworm, a dirty smelly head affliction which meant isolation in class and painting with a violet-coloured lotion. My early school years were marred by frequent illness. I was given a special school allowance of cod liver oil and milk and was excused all physical training ('Swedish drill.'). However, I was a good scholar and seldom, if ever, lower than the top form in class. I remember in the Standard 5 exam being given sixpence for dropping only one mark in eight subjects. The infant school teaching was interesting. We were given small tin trays covered with sand in which we finger-traced letters of the alphabet. Later we used slates and slate pencils. The sexes were separated from class 2 onwards. Girls in higher classes used to walk from Beauvale to Eastwood for lessons in cookery, washing and ironing.

Beauvale Boys School Standard 1 1932.

Harry Lindley was a long-serving headmaster around the 1910 years, and Sam Wood was a highly respected senior teacher until he retired to become mine host at the Sun Inn. Another teacher/publican was Mr Moon, landlord of the Moon and Stars. A master who smartened the minds (and backsides!) of several generations of boys was 'Daddy' Guy with his frequent use of the cane. Miss Bonser and Miss Brunnings took devoted care of the infants.

*Percy Cross
born 1906*

I spent all my schooldays at Beauvale and I loved it. I was five when I started, and I remember on my first day I walked home at playtime, thinking that was the day finished, and my mother had to take me back! I believe that Miss Grainger was the Infant head teacher and Mrs Corkhill the Junior head. Other teachers I remember are Miss Lineham, who walked from Cotmanhay every day, Iris Robinson, Marjorie Clay, Miss Wyld, Mary Hodgkinson, Ethel Longdon and Margaret Coe. I would love to have been able to take the scholarship exam for a grammar school in Nottingham but it was not to be, and I left Beauvale at the age of 14 to start work.

Mary Bend
born 1918

Beauvale Boys School 1946.
Back row (l to r): Mr Philip Birkin, Barry Hull, Peter Fry, John Davies, Arthur Flint, — Harvey, Billy Peggs, Albert Sadler, Russell Kerry, Glyn Turner. Middle row: Charlie Sisson, Geoff Duffield, Brian Hunt, Graham Embury, —, Leslie Parkes, Arthur Gaunt, Dennis Syson, Pat Smith, Roy Wadsley. Front row: David Wilson, Colin Lambert, Barry Peters, Noel Pratt, Bill Birkin, Malcolm Wilson, Colin Housley, —, Terry Syson, Derek Hill, —.

If parents could afford it the girls' uniform at Beauvale School was a black alpaca dress and white starched pinafore, with black boots and black stockings.

Florence Smith
born 1918

I had attended Beauvale School every day for a year and had won the Sir Lancelot Rolleston Charity prize of five shillings to be presented by Sir Lancelot himself. The day came and we sat in the hall; in walked this elegant man, every inch an aristocrat — frock coat, tall silk hat and silver-topped cane. I had been reading *The Knights of the Round Table* and here was my shining knight 'Sir Lancelot.' I went up to collect my prize but was so overwhelmed I forgot to curtsy and say thank-you (and I was reprimanded by the teacher). Miss Hodgkinson my teacher lived at Lynncroft on the brow of the hill. We often walked with her to school over the fields, Cow Closes, and carried some of her books.

A very dedicated teacher, she lived with her aunt Miss Mellors who had owned the Pottery. (The pottery was in ruins but the Pottery House was still there — they lived across the way.) Though very charming, Miss Hodgkinson soon had the children under control. If she was in a temper she would rush up and down, striking each desk with a wooden chair leg. You learned to put your hands underneath the desk, because it did sting if she caught you unawares.

I remember going with the art class to sketch Beauvale Priory and the fish pond. I could visualise the monks silently tilling the fields, tending the cattle — a hard monastic life. We looked in the tiny cells where they prayed and lived their lives, the earth floor and wattle roofs so bare. Much later I was given a book *The Breaking of the Storm* about the dissolution of the monasteries.

At eleven years old I left Beauvale and went to Walker Street School just across the road from where I lived, a very modern establishment where discipline was still strict. When I was 14 I left school on a Friday and started work the next Monday.

Enid Goodband (née Bailey)
born 1924

During the war and into the 1950s the Headmistress of Beauvale Girls' School (it was not 'mixed' in those days) was Miss Bullars. She managed to work under great difficulty and yet turn out wonderful results in the Intelligence Test (later the 11+) despite a shortage of textbooks and paper. We always had 'prayers' in the main hall each morning, and Miss Ida Stirland taught us to sing and understand basic music. There were percussion instruments forming a band, and there was an annual talent concert. Miss Mary Hodgkinson taught the upper class for many years, while Miss Coe taught not only the academic subjects but also basic hygiene and table manners.

Hilda Hill (née Skillington)
born 1937

We walked up to Beauvale School over the fields where Peters Close is now, except when the horses were in the field near the stile and then we had to 'leg it' round Main Street. There was no problem crossing over Dovecote Road because there were hardly any cars — not like today! At Beauvale girls and boys were taught separately. The girls' headmistress was Miss Bullars, and Miss Hodgkinson did the Scottish dancing. The girls were taught sewing and knitting. We all made a simple dress, but I never wore mine!

Pat Potter (née James)
born 1942

Beauvale Boys School Football Team 1949. Back row (l to r): Maurice Savage, Owen Syson, Peter Mann, Michael Walker, L Alan Godfrey. Front row: Stuart King, Harold Fletcher, Gordon Wilson, Norman Clark, Eric Hart, Brian Potter.

Greasley Beauvale School, a warm and friendly building, welcomed us on our first day of learning. Holding father's hand we walked from the stony unpaved Grey Street, through the jitty which bordered Captain Chambers' grounds to Hill Top, crossed the belisha crossing and hurried along Dovecote Road, familiarising the route we would take for the next six years.

A 'big' girl clanged the handbell at the edge of the iron railings, warning of the five minutes left to enter the playground and line up in neat rows class by class, waiting to crocodile inside. Our first day was quite unique as we had to meet the Headmistress Mrs Grey and register. I don't remember saying goodbye to Dad but I will never forget the coal fire blazing in the wide fireplace surrounded by a metal barred fireguard. Mr Dane the caretaker periodically fed the fire with coal. Over the fireplace a beautiful picture of the Nativity hung, giving a feeling of warmth and security.

It was January 1946 and most of our friends were well established in class; our attack of whooping cough had delayed our entry one term earlier. My brother and I were introduced to everyone as twins by Miss Harpham, a young and gentle lady who was soon to marry and become Mrs Clarke. We were asked if we knew any nursery rhymes and delighted the class by reciting *Jack and Jill* in unison. We were led to a table where the monitor filled Meggeson tins with pieces of chalk and a blackboard rubber, and each of those special treasures became our personal property. The war had just ended and our school equipment was in short supply or even non-existent so we did all our writing on a blackboard with chalk; even so, this was better than five years earlier when my brother and sister had had to burn their own wood to make charcoal with which to write. Then one day Miss West announced, 'I have some wonderful news, children, we now have some pencils and paper.' These were to be treated with great respect and we would only be allowed to copy our work onto the paper when our blackboard work was perfect!

Those were happy days with a learning assortment of percussion band, Scottish country dancing, singing together, musical movement to the radio, as well as the three Rs. There were drama productions and the annual maypole dance. I envied one of the boys' activities, that of gardening and bee-keeping with Mr. Brown. A team point was awarded to any boy stung by a bee!

To go to the toilet meant a trip across the yard to the row of outside small toilets. We always chose one and called it the 'fever lav' which everyone boycotted! At lunchtime we were allowed to play on the recreation ground opposite and my brother Ian once had the misfortune to fall into a cow pat. He was given a bucket of water and towel and told to stay outside until he was clean. At the age of seven we parted — Ian to the boys and I to the girls. We never shared the same playground again.

Our school hymn was *Fight the Good Fight* and each day closed with the prayer 'Lord keep us safe this night, secure from all our fears, may angels guard us whilst we sleep, 'til morning light appears. Amen.' Some of our friends passed the 11+ and would not join us as we moved on to the Eastwood County Secondary School on Walker Street.

Jean Duckworth
born 1941

A Century Remembered

My education or 'schooling' started when I was five years old, in the old school on Church Walk. From there I went to Devonshire Drive and, when old enough, to the Albert Street (British) School, under the headmastership of 'Gaffer' Darrington — a very strict but fair gentleman indeed. Schoolday memories allow for recollection of many happy times what with football competitions and snowball fights (in which the schoolmasters always joined) in the winter, and nature walks through the beautiful outlying countryside districts around Eastwood in the summer. I was considered by Mr Darrington to be a moderate pupil. One of his favourite questions was 'Which is the heavier : a ton of feathers or a ton of iron?' and I have seen many a boy afraid to answer for fear he was wrong. Schooling was very strict in those days, and if you misbehaved out to the front you would go and receive one or two strokes from the teacher's cane. If you had done something really bad off you went to Mr Darrington's room for at least four strokes with his cane, although I never managed to get as many as that!

Albert Street British School

The teaching differed from today in that the teacher took a class, or Standard, right through the whole range of subjects and did not specialise in just one or two. The headmaster often took the higher Standards for singing. I can remember only two of my teachers — Mr Coffey (and what a quick-tempered man he was), and Miss Truman, otherwise known as 'Katie.' She was one of the best and certainly the strictest of teachers I ever had. I stayed on at school until I was nearly fourteen (the school leaving age then was thirteen).

Kenneth Poynter
born 1909

At Walker Street in the early 1940s we were in segregated classes with boys to the left of the main entrance and girls to the right. The two floors of classrooms had wide staircases and long corridors. The playground was divided by a tall iron-railing fence which kept us apart at playtime. Each class had thirty or more children to one teacher and

Eastwood County Secondary School (Walker Street)

Form 3A of the Eastwood Higher Council (now the Comprehensive) School, Walker Street in 1933, the year it opened. Back row (l to r): Edna Worrall, Edna Sisson, Marjorie Chambers, Emma Thornley, Edna Riley, Joyce Bilby, Lucy Robinson, Jessie Meakin, Ivy Norman, Monica Humphries. 3rd row: Miss Enid Moult (teacher), Joyce Akers, Irene Fletcher, Nancy Rowley, Winnie Beaver, Joan Cheeseman, Freda Smith (1), Cicely Constable, Kathleen Hallam, Clara Heal, Eileen Constable, Doris Whittamore, Aileen —, Juanita Jacques, Sylvia Wilkinson, Joan Durant. 2nd row: Isabella Barker, Stella Marriott, Evelyn Lowe, Dorothy Smith, Cynthia Bradley, Rose Straw, Dora Neale, Betty Broadbent, Freda Smith (2), Edith Brown. Front row: Margaret Wykes, Monica Wright, Lucy Marriott, Maud Taylor, Laura Vamplew, Mary Purdy, Lilian Bradley, Enid Fretwell.

the teachers were nearly all women, the men having been called up into the forces. However, we did have a headmaster who took us for morning assembly. This was the only time the whole school came together, and we sat on the hall floor in tight groups with our teacher. We had a pep-talk, sang a hymn and said the Lord's Prayer. If the hymn was not well sung, we had to sing verses over again. *City of God, How Broad and Far* was one we learned by repetition.

Fred Skillington

Eastwood Secondary Modern School was active in music and drama, and Miss Wesson was particularly interested in Gilbert and Sullivan. During the 1940s and '50s she produced annual performances of *The Mikado, Iolanthe, Patience* and *The Gondoliers*.

Hilda Hill

When Headmaster Mr A H Scott, a real 'Dickensian' disciplinarian, retired in 1953 he was succeeded by Mr R F Cotes. Some of the teachers I remember include Miss Dove who taught needlework; Miss Williams, domestic science; Pat Clarke, girls' PE and games; Fred 'Basher' Bakewell, an incredible artist famed for his scenery at all the school drama productions; Mr Williamson, science; Mr T G Martin, a delightful man whose eloquence with the English language was portrayed in his spectacular productions *Yeomen of the Guard, Merrie England* and of course the famous Eastwood Pageant of 1951; Ethel Longdon, who assisted Mr Martin with those drama productions; Miss Richardson; Miss Truman; the genial Cyril Jackson who, when imparting his superb knowledge of maths, gained the fullest attention of his pupils with his warm wit and sense of humour; Noel

Kader, a South African and a student of Lawrence who lodged at the home of Willie Hopkin; George Phillips, woodwork; Charles Ross, metalwork; and last but not least Don Chambers who spent his whole teaching career at the school and is well known in the district as a lay preacher and a magician.

Mick Brown
born 1941

I attended the school from 1961 to 1966. Children travelled to Hall Park in special buses from a wide area of Nottinghamshire. The headmaster was Mr Cowling. I remember the girls' uniform was a maroon blazer with school badge, maroon striped blouse, plain maroon tie, grey skirt and cardigan, maroon purse belt, white socks, black shoes and navy raincoat. A beret had to be worn at all times to and from school (even if it was only gripped to the back of the head). In summer we wore a maroon and purple gingham dress. A straw boater was optional to the beret, but one or the other still had to be worn. White socks were worn until year 4, then we were allowed to wear tights or stockings in the final two years.

Hall Park Technical Grammar School (Mansfield Road)

Karen Clarke

In June 1973 I joined the committee of the PTA of the Eastwood Comprehensive Lower School as its secretary. It was decided to hold two educational and two social events, the proceeds of which could be used to fund whatever scheme the committee proposed.

Eastwood Comprehensive School

The first social event was planned as a Christmas 'get-together' for children, staff and parents on December 7th 1973. There would be entertainment ranging from old-time dancing to a disco for the children, various games from limbo to minto, treasure hunts, tombola, raffles etc., all for 10p admission. However, even after committee member Ken Bridge assured us that 'the tombola drum is in hand, the doll's birthday is sorted, and the old-time dance chappie is all fixed up,' it was to no avail for I received a letter from the Head Teacher Mr McNulty. He asked me to let everyone

The Upper Sixth form of Hall Park Technical Grammar (now Eastwood Comprehensive) School, Summer 1971. Back row (l to r): Clayton Wardle, Ian Purdy, John Walton, Graham Lowe, Alan Eyre, Steven Bull, John Wilde, Kevin Rowland, Michael Raynor. Middle row: John Baker, Alan Tinklin, Graham Fowkes, Judith Mee, Shirley Duffin, Pat Beard, Lyn Goodwyn, Philip Hodgkinson, John Clifton, Christopher Lowe. Front row: Julia Minkley, Rosemary Timms, Helen Keam, Winifred Gibbs, Valerie Bostock, Jean Louth, Margaret Comery, June Musgrove, Catherine Mitchell, Barbara Hooks.

know that the family evening would have to be postponed until further notice as the school building could not be used in the evenings owing to the fuel crisis.

I served on the committee until 1976 when both of my children had moved to the Upper School. In May of that year a 'Mini-Bus Push' was organised. The bus was pushed and pulled some ten miles around the Eastwood area by parents, staff and friends of the school in an attempt to raise funds for a new school bus.

Jean Brinsley
born 1937

In December 1976 a party of students from Eastwood Comprehensive School accompanied by staff members Mr Haining, Miss Kirkham and Mr Mackenzie went on an educational cruise around the Mediterranean on the *SS Uganda*. The itinerary included Italy, Egypt, Cyprus, Turkey and Greece. We flew from Gatwick to Naples, and the drive from the airport to the ship took us through the poor part of town which we all thought was quite dirty and scruffy. Our first glimpse of the ship was also a bit of a shock, not as big as we thought it would be and a whole lot rustier!

Our first morning was spent on an excursion to the ancient ruined city of Pompeii. What I found amazing were the bodies of the villagers and animals who had been caught in the path of the molten lava and preserved where they fell. The next four days were spent at sea, trying to stave off sea-sickness while we crossed the Mediterranean from Italy to Egypt. As it was an educational cruise we had lessons during the day and also lectures by the formidable Miss Breeze on the places we would be visiting later in the trip. Our first port of call was Alexandria, and we travelled from there to Cairo by coach. We were all saddened by the pathetically thin children and animals we passed in the villages, and amazed by the incredible number of passengers that Egyptian buses could carry both inside and out! The Pyramids and the Sphinx were a spectacular sight, and it was hard to comprehend quite how long they had been there. We had all been told that we could ride on a camel if we wanted to, but to be sure to pay only half the money at the beginning of the ride and the remainder at the end. Unfortunately one of the chaperones did not heed this advice and had to be bailed out by her husband before she disappeared into the sunset! There were many souvenir sellers at the Pyramids and most of us ended up buying statues of Nefertiti which our parents later found would make excellent door stops.

Our next port of call was Cyprus where we visited Greek and Roman ruins and a fruit packing factory! Two days later we arrived in Turkey and visited the ruins at Ephesus, grimaced at the taste of real Turkish coffee and stocked up on Turkish delight. Santorini, one of the Greek islands, was next on our list of places to visit. It had been formed as a result of a volcano erupting, and we found to our horror that there were 500 steps to the top. Most of us walked but some people paid to ride up on a donkey. The following day we arrived in mainland Greece and had the opportunity to see the Acropolis and the Parthenon which were quite spectacular.

Our journey ended at Brindisi and we flew Dan-Air back to London, finally travelling by coach home to Eastwood. It was December, and after two weeks in the sun I found it very difficult to adapt to the chilly weather. I will always be grateful for the experiences I had on the *SS Uganda* as it served as the spark for a love of travel which I still have today. I have been living overseas for the past ten years. Unfortunately the *SS Uganda* did not fare so well. She served as a hospital ship during the Falklands War and then as a transport ship. In 1986 she was sold for scrap, was grounded and capsized during a typhoon in August 1986 while waiting for a breaker's berth in Kaohsiung.

Susan Jackson (née Lord)
born 1962

The cast of the Secondary School, Walker Street, production of The Scarlet Pimpernel in 1950, directed by Miss E Longdon and Mr T G Martin.

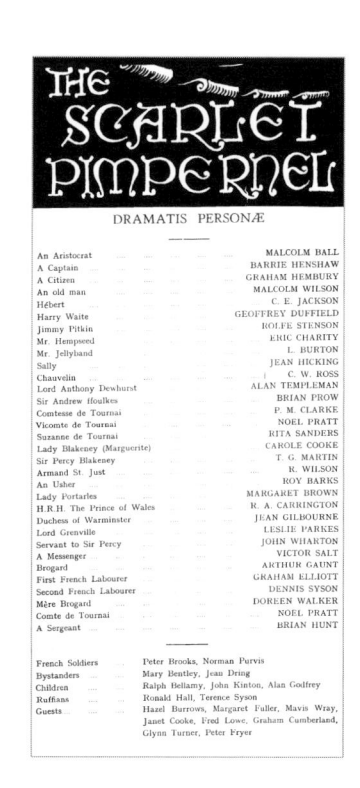

I was on the board of governors of Eastwood Comprehensive School from 1974 to 1977. As well as governors' meetings I was lucky enough to attend various other events. Having been chosen as one of the two schools to represent the Midlands in the BBC Radio programme *Top Of The Form* a team took on Oswestry High School for Girls in the first round. The recording took place on October 14th 1975 with an audience of pupils, parents and teachers, and the Eastwood team — Susan Watson, Annette Todd, Stephen Madeley and Melvyn Oldfield — beat Oswestry by 47 points to 39. This left only eight schools in the competition, but sadly in the next round on November 4th Eastwood was beaten by Paisley Grammar School, Glasgow.

Jean Brinsley

Eastwood Comprehensive School was twinned with the Marie Curie Gymnasium in Neuss, near Dusseldorf, and in 1977 an exchange was arranged with their students. The intention was that they would practise their English in England, and we would practise our German in Germany. However, the reality was that they were far more proficient at English than we were at German so English ended up being spoken most of the time!

The German students came to Eastwood first and then we returned with them to Germany. We were accompanied by Mr and Mrs Lambert and Mr Mann. The trip got off to an inauspicious start by being brought forward by a day at the last minute owing to a seamen's strike. This meant that by the time we boarded the ferry all the seats were taken and we had to camp out by the men's loos. From Ostend we travelled by train and were further delayed when we lost several of our party at Brussels station when they forgot to get off the train!

I stayed with the Uhlenbroich family, and when they found out that Eastwood was a mining town it was as if they felt they had a mission to show me every 'braunkohl'(brown coal) mine in the region. They even managed to find a museum of opencast mining to take me to! We went to school with our penfriends and were horrified to find that it started at 8.15 a.m. We were dispatched to help out in the English class and the German children found our accents very funny, saying that we didn't pronounce the words properly. It turned out that their English teacher was in fact an American. After that we did French and music classes, then English again and to finish the day a nice film on brown coal!

The school arranged a trip to Bonn where we visited Beethoven's house, the parliament building and a castle, stopping on the way back to see an opencast mine! A second excursion was arranged to Koblenz where we took a trip down the Rhine and then climbed for two and a half hours to the top of Burg Eltz, a picturesque castle on the top of a very high hill.

On the return journey we again managed to miss our trains with alarming regularity and finally arrived in Nottingham at the ungodly hour of 1.45 a.m. I really enjoyed the opportunity to stay with a German family, as it provided an insight into their daily life which was very different from what I was used to.

Susan Jackson

Chapter Three

Our Working Lives

The main employment in this area for men was coal mining. Women did work in a variety of factories including Wolsey hosiery at Kimberley and the Compressed Leather works at Giltbrook. Many women went to work in factories in Nottingham. A few went into service at country mansions such as Watnall Hall. When I left school I spent a little time at a cabinet factory, then started at Donnelley's as a joiner apprentice on a wage of five shillings for a six and a half day week

Ken Marsland
born 1924

Long Days at the Laundry

Employees of the laundry at Bailey Grove in the 1920s, including Nora Reeve (front row, 2nd left), Edith Guyler (5th left) and to her right, Ivy Patrick; Dorrie Steel (back row, 2nd right) and to her left, Dorothy Smith; 6th left on the third row up is Miss Colson whose father was the Eastwood town crier

I was 14 years old when I started work at the Bailey Grove Laundry, working from 8 in the morning until 8 at night. On Saturdays we had to stay until the work was all cleared ready for the van drivers to finish their delivery. I operated two machines in the pressing unit. Each girl had a box filled with damp clothes which had to be pressed to perfection — or back they came! As the pile in the box got lower, more clothes were put in. It was hard work for a girl of 14, and for all those hours my weekly wage was 11/3d. We had a ten-minute break in the morning, and 45 minutes for dinner. In summer I cycled the mile and a half home to Heanor, bringing back with me some sandwiches for the 30-minute afternoon tea break. In the winter I travelled by bus; the fare from Eastwood to Heanor was twopence.

When I was 17 I was put on the shirt unit, still operating two machines — one for the collars and cuffs, and the other for the body of the shirt. I was by no means 'the fastest gun in the west' but I was certainly the fastest in the shirt unit, and for that I was complimented. Our workload became even heavier when the American forces moved into Kings Mill Hospital at Sutton. They used to bring their laundry in themselves, and collect it, so we saw rather a lot of them — and also their chocolate and tinned fruit!

I have said that in summer I cycled to and from work. When I was on my way home one day the father of my cousin Jean saw me. He often waited at his front door on Station Road at Langley Mill, just to wave to me, but I did not have time to stop. Having seen me on one occasion, he told my mother that people could see up my clothes as I cycled so I asked her to buy me some shorts. However, in those days it was unheard of for women to wear shorts and it got me into trouble at work. I was banned from entering the laundry, so I decided to carry a skirt in my cycle bag and slip it over my shorts when going into work!

Betty Richardson (née Pollard)
born 1922

1935 advertisement

The Slaughterhouse

When I was ten I was allowed to leave my classroom at the British School on Albert Street on Thursday afternoons five or ten minutes before the end of the lesson. This was to enable me to take Herbert Johnson's tea down to Barker's slaughterhouse at New Eastwood. Here Mr Johnson did the killing, cleaning and cutting up of pigs which would be sold at the weekend at Barker's Pork Butchers shop on Nottingham Road (almost opposite Victoria Street). I used to help put the rope around the back legs of the pigs and drag them out of the 'keep' into the slaughterhouse. Here they were fastened to a pulley wheel and pulled to a certain height head-downwards. At that time there was no such thing as humane killing, and the method used was to cut the

Robert Frederick Skillington (sitting 3rd from left, without cap) with a group of fellow bricklayer's labourers. Born in 1875, he lived in New Eastwood and died in 1926

pig's throat lengthways while I caught in a bucket as much of the blood as possible. This was later used to make black pudding etc. I remember one incident when, just as Mr Johnson had cut the pig, the pulley rope broke and the pig fell to the floor, knocking over both me and the bucket. The pig ran out of the slaughterhouse and nearly reached the street before it dropped down dead. It took five or six of us to carry it back again.

Kenneth Poynter
born 1904

Fetching the Washing

My mother used to do the laundry for Mrs Hartley, the Eastwood undertaker's wife. On Monday mornings I had to go with a wooden pushchair to fetch the basketful of washing and later take it back, aired and ironed. For this my mother was paid 1/6d, and when the Hartleys moved to Langley Mill I had to go all that way and back – still for 1/6d.

Mary Bend
born 1918

The Noisy Factory

Two of my mother's sisters worked in a hosiery factory on Radford Boulevard in Nottingham. My mother, brother and I would go and meet them from work on Saturday. In those days factory hands had to work on Saturday mornings. We got off the bus at Bentinck Road Schools and walked down to the factory, but the minute the factory door opened I was terrified of the sound of all the machinery and all the noise, and I would not go inside. My mother and brother used to go in but I waited outside — it must have been safe to do so in those days — until they all came out after knocking-off time. My mother told me years later that she had thought to herself, 'I shall never be able to send that child to work in a factory' — which was a very good idea, actually!

Nowadays as I go to the Blind Centre off the Alfreton Road I always see those lovely Victorian houses. It was to one of those four-storeyed houses that one of my mother's sisters went as the maid of all work, and I can remember visiting her. She had her living quarters in the basement and slept at the top in the attic. All those stairs — the work must have been horrific, carrying up all the coal and everything else. She went there at the age of 14.

Vera Musgrove
born 1918

Starting Work in 1974

I was on the board of governors of Eastwood Comprehensive School from 1974 to 1977. I still have a copy of a report presented at one of the meetings which listed the first jobs taken up by pupils leaving the school in 1974 :

Girls: Police Force 1, Hosiery 23, Shop assistants 1, Clerical 21, Banks 5, Hairdressing 2, Hotel work 1, Laboratory assistant 1, Trainee optician 1, Receptionists 2, F.E. College 13.

Boys: Police Force 2, Hosiery 3, Office/Clerical/Sales 22, Engineering 23, Electricians 8, Building 14, Langley Pottery 9, Birnams 3, Mining 6, Printing 4, Chefs 2, Services 3, General factory work 3, Gardener 1, Seaman 1, Jockey 1, Signwriter 1, Farmer 1, Piano tuner 1, F.E. College 4.

Jean Brinsley

A Life on the Buses

My father was a policeman, and in 1934 we came to live at Underwood. Our house was next door to the Midland General Omnibus Company's garage. With the coming and going of the buses and the clanking of doors we soon realised that we were living right against a very busy industry. I was 18 years old at the time and a motorcyclist, so I did not use the buses. I worked for several years at the pipeyard and brickyard at Jacksdale until 1937 when I applied for employment with Midland General. I was interviewed at the head office at Langley Mill by Mr Laing, the Traffic Manager, who set me on to be trained at Underwood as a bus conductor.

A Century Remembered

Bernard Pass (right), pictured in conductor's uniform in 1938, worked for the Midland General Omnibus Co. and its successors for 43 years

However, he made it quite clear that while I was being trained the company would pay no wages!

Underwood garage operated three main services: routes B3 and C5 Alfreton to Nottingham, and B4 South Normanton to Nottingham. There were also various colliery and school services. I trained on service buses with a variety of conductors. Once the system had been explained to me I was allowed to take the money and issue tickets. One conductor emphasised that I must be very careful when handling money, particularly giving change, because any shortages in takings would be stopped from my wages. Although the pay was poor — tenpence ha'penny an hour — and with no guaranteed week, I enjoyed the work.

Of course it was not all plain sailing. In those days Nottingham was prone to winter fogs, really thick ones. I remember on one occasion conducting a double-decker to Nottingham. At Cinderhill we ran into fog. By the time we reached Stockhill Lane the driver could not see to drive without assistance so I had to walk in front of the bus, its headlights on, and guide him to Huntingdon Street bus station.

In 1939 I joined the RAF and served for the next six years. I returned to the MGO in November 1945 and resumed my duties as a conductor. After a few weeks the Traffic Manager offered me the position of Inspector which I accepted, and I was based at Mount Street bus station in Nottingham. (Also, in my own time, I entered the driver training school at Langley Mill. I obtained a PSV licence, which was very useful as I could move buses when I felt it was necessary to do so.) It was very busy work; not many people had cars so there were plenty of passengers. At the afternoon peak double-deckers were departing fully-loaded every few minutes.

1947 was a terrible winter, with heavy snow in January and continuous heavy frost day and night for many weeks. It was very difficult for the drivers, and sometimes impossible to keep to the timetable. In 1949 I became a mobile inspector, a new idea by the management. I was allocated a small van and a driver

Page 47

called Walter, a very good man to work with. We travelled the company's area for many years, all year round and in all types of weather, and never had any trouble except for the occasional puncture.

One of the benefits of having a mobile inspector was that a bus could be stopped in many parts of the company's area where the crew never expected to see an official. The inspector would board and check the passengers' tickets. Of course the majority of passengers are honest but a few pay a smaller fare or travel further than they should. I remember an amusing incident when I boarded a bus at North Wingfield and checked the tickets. I came across a woman with a little girl beside her. Her ticket was OK, so I asked if she had one for the girl. 'Oh no,' she replied, 'she's not three yet.' The girl piped up, 'I am, Mum, I'm four!' The woman looked very red and uncomfortable and I said, 'I think you'd better pay for her,' so I signalled to the conductor to come and collect the fare. I also told her that she was committing an offence and could get the conductor into trouble. I told the conductor that I would not report him but in future to be more alert.

MGO was very keen on timekeeping. If a bus was three minutes late departing the timetable point the driver would be expected to submit a report on the reason why. If a bus was observed by an official leaving a point before time, there was no excuse for this and the crew would be disciplined.

In 1964 I became Supervisor of the depots at Underwood and Alfreton, and two years later Superintendent at the Langley Mill depot. This was a busy job but very interesting. In 1970 I was sent to Mansfield District as Superintendent. I was there when Trent took over the MGO group companies and in 1973 when East Midland took over Mansfield Traction. I was then sent to Derby as Area Manager, where I was in charge of the six depots throughout Derbyshire.

Mattresses being manufactured at Birnam Products Ltd factory at New Eastwood. Production of mattresses and furniture interiors ceased in 1993.

I retired in 1980. Midland General was a remarkable company, operating efficient services with well maintained buses, good timekeeping and cheap fares. I worked for the companies for 43 years, held many responsible positions and had a very satisfactory life, including the last few years with Trent.

Bernard Pass
born 1915

The New Junior

On August 5th 1959 I arrived at the Eastwood branch of Barclays Bank to commence my employment there. I was greeted at the door by the manager Mr George Noon, 'Good morning. You must be Miss Lockett, my new junior.' As I entered it was the first time I had been inside a bank.

The duties of the junior were to answer the telephone, fill the inkwells, change the blotting paper, prepare statements for the customers and do the errands in the town. Those were the days of mental arithmetic and handwritten ledgers. Cheques were not printed with the customer's name, so sorting them into alphabetical order by reading the signatures was quite a challenge! I especially remember Dr Gladstone's signature. In the 1960s some of our business customers were Bricknell & Williamson (high-class grocers), J H Skelton (the chemist), the Manners Brick Company of New Eastwood, Kenneth Clarke (jeweller), J W Bygrave (builder and undertaker), H S Cockburn (veterinary surgeon) and F R Chambers Ltd (beer, wine and spirit merchants).

Rose Chrich (née Lowe), a teacher at Beauvale School in the 1920s

When the Head Office inspectors paid their annual unannounced visit it was the time of checking to see if all was correct in the books and in the way business was conducted. I was in awe of them the first time they arrived in their dark suits, bowler hats and carrying umbrellas — the real City men! The end-of-year balance necessitated working overtime, as every account was checked and ruled off, and a new page prepared for January 1st.

I remember how heavy the bags of coins were before decimalisation in 1971. Blue bags contained £5 of the old pennies and green bags held £20 of threepenny pieces. The half-crown was my favourite coin in those days. We had two sub-branches, at Jacksdale and Kimberley, and a clerk was sent to those accompanied by a guard who was a retired man from Eastwood. Happy times!

Doreen Lockett
born 1943

The Demise of Mining

In 1868 Barber Walker & Co. sank two shafts at Moorgreen, one producing bright soft coal and the other hard coal, and output commenced in 1871. It had been in production for only nine years when disaster struck. A fire destroyed the headgear and the winding rope of the up cast shaft (there must always be an up cast and a down cast to give a circulation of air). In 1963 production reached an all-time high of one million tonnes. At one time there were 1300 people employed there, but a general decline in both production and manpower forced its final closure in 1985. The site was outcropped and the transformation is a silent tribute to the personnel who worked there. The site is now called Colliers Wood. Some of the old workshops have been transformed into factory units to remind us of days gone by.

Moorgreen Colliery in the 1970s. It closed in 1985.

New London, Digby, Woodpit, Speedwell, Kimberley, Babbington (Swingate), Cossall, Babbington (Cinderhill), Moorgreen, Underwood, Brinsley, Pye Hill, Loscoe, Coppice, Woodside and Langley — deep coal mines which for much of the twentieth century gave employment for thousands of men in the Eastwood area are now a distant memory.

Ken Marsland

My Number Six Shovel

John Smith and his wife Mary (née Fisher) lived at Grosvenor Road and had eight children. The six sons all followed in their father's footsteps as miners. John was a 'butty' (contractor) at High Park Colliery and died as a result of a head injury in 1921, aged 57. Mary died in 1954 at the age of 88.

*In my shed there is a shovel, not a very pretty thing.
It is dirty, old and rusty; once I used it with a swing.*

*Then, it had a shiny surface with a polish on the wood.
Then, it had a new stamped number and it felt both firm and good.*

*Carried proudly underground, it had a task to do
Along with other similar tools that also were brand new.*

*A 'stint' of coal was waiting there which had to be removed.
The quality of those working tools was soon to be approved.*

*The end of shift would prove the tale; the coal had been removed.
The shovel was much dirtier now but its worth and 'temper' proved.*

*It had a hole drilled in the pan to fix it to lock and chain.
The tools waited in the dark until the shift came round again.*

*It did its duty many months until replaced again.
I took it home to rest while another shared the chain.*

*As every working miner knows, tools are important to his trade.
Without good tools he'd soon be lost, and find out it was to his cost.*

*The mine has long been closed, the shafts have been filled in.
The coal that once we shovelled has long gone in the bin.*

*The tools that we once used have become museum pieces,
But I still have a number six; my hands still have the creases.*

*When I pass by the mine site, I feel a total stranger.
But when I see my number six it reminds me of the danger.*

*Fred Skillington
born 1931*

Shovels were numbered according to size of pan 2-4-6. Coal stripping needed a large flat shovel to clean out the undercut coal prior to shotfiring. When I worked at Moorgreen Colliery in the 1960s tools were bought from the resident blacksmith who also sharpened pick blades for the next shift.

Fred Skillington

On the day in 1932 that I was to leave Beauvale School my teacher Miss Coe told me that she had got a job for me in the offices at the Wolsey hosiery factory in Kimberley. However, because since birth I had had problems with my sight, my mother decided that it would not be suitable employment. I had a cousin who worked at the Bairnswear factory on Stoney Street in Nottingham and she offered to take me to see if there was a job. I went in fear and trembling — I was only 14, still a child really. Obviously my cousin was well thought-of because the manageress who interviewed me said, 'If you are half as good as Irene, you'll do for me,' and so I was given a job.

I was employed on cutting out, and I really enjoyed it there. It was a long day, leaving home at 7 in the morning and not getting home until 7 at night. For a 48-hour week, including Saturday mornings, I was paid 8/4d. Just over half of that went on bus fares (they were trolley buses then), and I paid sixpence for a penny cup of tea every day. At the end of the week my mother allowed me sixpence for pocket money, so if I wanted to go to the pictures, which cost sevenpence, I got only fivepence the next week!

We had a half-crown a year pay rise, so it went from 8/4d to more than ten shillings. Then we went on to piecework, which meant that we were paid for the amount produced. The rate was a penny farthing a dozen for cutting out backs, fronts, sleeves and collars etc. We were regularly doing 100 dozen, and I think I never earned more than £3 a week. I finished working in 1943 when I was expecting my first child.

Mary Bend

Working at Bairnswear

A reference for Rose Chrich (see photograph on page 49)

A Century Remembered

The Pit-Head Baths

Working in the canteen of Moorgreen Colliery in 1970. On the right is Mary Lees.

With the advent of the provision of showers for the washing away of pit dirt, the lot of miners' wives changed for the better. Gone now were the days of the tin bath hung on a nail on the house wall and the heating up of water for the routine bath in front of the fire in the kitchen. Back scrubbing was now just a memory. The miners now had a key for their own clean locker, and on arriving for work would undress completely, put everything in the locker and lock it in. Most carried a sponge, soap and towel and went into the next area of the locker room to the 'dirty' lockers. These stored the working clothes from the previous shift. If they had been put away wet then they would now have dried hard — 'stiff as boards' we would say as we banged the dust out of them! After work the reverse would happen. The dirty clothes were left in the locker and then the miners took a quick shower, washing each other's back with a sponge or flannel. After putting on clean clothes they would go for a drink in the canteen alongside the baths.

Fred Skillington

Working for the Co-op

I stayed on at school until I was nearly 14 years old (the school leaving age at that time was 13), and then I started work with the local Co-operative Society in their boot and shoe repairing department on Cromford Road, Langley Mill. After about fifteen months working there I was transferred to the grocery shop at Old Brinsley which at that time was managed by Mr J W Marson. I stayed there for six happy years.

Although this was only a very small store we had our own phone line, both internal to other departments and also linked to the national telephone network. How strange it was to watch commercial travellers instantly able to get in touch with their head office using this medium. I vividly remember one chap coming in and ringing up his head office in Scotland and being connected within a couple of minutes to that distant part of the country. At that time it was a real novelty!

Kenneth Poynter

Two Early Hours in the Life of a Railway Lad Porter

The alarm went off at 4.15 a.m. and I could hear my father getting up to make the fire before setting off for work at Brinsley Colliery. I thought I'd just have a doze for half an hour ... 'Ted!' — it was my father calling —'It's a quarter to five!' Blimey, I thought, that half hour's soon gone.

At last I'm ready to go with food basket packed, and on a dark raw frosty November morning at 5.15 I set out with a shiver and I wonder who first started these early morning shifts. It is now 5.35 as I unlock the porter's room at Eastwood Station, make the fire and then start out with keys, hand-lamp, paper, firewood, basket of coal, a duster and a grim determination to have all rooms unlocked, three fires lit and dusting done by 5.50 a.m.

Phew! 5.51 and I've done well. I dash up the steps from the platform to issue tickets for the 5.56 down passenger train. 'Es'wood! Es'wood!' I yell as the train draws in. 'Tickets please!' 'Any fish, Guard?' 'Hurry up there!' I try to talk to three people at once and in one breath.

'Ry forred, Guard!' I shout. Pheep! goes the guard's whistle, and then it's 'Righty away!' from the fireman to the driver, and with a 'pop' on the whistle the train draws out of the station, leaving me scratching my head and moaning 'fish, fish!' I fetch a four-wheeled truck and trundle a ton and a half of fish from the water crane to the archway leading up to the platform.

It is now 6 a.m. and the end of a busy twenty minutes after being in turn station porter, booking clerk, ticket collector, platform porter, and parcels and fish porter.

Edward Painter
born 1911

Edward Painter started work with the LNER as a lad porter at Pye Hill Station in 1927.

Maid of all Work

My great-grandfather John Harris built two houses on Mansfield Road at Underwood. My grandparents lived in one and my great-grandparents in the other. When my mother left school at 14 she simply moved next door to become the maid of all work. She learned from her grandmother all the usual household skills — cleaning, cooking, washing, ironing, sewing and mending.

I never pass Durban House at Eastwood without thinking of my mother. My great-grandfather was a 'butty' (contractor) in the local mine and it was part of my mother's job when a teenager to walk from Underwood along a lonely country road to what is now called Durban House, the colliery company offices. Here she collected, mainly in sovereigns, the men's wages. It was a round trip of eight miles. She walked alone, unescorted, and was never molested. On a Friday evening my great-grandfather and his fellow workers would sit round the kitchen table and share out the money. My mother saw all this and from it got her first experience that money needed to be budgeted.

Vera Musgrove

'It's a Grasser'

Moorgreen Colliery

All is in silence where black coal lies sandwiched between layers of grey rock. Then a shaft is sunk to the coal reserve and a tunnel reaches into the black fossil fuel. The rock roof is supported by stilts of wood or girders and the pit bottom extends. As a shift is completed, the miners gather to be lifted back up the shaft in the cage. The miners have battery lamps and these are turned low to a pilot light.

The cage arrives with stealthy silence and the bells ring to mark its arrival. A 'bantle' of sixteen men then go up the shaft and the cage travels almost silently as do the men. Near the shaft top is a large extractor fan which draws bad air out of the pit. The noise of this fan is the signal of the end of the ride and once above the fan's tunnel, the air changes to the normal above-ground atmosphere. Sometimes the air is wet and cold, sometimes warm and sweet. If the air is sweet the men break their silence and say, 'It's a grasser.'

Fred Skillington

Members of the Eastwood and District Trades Guild on a visit to Fort Dunlop, Birmingham in 1935, including (front row, standing, l to r) Madge Wesson, H Robinson, Elisha Hopkin, George Gascoyne, Will Darrington, Sam Wood, Aubrey Machin, Arthur Neville and Percy Rolling. 'Jakey' Booth is between Messrs Neville and Rolling. On the far right of the back row are George Cliff, Bernard Johnson and Nigel Johnson. The group of ladies standing in the centre include Mary Mather, Maud Hartwell and Lucy Chambers. Immediately above and to the left of them are Arthur Hartwell and George Hawksworth. Seated on the far left of the front row are Miss Chrich and Madge Neville, and standing on the extreme right is Mary Clarke.

Chapter Four

Sundays at Brinsley and Underwood

Six Days Shalt Thou Labour ...

My father grew up at the old Wesleyan Chapel in Brinsley and as a child I attended many events there. I remember particularly the Sunday School anniversaries with the children arranged in tiers on the raised platform. They would be conducted by Uncle Tom, my father's elder brother, who wrote many pretty hymn tunes for the children to sing. On the front row would be my Grandma Musgrove, resplendent in her Sunday-best hat, her chest swelling with pride.

Later, when we moved to Underwood, we attended St Michael's. I hated Sunday because you had to put on your best clothes. In fact I changed my clothes six times on Sundays. First I went to church with my father and brother who were in the choir. I came home, took off the best clothes, put on the old ones to have lunch, got dressed up again and walked with my brother to Underwood School for Sunday School. I came home, took them off again, put them on once more after tea, and this time with the whole family walked back to church for evensong.

The morning service was usually Matins but one Sunday a month it was Sung Eucharist. I used to watch it all taking place, and when I could read I would follow the service in the prayer book. In the Communion service it said 'And the people shall go up in order to the altar,' and I thought that meant those rich people at the front went first and we lesser fry followed on behind. This idea was further cemented when we used to sing 'The rich man in his castle, the poor man at his gate, God made them high or lowly, and ordered their estate.' That set the scene for my politics for life, I think.

We all sat in our own place in church. On going into

Young members of Eastwood Baptist Church enjoying a party in 1951. In the foreground, sitting (l to r) are Leslie Parkes, Donald Wilson, Barry Sheffield, Malcolm Wilson, —. Facing them on the front table are Rosemary Snooks, Mary Bentley, Harold Harwood, —, Pat Timmins, John Cliff. Standing are Eric Godfrey and Roy Bentley, and at the far right of the back table are Kathleen Flett, Mac Minkley and Peter Clarke.

Underwood Church not so long ago I was horrified to find *V. Musgrove* scratched on the pew, very small. At some point I must have been bored! I remember the pew occupied by the Lowes, a large family with six or seven children. The mother sat at one end of the pew, father at the other, the children between them. One by one all the children disappeared. Each had died of tuberculosis — it was such a shock to me. I knew them all, and one by one they died — a sad memory.

Vera Musgrove
born 1918

Hill Top Sundays

Sunday was well observed at Hill Top, not so much in holy worship as in an air of quiet reverence. The sound of silence prevailed. There were none of the weekday profanities and punch-ups, no 'working' activities. The only gardening allowed was the gathering of vegetables for Sunday dinner. No washing could hang on drying lines. There was one tram per hour and scarcely any other traffic. And of course there was no Sunday sport.

Many men took their wives to bed after Sunday dinner, while younger chaps lazed the afternoon away chatting in small groups. They seldom stood, but squatted on their heels, the same position they worked in hewing coal in those low-roofed galleries. I remember how the Sabbath day was also 'rest day' for the farmer and his labourers. They were seldom to be seen, and so children had the freedom of his fields and hedgerows for the delights of chasing rabbits and birdnesting, exciting Sunday afternoon iniquities.

There were other temptations in those fields. We kids always made a detour — on our parents' instructions – around the groups of fifty or more men, all looking guiltily furtive over their shoulders. These were the Sunday pitch-and-toss schools where foolish men gambled their hard-earned wages on the toss of a coin. Other men were posted around them watching for interference by the police.

Percy Cross
born 1906

A Century Remembered

The Salvation Army

The Salvation Army had premises on Victoria Street, until about 1939. When I was young the Rowley family were much involved in it and I think Mr Rowley, who was a greengrocer, was the Captain. I do remember them standing at the junction of Nottingham Road and Victoria Street on Sundays.

*Winifred Stoakes
born 1909*

Salvation Army members Annie Barnes and John (Jack) Burgoyne on their wedding day in Eastwood in 1910.

The Hill Top Mission Church

We lived on Castle Street, and when I was three I was taken by my Mum to the Mission Church at Hill Top (where the Assemblies Of God church is now) for Sunday School. Mrs Holbrook was my teacher and I looked on her like a grandmother. We had stamp albums and each Sunday we were given a stamp depicting the parable she had been talking about. At the end of the year we each received a prize if the album was full. Each first-year child received a Bible.

Sunday School was at 10.30 and 2.30. We had some lovely times. There was the Sunday School Anniversary when we were all decked out in new dresses and hats. Later the girls joined the 'Little Cheerfuls' under the supervision of Miss Kerry Brown and Mrs Schofield who taught us how to knit and do all sorts of useful things. As we grew older we formed a women's group called the Band of Cheer.

As I grew up I went to the other services, joined the choir, played the harmonium and became a Sunday School teacher. At that time the Mission Church was

Captain Fox served the Mission Church from 1926 until approx. 1932.

Page 59

led by a succession of officers from the Church Army, including Captains Hobson, Brown, Fox and Weir, and more recently Sister Palmer. In fact my daughter Janice later became a Church Army Sister and married a Captain. Until 1915 the Mission was part of the parish of Kimberley but was then transferred to Greasley. When I was about 19 Mr Eagle came as the curate and he officiated at my marriage to Cyril in 1942 at Greasley Church.

The Mission was in two houses which we rented and when the owner wanted us to buy it we decided that it was not worth the £100 being asked! For a while we met in a private house on Lynncroft, then the Vicar of Greasley, the Revd Cyril Pegler, rented a schoolroom from the Methodists. In 1964 the chapel from the former RAF camp at Watnall was bought and became the Mission Church on Edward Road which is still in use today. The land on which it stands was being used as allotments but the owner Lady Cowper gave it to us on condition that there would only be a church building on it.

Mary Bend
born 1918

Officers of the Church Army preaching at Hill Top in 1929. Mary Smith, aged 11, is just left of centre with her back to to the camera. Among her friends in the photograph are Bessie Duffield, Melba Gregory, Ida Chambers, Eli Priest, Lily Norman, Addy Worrall and Annie Carlin.

Visiting the Relations

As a young girl living with my parents at Langley Mill, Sunday afternoons were often occupied visiting my father's many relations in Eastwood. We would set out from Langley Mill and walk along the canal towpath. We crossed the bridge over the canal and climbed the stile at the bottom of the fields leading up to Cockerhouse Lane. The path ran through the middle of the field, and at the top on the right hand side was a row of small cottages and on the left a large white house standing out among the trees. The walk along the leafy lane brought us out onto Nethergreen and then onto Greenhills Road until we came to Mill Road (or Cabbage Stalk Lane as my father always called it).

Half way up on the left hand side were some council bungalows where my grandparents lived and this was always our first place to visit. From there we took a path through to Lynncroft where at the top lived Uncle Walter and his family. Half way down lived my great-grandmother Carlin and my great-aunt Elsie. I always found visiting them particularly exciting because they had one of the old 'privies' which had two seats (so you could sit side by side!) with the wood of the seats varnished. At that time there were still fields at the bottom of their garden. Then we went on down to visit another aunt and uncle and their daughter Honoria. After that we turned left onto Walker Street and our last visit to another aunt and uncle who lived opposite the school. We would go back by the main road arriving home in time for tea before going to church.

Jean Brinsley
born 1937

St Mary's Parish Church, Eastwood

My mother was a great worker for St Mary's, sewing, baking and making large quantities of pickles and preserves etc for bazaars and garden parties. I helped her deliver the parish magazines to Nethergreen, Greenhills Road and Lynncroft, and we sold threepenny and sixpenny tickets to be saved up to enable poorer people to spend them at the Christmas bazaar. Garden parties were held in the grounds next to the old Rectory, and sports took place in the adjoining field.

Rose Keech (née Straw)
born 1919

The Hill Top Church of Christ

The now-empty chapel on Dovecote Road was originally known as the Christians Meeting House, and then before it became the Christadelphians' meeting place was the Hill Top Church of Christ. I attended there during my schooldays in the 1940s and '50s when John Diggle was the Superintendent and Miss Winnie Sheldon (later Mrs Diggle) was my Sunday School teacher. Miss Enid Bonser played the piano, and she later married Geoffrey Clifton who assisted with the Sunday School.

Civic leaders Herbert Knapp and Charles Limb and their families were staunch supporters and worshippers, and Mrs Beaver was the caretaker. Prizes were awarded annually for attendance and also for reciting the 'golden text' each Sunday, a verse or sentence from the Bible to be learned by heart.

Every Wednesday evening we met for Sunshine Corner whose signature tune was 'Sunshine Corner, it is very fine. It's for children under 99. All are welcome, seats are given free. Eastwood Sunshine Corner is the place for me.' It consisted mainly of Bible study and learning short 'choruses' such as *Jesus Wants Me For A Sunbeam* and *Root Them Out* ('All those little bunnies in the field of corn — envy, jealousy, malice, pride — don't let those bunnies in your heart abide.')

Hilda Hill
born 1937

Church Of Christ Sunday School outing to Wicksteed Park, c.1949.
Back row (l to r): Geoffrey Clifton, — , John Diggle, — , Enid Bonser, — , — . Middle row: — , Ann Mellors, Barbara Riley, Hilda Skillington, Jean Mann, Margery Burgin, Joyce Langley, — , Albert Nash.
Front row: Roy Clay, — Nash, Billy Holmes, — , Joan Sweet, Jean Price, Pat Cauldwell, — , — , Eva Langley, Margaret Higton, Pat Holmes.

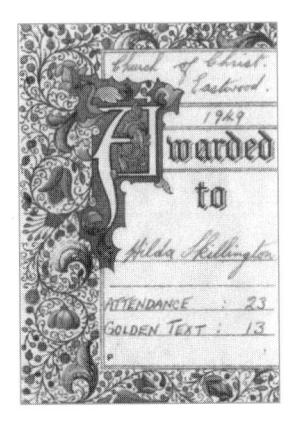

A Century Remembered

The Congregational Church

I attended the Sunday School at the Congregational Church on Albert Street. I wore my best clothes. On Sundays we were not allowed to play any games, and only essential housework such as cooking could be done.

*Sybil Griffin
born 1905*

Members of the Congregational Church on an outing to Codnor Park Monument in 1921. The minister (standing far right) was the Rev Sidney Butler. Sitting centre front are Winifred Brittain, aged 13, with Edna and Gwennie Clements.

My mother was a strong Congregationalist. Her parents and grandparents had founded the church at Riddings, and of course when they moved to Eastwood they attended the Congregational Church which was regarded as very go-ahead. Morning service was at 11, and Sunday School at 10 and 2 o'clock. There was also an evening service, but if you were lucky you were allowed to stay home and not go with your parents to that! I recall two of the ministers, Mr Reid and Mr Finnis. If you had not been in church on Sunday they were down at the shop on Monday morning to see if you were not well and where you were.

One of the great occasions at every chapel was the Sunday School Anniversary. We progressed from sitting on the bottom row of the platform until at the age of 12 or so we reached the top row, and we felt very important when we were up there. Twice a week we had to practise the songs with the choirmaster. The Anniversary was always held in the summer, and the girls wore their best summer dresses.

Winifred Stoakes

I have happy memories of the Congregational Church. There were more than 100 children in the Sunday School, and we all piled onto the platform on Anniversary Day. We did street collecting in the morning and then had three services. The Revd James was the minister and his wife had charge of the Pilots, an active youth organisation. We had prizegivings, Christmas parties and outings to places such as Drayton Manor Park.

David Richmond
born 1938

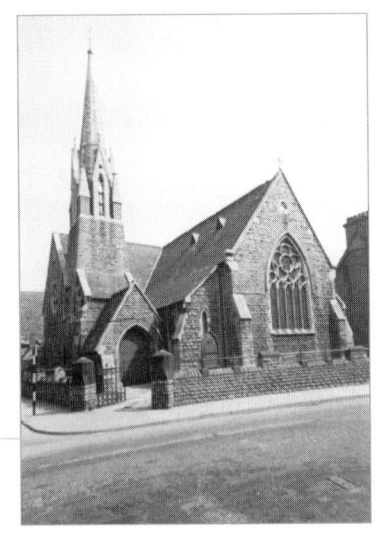

Eastwood Congregational Church at the corner of Albert Street and Nottingham Road (with the former British School behind) was opened in 1868 and demolished in 1971.

Pennies for Heaven

When one of my sisters got so carried away in religious fervour by the poignancy of a Pentecostal chapel sermon, she put her whole 'Saturday penny' spending money on the collection plate. My indignant mother rushed to the parson's house and demanded the penny back, but the request was equally indignantly refused. In reprisal mother withdrew all family patronage from 'Pentecost' and several other families followed suit in sympathy. A prominent Eastwood lady called at Cross's house two weeks later with a penny and apologised on behalf of Pentecost. Mam stuck her nose in the air saying, 'No thank you very much. I don't want charity. I want that penny handed over by the parson himself with his personal apology!' She did get the penny back although it was many weeks before the parson admitted defeat. That 'Pentecost penny' feud lasted nearly three months.

Percy Cross

Newthorpe Common Methodist Church's Year

The 'Crusaders' children's group from Newthorpe Common Methodist Church on an outing to Newstead Abbey in 1959. Back row (l to r): Brian Fearn, Lesley Etches, Peter Clarke. Middle row: Marlene Pazzura, Sylvia Ellis, Glenis Ward, Kathryn Bull, Dorothy Bull. Front row: Christine Jones, Jean Kirkham.

Newthorpe Common Methodist Church's year began in February with the Men's Effort, a concert and sketches on the Saturday and special services on Sunday, the men's voices in harmony in the choir. In March came the Ladies Bright Hour Weekend: special services on the Sunday and a Rally of local churches with a 'roll call' on Monday afternoon. The Sunday School children were practising in May for the Anniversary services the following month. In July flower services morning and evening filled the church with floral decorations in pretty vases and jugs. September brought the Harvest Festival weekend: Saturday evening was busy with a hot pie supper for up to 150 people, and the Sunday services were full of colour and spectacle. November saw the Choir Weekend flourish with special events and the rendition of anthems and cantatas, and the year ended with the Church's Birthday with the usual services, nativity and guest preachers.

Stella Burrows (née Meakin)
born 1924

The Sunday School Anniversary

The Sunday School Anniversary day was the highlight of the local chapels' year. Each Sunday School had its own special Sunday, and adult choir members were borrowed from each to help the others. At Newthorpe Common Methodist Church in the 1940s and '50s our day began with the older scholars and helpers arriving early to collect their tins and scuttling off to their designated street to collect money for the 'Chapel Anniversary.'

As children our preparations began weeks before with singing and recitation practice and the power struggle to see who was tall enough to stand on the top row of the platform. We achieved this by craftily raising our feet slightly within our shoes so as not to arouse suspicion — strange how each child suddenly grew one inch taller! Then there was the Anniversary dress or suit to buy, and this garment would be worn every Sunday thereafter for a year as 'best.' The Saturday night before the big day was equally exciting, waiting for Mother to produce the rags which would make ringlets in my hair. These were stoically endured all night in order to look pretty the next day.

The big day arrived. All the girls gathered at the Sunday School wearing headscarves to hide the tell-tale curlers and rags. Off we went to march through the streets, stopping at every corner to sing. The boys were swooped upon by Willie Templeman to carry the portable organ which was set up, played, then packed up for the next venue. Residents appeared at their doorsteps to cheer us, wish us well and put money in the collecting tins. Our teachers, Mr Limb and Mr Kirkham, took turns to shout the Gospel and invite the friends to 'support the children.' Some older folk still called the occasion 'the sermons,' and everyone seemed to be as happy and excited as we were. Our route took us down Newthorpe Common, up Nottingham Road to Hill Top and ended at Chapel Street, New Eastwood (the original site of our Tents Chapel).

There was just enough time to rush home for a quick dinner, change and be back at Sunday School for the afternoon service which was repeated in the evening.

Newthorpe Common Methodist Church Sunday School Anniversary Day, c.1959.
Back row (l to r): Billy Templeman, David Kirkham, Dorothy Bull, Susan Tomlinson, Glenis Ward, —, Barbara Wheeler.
6th row: —, —, Jennifer Lord, —, —, Elvia Howitt, Jean Hill.
5th row: —, —, Lynn Carlisle, —, —, Sherida Leivers, Lesley Etches.
4th row: David Cooper, Freddie Watkinson, Ann Dolby, Margaret Davies, Christine Jones, Jean Kirkham.
3rd row: David Rowley, Peter Cooper, Peter Clarke, Gillian Spencer, —, —.
2nd row: Malcolm Jones, —, Joy Smith, Christine Clay, Sylvia Ellis, Christine Webster, —.
Front row: Dorothy Watkinson, Carol Clay, Susan Price, Annette Mellors.
Leaders: Bill Limb (left) and Douglas Kirkham.

The chapel was filled with grandparents, aunts, uncles and friends. The hand-built wooden platform was crammed with neatly dressed, well behaved children who sang under the strict but loving tuition of their conductor, Eric Templeman. The money collected went towards Sunday School prizes and the annual outing. Everyone who took part in the Anniversaries will remember with happiness their Sunday School days.

Jean Duckworth
born 1941

Newthorpe Common Methodist Church Sunday School outing to Drayton Manor Park in 1962.
Back row (l to r): David Kirkham, Billy Templeman, Tom Farnsworth.
3rd row: Eric Templeman (holding Kathryn Bull), Vera Kirkham, Betty Farnsworth, Doris Bull, —, Mary Templeman, —, —, Jean Leverton, —, Jean Holroyd, Miss Wilson, Dorothy Smith, Mrs Twells, Douglas Kirkham, Margaret Uren, Charles Uren.
2nd row: —, Billy Hayward, John Mellors, —, Susan Bull, Audrey Gibson (adult), Glenda Birch, Susan Tomlinson, Cynthia Horridge, Mrs Brown, Mrs Tomlinson, Brenda Clark.
Front row: —, Ian Moseley, Steven Scott, Susan Scott, Sandra Smith, Jane Gibson, Jenny Kitchen, —, Peter Kirkham, Neil Farnsworth, Christopher Uren, Jane Inger, Mary Holroyd.
Kneeling (l to r): Jean Kirkham, Janet Kitchen, Christine Webster, Ann Farnsworth

I wish I were a fairy
I wish it oh so much
When all collection boxes
I with my wand could touch.

Then every big brown penny
I'd turn to half a crown.
Then we should have the biggest
collection in the town.

But since I'm not a fairy
But just a girl so small
And can't turn pence to silver
and have a wand at all.

I want you please remember
To raise the funds we need
Will require every effort
These little lambs to feed.

It costs a lot of money
To give us all a tea,
And then there are the prizes
To buy besides you see.

So now I leave it with you
To do your very best
And each one give a bumper
To set our minds at rest.

You all can be a fairy
And use the magic wand
To make this year's collection
The greatest in the land.

A collection piece written by William Templeman for the Newthorpe Common Methodist Church Sunday School Anniversary 1941

Jean Kirkham

Chapter Five

Hard Times

I was born into a desperately poor family. Nine months after his marriage in 1901 and three months before the birth of his son, my father started having epileptic fits. No cure, or effective treatment, was known in those days so his work was only intermittent. After the birth of her son, mother had rheumatic fever which seriously damaged her heart. However, with no help from the State, she cleaned and washed for other people, father often accompanying her. I was the last of three children. What a wealth of love was bestowed upon me from the family, especially my mother. Our house was ever open and people came with their problems. My mother's would be greater but still she listened and helped. Her creed was instilled into her children — consideration for others and good manners will get you what money won't.

Of course money was important then, as there was never enough to pay all the bills. Many weeks the only contribution would be the lodger's board and my brother's small wage from the pit. I learned early to help out, but was always grateful I wasn't sent to the pawn shop. It was a sad circle: Monday morning would see my brother's best suit go and my father's black one, if it wasn't already there. Then with the money I paid the Co-op grocery bill and the rent, and mother paid the weekly clothing club.

In the days of short-time working many men were employed on a day-to-day basis. I remember my brother walking to the pit not knowing if he would be kept on. He was usually lucky. Then on Saturday morning I would be sent to perhaps three different addresses, sometimes a mile apart, to collect the money for each day's work.

Friday afternoon saw me at the blacksmith's with my brother's pick blade to be sharpened ready for Monday morning. I would have done anything for him. I was so sorry he had to work so hard. When he was 16 he told his employers he was 18, the age necessary to work on the coal face and so get more money.

Alice Geeson
born 1912

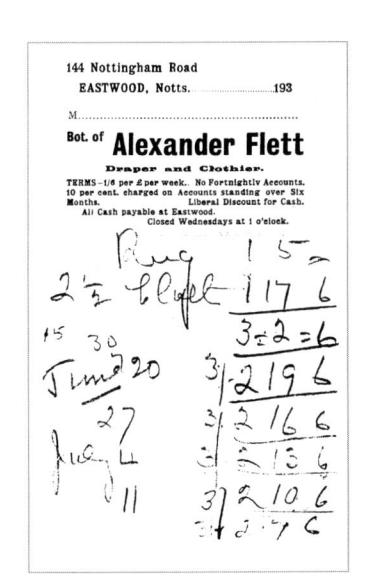

People are much better dressed today, especially the children. When I was young I have seen children of my own age going to school in very tattered and torn clothes, and often hardly any shoes on their feet.

Kenneth Poynter
born 1904

Any ordinary family might have prospered over the years with our shop at the corner of Nottingham Road and Dovecote Road which did quite a good trade. However, with my parents' lack of education and business acumen and with having 14 children, we always struggled to make ends meet. I remember us being twice thrown out onto the street because we could not pay the rent of 3/6d. Mother and father, huddled in overcoats, spent the night on the pavement with the furniture, while we children slept on chairs or on the floor of the Christians Meeting House on Dovecote Road. The Eastwood pawn shop was a God-sent blessing in so many crises. We had three items for regular pawning — a nice wall clock, a blue serge man's suit (too precious to be worn, and kept wrapped in brown paper in mother's drawer), and three blankets. They went back and forth like yo-yos for many a year!

There was a woman on Raglan Street who had a 'pool' of men's and women's black mourning wear for poor folks — free of course. They were worn for the sad occasion then returned for the next customer. What did it matter if a man's trousers were four or five inches short in the leg? Or his hat was too large or too small (it had to be worn, not carried)? Or his wife hobbled along in odd shoes that didn't fit? Nobody laughed, for they understood.

Percy Cross
born 1906

Making Ends Meet

The British School on Albert Street also served as an unemployment and benefits office in the 1920s.

'Bits and Bobs'

My father was a miner, but not in good health, and he never knew what it was to make a whole week's wages. My mother, as well as doing the regular weekly laundry for Mrs Hartley, the Eastwood undertaker's wife, was glad to earn extra money by doing 'bits and bobs.' After Mr Hartley died, she would do decorating for his widow, the payment being 1/6d for painting the walls and ceilings. She also cleaned for Mrs Hayes at the Lord Nelson pub, doing all the dirty jobs like cleaning spittoons and toilets, again for 1/6d — this seemed to be the regular rate. When my grandmother came to live with us, we had only half a crown a week 'parish money' for her keep. However, although we never had anything to spare we were always kept clean and we had all the basic necessities.

Mary Bend
born 1918

Helping One Another

In 1918 I went to work at Brown's chocolate factory in Castle Gate, Nottingham. (One of the directors, Mr Ball, was related to Albert Ball VC, the airman.) I became an overlooker and was allowed to bring home chocolates and Easter eggs to sell cheaply to family, friends and neighbours. These were eagerly looked for as times were hard and luxuries few.

It is something of a cliché to say that people were more neighbourly in those days but I do remember Greenhills Road being like one big family. With no help from the State, sickness, bereavement or loss of work for the breadwinner meant real hardship. Neighbours all rallied round to help with cooking, washing, ironing, caring for the children etc., and no-one went hungry. I remember my father coming home and then taking the freshly baked bread to give away, and my mother having to start baking more.

Nellie Wilson (née Straw)
born 1903

Hill Top Sundays

On Sunday afternoons in midsummer heat Hill Top square had its drowsy siesta-like atmosphere broken by a straggle of beggars and tramps (and a few Sunday trading opportunists), all acceptors of kicks and charity. Some of them looked cringing and beaten, others still clung to a bit of respectability and defiance. There were several shabby armless or legless soldier veterans showing off their medals (and the nation's ingratitude to its heroes). And I cannot forget my feelings of pity for a dirty old woman who clasped a baby tight-wrapped in her shawl, with two other ragged kids clinging to her skirts as she sang tunelessly and feebly — until Mam told us she was a fake from Kimberley, who ought to be in prison because the 'baby' she held was just a bundle of rags. To all these desperate appeals for charity our mother changed her favours each week, but her expenditure seldom varied — six ha'pennies for the lucky half dozen.

Percy Cross

The 1921 and 1926 Strikes

By 1921 the colliers were demanding more wages, better working conditions, less hours etc., and the mine owners were reluctant to grant any new additions to the existing conditions. At this time coal cost from 14 shillings to £1 per ton, delivered and tipped on the street as near to your home as possible.

1921 was a trying time for all — the colliers and their families, tradesmen and civil authorities alike. Conditions became very bad; there was no coal to deliver and all the miners' allocation of coal was stopped. In due course quite a number of the miners around the district decided to start 'outcropping' (a form of surface mining) in the fields at the bottom of the 'common gardens' or allotments. These fields belonged to the Rollings, a local landowning family, who kindly gave permission for this operation to be carried out. The miners dug deep down until they reached the 'bastard' seams of coal which were of very inferior quality. Nevertheless it was coal and the old people in the area were glad to use it.

My father and two or three of his pals decided to sink a shaft and get what they could. Many of these shafts were sunk in a position to serve two or three streets in their immediate area. My father and his friends were thus able to see to it that the elderly people in Queen Street, where we lived, and several streets around had a plentiful supply. It was my job, along with one or two friends, to see that these people had at least a bit of coal to keep them going. I went to see Captain Chambers about borrowing the Boy Scouts' trek-cart (a hand-pulled cart for transporting the Scouts' camping equipment etc.) I was a member of the Cadet Corps at that time so permission was given to use the cart. We took quite a number of bags to the elderly before our respective fathers took any for themselves, and we did so on the understanding that 'we must not, under any circumstances, accept anything, neither money nor kind, from the old people.'

Kenneth Poynter

I cannot remember the 1921 Strike, but my mother told me that she stood for hours in a queue for perhaps half a pound of lard, only to find out there was nothing left when she reached the front.

Mary Bend

In the evening we would often pass the time by going for long walks, sometimes until past midnight. Whole communities would walk together and I well remember listening with my father to the sound of men singing in the distance. It turned out to be miners from the Buildings area of Eastwood on such a walk. The singing, needless to say, was not because they were drunk — they had no money for public houses — but was for companionship, and it sounded just like a church choir.

The local Co-operative Society helped many a miner's family during this difficult period. It affected the tradespeople so much that employees of the Society, including myself, had to have a week or two on the dole in rotation on account of the trade being badly hit. I had to go to the Midland Bank every Friday dinner time for £40 or £50 worth of change. I remember Mr Daniels the manager saying, 'Don't let anyone stop you on your bike whilst carrying so much money.' I think he was afraid of the miners waylaying and robbing me. That's how desperate times were getting.

The miners had no coal allocation during this time (April), but fortunately that particular year provided one of the earliest warm springs which helped some. Even so we still had to be able to cook our meals. Because we had such a small amount of coal to heat the oven my father bought us our first gas-ring, another modern miracle and an aid which I thought was absolutely marvellous.

Although the first strike did not last long it was to be the forerunner of a further series of social changes. More and more demands were being made by the ordinary worker. After the end of the Great War he had been promised so much and this did not seem to be appearing. He now thought it was high time that things got moving. Pressure was mounting between social groups, and the old unquestioned obedience of 'mister' to 'master' was no longer being taken for granted. The miner had something to say and now he was going to speak out.

Kenneth Poynter

I remember in the 1926 Strike that we children from Castle Street were able to go on Saturday dinner times to the General Havelock pub at Hill Top (where the Man In Space is now) to be given a basin of soup by Mr and Mrs Fish, the licensees. Also Beauvale School used to supplement our diet once a week with potted meat sandwiches and a mug of cocoa.

Mary Bend

A Century Remembered

A mine shaft dug at the rear of the Lord Raglan on Newthorpe Common c.1913.
Standing (l to r): Jakey Booth, Mr Burrows, Mr Wesson, J Lawson. Sitting: Mr Wright (the owner), Mr Beresford, T Hazeldine.

Towards 1926 trouble was again approaching. The majority of workers were again becoming dissatisfied with their wages and working conditions. They were beginning to want better and safer conditions for their respective labours, shorter hours per week, and certainly more money in their pay packets. This time however they had the unions to help them fight for their rights, and they were determined to stick things out no matter what the cost.

On May 1st 1926 a general strike was called, and this brought everything once again to a standstill. It was a long and bitter struggle for everyone, with everywhere the sight of queues forming for essential commodities. Shopkeepers were losing trade and as a shop employee myself I occasionally, along with my other workmates, had to take a week off without wages. I was working for the Co-op which was considered a 'good' job, having a full week's holiday with pay. However, at least I was working although some of those people out on strike were not too sympathetic for me. My pay at this time was approximately £2 10s and because of the fluctuations and instability of money I was sometimes paid in gold coin (sovereigns or half-sovereigns).

As they had done in 1921 the miners started outcropping again, only this time on a much larger and better organised scale. They were now able to drive footrails, i.e. digging down at an angle to enable a person to walk down to the coal face. My father took me down one of them and it was very interesting for me to see how the men used timber to hold the roof and sides from caving in. The working conditions were considerably better than in the vertical shafts dug in the 1921 strike.

Kenneth Poynter

Devonshire Drive School seemed a huge building to a five-year old, away from the security of home for the first time. One day in 1926 our teacher lined us up, two by two, and told us to put on our hats as we were going for a walk. We went about 200 yards to Church Walk into a building known as the Old School Room (where Plumptre Hall now stands). It was very dark inside as the windows were high up. Wooden tables had been set up, and some ladies gave each of us a blue paper bag — the sort that sugar used to be sold in — containing a slice of cake and a jam sandwich. Of course this was a welcome treat as food was in short supply, with most fathers being off work because of the Strike. I remember one of the ladies was Sister Hurst who belonged to the Church Army.

We also went to the old Rectory on Ivy Lane off Church Street where the Revd and Mrs Ives ran a soup kitchen. There was also one at the Sun Inn, courtesy of Sam Wood, and believe me that soup was very welcome for many families. Most men were digging for coal — anywhere, even in their own back gardens — as fuel for cooking and heating. Any surplus coal was sold to local businesses and the money divided amongst the men to buy other necessities.

Ivy Attenborough (née Williamson)
born 1921

During the 1926 General Strike Joe Hardy, landlord of the old Palmerston Arms on Greenhills Road, prepared coppers full of soup for the local children. They waited in long queues with their bowls to take the soup home, and even if they didn't really need it they went along for the fun! Tea and sugar were distributed in the old boys' school near St Mary's Church.

Rose Keech
born 1919

The old Palmerston Arms on Greenhills Road whose landlord provided soup for local children during the General Strike and at other times of hardship.

Times were difficult for my parents, my father being a miner, and I helped out where I could. I had been very interested in photography for some time, having my own camera and doing my own developing and printing. However, in order to help my father out, I advertised my camera for sale in a magazine and eventually sold it for £1 10s, giving the proceeds to him. Many of the miners were helped out in this way and for example would sometimes be given a 'facer' to enable them to get a drink. This consisted of a small sum of money, perhaps a shilling, enabling them to buy their first pint at the bar. They would then often be treated to their second pint by businessmen, local shopkeepers who knew them, also drinking at the same pub. The miners continued their strike until November 1926; it was a very trying time for everyone, and a great relief when it came to an end.

Kenneth Poynter

Parish Money

At the time when we married, my husband Jack was only working one week in three, with unemployment money of £1 6s plus two shillings for our baby when she arrived. Although Brenda was born at her paternal grandmother's home we moved soon afterwards to my mother's. By this time Jack was totally unemployed and my mother said that if we lived with her and did the work she would not take any rent from us.

However that didn't last. Mother had been receiving six shillings a week 'parish money' in addition to her ten shillings pension. A form was filled in every six weeks stating the names of people in the household. When our names were added without a financial contribution the officials queried it. I told them my husband was unemployed and I did all the work. They replied, 'Well, you would have to pay rent if you lived elsewhere, wouldn't you?' So my mother's six shillings was taken from her.

Luckily Jack was unemployed for only seven weeks and had been working for one week as a coal lorry driver when a councillor told me of a vacancy for a driver on the council refuse lorry. I was on cloud nine and pushed the baby in her pram to his place of work, weaving dreams all the way about the extra money. He had only ten minutes to reach the Council offices but he made it, leaving me with my continuing dreams.

Alas the bubble burst! The wage of £2 8s for working from 6 a.m. until 4 p.m. Monday to Friday and 12.30 Saturday was just a pittance. Still it was regular and better than the dole. I think those years were the hardest of my life. Three people going out to work and coming in at different times. Through illness my mother was mostly in bed, and there was the baby. The work was hard; electrical equipment was still in the future. So much scrubbing, blackleading and washing. I was worried about my mother's worsening condition, but when she managed to get downstairs I was the happiest girl in Eastwood. With her presence in the living room I could cope with anything.

Eighteen months passed, and we knew a change had to be made. The doctor had said that mother's bed must be downstairs, and Jack and I lived in the front room from teatime onwards. Council houses were being built and we were promised one in the next batch, with an increase of two shillings a week towards the rent. So on my 21st birthday plus one we moved into a new council house where we spent eleven happy years. When I felt sorry for myself about the state of the garden and house and having little furniture and no floor coverings, Mother — ever practical — said, 'Be thankful. You have a new house for a birthday present,' which of course was true.

We had the security of a regular wage, even if it wasn't big. I had a book at the Co-op for groceries. The butcher, greengrocer, milkman and baker called and I paid all this on Saturday. I managed to keep solvent. We paid a shilling per week to a clothing club, a

Alf Lees standing at the cab of a Basford Rural District Council refuse lorry in 1935, similar to the one driven by Alice Geeson's husband. (Basford RDC served the area surrounding Eastwood and, along with Eastwood Urban District Council, became part of Broxtowe Borough Council in 1974.)

shilling on furniture, a further shilling on a mutuality for coal, and sixpence per fortnight to the Foresters Lodge which gave us a half day at the seaside besides paying doctor's bills.

Mother ran a Universal Club, members paying a shilling a week for something in the catalogue on a 'draw' basis. She was thrilled to do it, especially on the night when the names and numbers were drawn. With these draws I had oil-cloth for three floors and stair carpet. Come Saturday night and my purse held six pennies for the penny slot of the gas, but it didn't matter. We had each other and our daughter.

Alice Geeson

A Compensation Man

My father was a banksman at Digby Colliery. At the age of 15 he suffered a fractured skull so he then worked on the screens, and later in the lamp cabin at New London Colliery. After the 1926 general strike he was on a three day week and was not eligible for dole money. Digby closed in 1927 and New London in 1937. The colliers had to seek employment elsewhere mostly at other pits, but Dad being a compensation man was unable to go to other employment and was awarded a lump sum. He then found alternative employment. Retired personnel were eventually paid a pension of ten shillings a week, but if they were caught doing other work their pension was taken away from them. There were virtually no social services.

Ken Marsland
born 1924

Signing On

I remember being unemployed in Eastwood during the 1980s and having to visit the Unemployment Benefits Office situated in the Percy Street Baptist Church, before operations were centralised at Heanor. Walking through the front door, the clients were directed into the side hall where a rank of desks manned by stern-faced clerks was laid out. Access to other areas of the church was denied by a stack of chairs blocking the passageway, and often the directional signs were crudely hand-lettered in marker pen or biro and emblazoned with huge arrows. Behind the desks were placed tables with filing-cabinet drawers arrayed in neat lines. These held the client details in small cardboard files, set out in alphabetical order by surname. Next to these was the telephone, the link to the main office at Heanor.

The Benefits Agency was only present in the church each Wednesday from 9.15 until 12 noon. If one was delayed and missed the deadline, the single option was to dash up to Heanor before the claim was discontinued. The difficulty and confusion encountered in re-opening the claim had to be seen to be believed and was best avoided if possible! I wonder if this was purposely planned to encourage good timekeeping?

The length of the queue tended to grow and shrink according to the time of year or level of unemployment. Occasionally the line would stretch almost to the front door, while at other times I had instant access to the clerks — always a relief! The people stood in silence with bowed heads and glazed eyes, although sometimes a couple of young men would meet and their loud voices, peppered with expletives and local slang, would fill the church hall. It was very common to see graffiti scribbled by bored people on the walls, notice boards and window panes. All in all, the atmosphere was quite demoralising.

The fact that the office was almost on our doorstep proved very useful, and I well remember the disappointment and grumbling when the posters announced that we would have to journey to Heanor to sign on. The general feeling was that Heanor was such a long distance to travel and could only inconvenience the claimants — never mind that the service would be improved!

Carl Richards
born 1968

Chapter Six

'We Shall Remember Them'

For King, Queen and Country

Most of my family lie at rest in Greasley churchyard but one grave is missing, that of my brother Bobby who 'lies forever in a foreign field,' a casualty of the First World War. Bobby was my opposite — happy-go-lucky, noisy, good at games. In my infant school years he guarded me from rougher elements. Offered a good training as a boot repairer by our neighbour Sam Riley, Bobby preferred 'a man's life' with his brothers down the pit, but it was not to be for long.

One of the graves in Eastwood Cemetery maintained by the Commonwealth War Graves Commission. Gunner 996396 John Thomas Wharton of the Royal Artillery died on 10 September 1940, aged 29. At his funeral eight comrades from his regiment acted as the bearer party.

Since the outbreak of war in 1914 the sight of soldiers in khaki, long columns of marching men, horses and guns passing through our village day and night had excited Bobby's imagination, and he was only just over 17 years old the day he burst into our home to say that he had 'joined up' in Nottingham and that he would run away if anyone tried to stop him.

Those were days of grave emergency. The war news was bad, with the Germans already shelling Paris and the sound of gunfire audible from the south coast, and the call for more and more cannon fodder was urgent. Bobby was whisked off to Ruddington Camp for the briefest of training, then he was 'over there' and in the front line in a matter of days. There was no embarkation leave for family goodbyes — the guns were calling. In fact we never saw the lad in his uniform. The only letter of his to reach home arrived several days after the dreaded buff envelope marked OHMS containing the message 'The King regrets that your son Robert must be presumed missing, believed killed.'

What heartache Bobby's letter caused — a letter from the dead, written in France. In it were no words of remembrance, no hint of homesickness: 'I am a Lewis gunner ... I've already made good friends ... the grub is fine ... we are already in range of the German "Big Bertha" gun ... we'll be moving up to the front any day now … the chaps all think the war will soon be over.' How sadly prophetic that was for Bobby. Mother had had the letter read out to her several times, and the next day when we were alone she asked me to read it again, slowly. When I had finished she snatched the letter from my hands and threw it on the fire, silent tears of anguish, grief and bitterness in her eyes.

Percy Cross
born 1906

My uncle, John William ('Jack') Saxton, was the second son of Kate and Samuel Saxton, a grocer and ale and stout merchant of Church Street, Eastwood. By 1914 Jack had six brothers and seven sisters. Two of them died in infancy, two brothers served in the war and survived, and one sister died in the great flu epidemic of 1918 while she was nursing wounded soldiers in Eastwood. Jack married Kate Winterbottom of Beauvale at Eastwood Church on January 15th 1906, and they had two sons Claude and Eric who were aged eight and five in 1914 at the outbreak of the First World War. Jack became a sapper in the 249th Field Company, Royal Engineers, but was killed on October 22nd 1917 at Ypres in Belgium. He is buried in the Duhallow A.D.S. Cemetery and his name is listed on the Eastwood War Memorial. His wife remarried and moved with her sons to Troon in Scotland, and many of their descendants still live in that area.

Margaret Chambers (née Braithwaite)

Gunner John Thomas Wharton

Sapper John William Saxton

The Womens' Land Army

Vera Kirkham in her Women's Land Army uniform.

After leaving Walker Street School in 1934 I worked as a machinist at the Vedonis factory at Basford. In August 1941 I volunteered to join the Women's Land Army, which I chose in preference to munitions. Having attended an interview at an office near Marks & Spencer in Nottingham and passed the medical, I was fitted for my uniform — dark green pullover, brown cord breeches, top coat and felt hat. This was the 'walking-out' uniform; the everyday working wear was dungarees and boots!

My first posting was to Kinoulton, south of Nottingham, where I lived with thirty other girls, four or six to a dormitory, in a hostel at Manor Farm, a lovely old four-storeyed house. This was my first experience of living away from home. The day began at 6.30 with the breakfast bell, and then with a packed lunch provided we were sent out to one of six or seven local farms as required. The work was varied: hoeing, sugar beet, and heavy jobs like machine threshing the corn, often working in the chaff hole — a very dirty job. It was very tiring work but I loved being outside in the fresh air.

After a year and a half I was moved to Surfleet, a small village near Spalding, where I worked on a fruit farm. It was a lovely job in the summer climbing the trees and picking plums and pears, as well as raspberries and gooseberries. We sorted them ready for storing or to send to the markets. We worked long hours in the summer into the evenings, but in the winter we did a lot of pruning and 'sticky banding' the trees to catch insects. At Surfleet we were billeted in various houses, including the village post office, and I still keep in touch with one family I lived with. I cycled everywhere, to and from work, to the cinema in Spalding and village 'hops.'

At a farm near Spalding I learnt to work with horses, harrowing or flat rolling. It was lonely but very peaceful, just me and the horse, who seemed to know by instinct when it was 3 o'clock and time to go back home to the stables for food and water! At Spalding I lived in the WLA hostel. Apart from food rationing we were hardly aware that there was a war on. I returned home to Eastwood in 1945 when the war ended, having enjoyed my four years in the Women's Land Army.

Vera Kirkham (née Meakin)
born 1919

A happy group of Land Army girls with their foreman, taking a break from picking plums on a farm at Surfleet in 1944. Vera Kirkham is 2nd from the right on the front row.

A Century Remembered

RAF Watnall 1940-1961

RAF Watnall was a highly secret and important site. It was not an airfield but a very important RAF station for all that. Building of the underground section began as early as 1938 but was not ready until 1940, when No. 12 Group HQ moved to the site from Hucknall. The office block and billets, which were of timber construction, were situated on the west side of the main road; on the opposite side were the workshops, transport and stores etc. The officers' quarters, also timber buildings, were in the grounds of Watnall Hall to the north of the main site. On the east side were the officers' mess, headquarters and the operations block (60 feet below ground). This base had a direct link into the main defence telephone and teleprinter network with direct lines to all operation HQs.

In 1941 work started on a second operations block to the south of the main site on the old Watnall Midland railway station, utilising the tunnel as the underground base. I worked on this site erecting the shuttering for the concrete roof and walls which was a yard (1 metre) thick. The plotting station was transferred from the old church to this site and was known as the Filter Block which housed the top-secret equipment. Through this filter block, which became operational in 1943, came the information received from all the radar and ground control interception stations. Also here were the Air Traffic Control building, guard room and two ejector chamber buildings, all solid brick built.

After the war No. 12 Group HQ moved to RAF Newton in 1946 when the operations block closed. The filter block continued to be used. In 1950 the buildings were updated and the site was used during the top-secret 'ROTOR' programme throughout the 1950s.

RAF Watnall closed in 1961 but the filter block remained in a state of readiness. The heavy metal doors were welded shut, but soon thieves broke in through the venting duct and stole brass and copper nuts and cables. Fires were started and classified documents disappeared — inside the building was a telephone directory of all the secret sites in the UK. Now almost all the RAF buildings to the west of the

John (Jack) Gregory, father of Leila Keam, served in the First World War in the Rifle Brigade and was a prisoner of war in Germany for three years.

main road have gone; on the east side where the operations block stood is now a HGV testing centre, and to the south the former Weather Centre (the Royal Observer Corps site in the war).

As a young apprentice joiner I worked on the first plotting station (the old church), the filter block, and on the erection and finishing of the Log Cabin behind the Royal Oak public house. The Cabin was built to accommodate the extra custom generated from the adjoining camp.

Ken Marsland
born 1924

During the Second World War groups of people got together and collected money – 'comfort funds' – to buy items such as toiletries and wool (to knit gloves, scarves and balaclavas) for making up as parcels to be sent to the troops. The soldiers serving abroad were grateful to receive the parcels as they brought a little touch of their home town to them. I received one from the group in Newthorpe and smiled when I opened it as it contained the woollen items mentioned above. I am pleased to say that they also came in very useful when I returned home in the awful winter of 1947. On behalf of everyone who received a parcel I say a big thank-you.

Ken Marsland

Comfort Funds

PUBLIC NOTICES.
EASTWOOD COMFORTS FUND.

GARDEN FETE

At THE GRANGE, EASTWOOD
(By kind permission of Mr. and Mrs. C. W. Phillips).
WEDNESDAY, JULY 26th, 1944.
To be Opened at 2.30 p.m. by
MRS. C. W. PHILLIPS.

SEVEN STALLS OF USEFUL AND MISCELLANEOUS ARTICLES, CROCKERY, FANCY GOODS, AND GARDEN PRODUCE.
PUNCH AND JUDY PERFORMANCES at 3.15, 5, and 7 p.m
DANCING DISPLAYS, by Betty Rose and Pupils, 4 & 6 p.m
ANKLE COMPETITION (with Stockings), 4.30 p.m.
CHILDREN'S FANCY DRESS PARADE, 5.30 p.m.
PYRAMIDS AND P.T. DISPLAY by Lads' Club, 6.30 p.m
WHIST DRIVE (Voucher Prizes), 7.0 p.m.
SIDE-SHOWS will include—
Bowls, Racing Motors, Darts Competitions, Roll-em-In-, Roulette, Table Skittles, Treasure Hunt, etc.
REFRESHMENTS AT MODERATE CHARGES.

ADMISSION—2.30 to 5.30, 1/-; After 5.30, 6d.; Children, 6d.
If wet, the Event will be held in Eastwood Miners' Welfare.

The Comforts Fund provided parcels which were sent to the troops.

For Douglas Kirkham On Leave From The Army, 1941

It is about three weeks ago when I came home from toil,
My wife came running up to me, she seemed all of a boil.

She said, 'Have you not heard the news? Doug Kirkham's here, that's that.
I've seen him there down Eastwood way, and he wears a great big hat.'

I then did say to my dear wife, 'Look sharp and get my dinner,
Cos if Doug Kirkham comes up much, we are sure to get much thinner.'

So for the present leave the news. A word about his mother —
She's had a very trying time, with one thing and another.

A lot has happened in four years, for him as well as we.
Some have come, and some have gone to their eternity.

So let us all as friends and kin join in a song of praise
That he's been spared to come back safe and renew those happy days.

When he again from us doth go to a place we cannot tell,
Let's hope the journey won't be long, so he can with us dwell.

So now that we have had our fill of trifle, cakes and tea,
Let's all unite in games and song as one big family.

And when it comes to Auld Lang Syne and we go our several ways,
Let's thank the Lord for this grand day of reunion and praise.

Written by William Templeman and read at a celebration at Newthorpe Common Methodist Church for the homecoming of Douglas Kirkham, a local preacher for 50 years until his death in 1999.

Jean Kirkham

The Bevin Boys

Towards the end of the Second World War there were some Bevin Boys working in our area who came from Surrey. Three of them, who at home had belonged to a Christian group called the Guildford Crusaders, started a Bible class for young people which was held at St Mary's Mission Church at the bottom of Church Street, New Eastwood. For added interest there were games and outings including walks and cycle rides, and get-togethers for shared meals. Recruits were gained from the church and from the Lads Club, both at the top of Church Street. The first meetings were held at the hostel where the Bevin Boys lived down Derby Road. The hostel was a former Army camp, just above the Co-op Model Dairy. It had previously housed some prisoners of war who were employed on local farms, and was later to become a mushroom farm before its eventual demolition. The industrial estate stands on the site today.

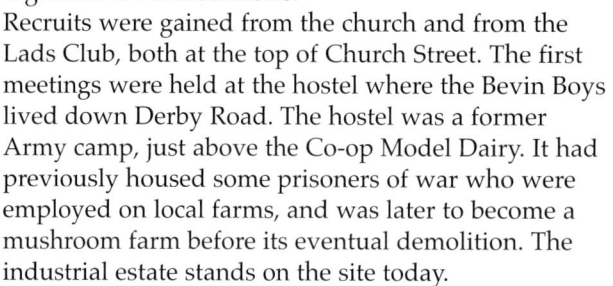

The Bevin Boys were recruits who were conscripted to work in the mines as an alternative to joining the armed forces. Ernest Bevin, the Minister of Labour, faced a nation demanding more coal, so with his usual far-reaching power he directed men into the mining industry, regardless of their suitability or education. From a small nucleus the class grew with some fifteen local lads enrolled. When the Bevin Boys were demobbed to return to 'civvy street' Ron Bestwick from St Mary's Church continued the work and it flourished under his leadership. The Guildford Crusaders kept in touch and in 1948 we got an invitation to go to their annual camp at Portscatho in Cornwall. Some of us managed to get time off work, and in August we found ourselves in deepest Cornwall. Outings were arranged and we visited many famous sites, travelling in an old Bedford Duple bus — I remember Padstow, St Ives and St Just-in-Roseland. These trips entailed long journeys up and down steep narrow winding roads, with the packed bus barely able to climb some of the hills, but the view from the

John Harwood (far right) was one of three Bevin Boys working in the collieries who started a Bible class which met at the old Mission Church in Eastwood. When they returned to Guildford after the war Ron Bestwick (far left) took over the leadership. The local lads on this photograph taken c.1948 on the slope of a hill just above the church at the corner of Newmanleys Road and Church Street include: Back row (l to r): — , Ron Carlisle, Fred Skillington, Kenny Semper, Gordon Leverton, Ron Smith, Kenny Hemsworth. Front row: Kenny Aldred, — , Leslie Turner, Norman Day, — , — , Keith Bentley(?), Barry Daft (wearing a Henry Mellish School blazer). The railway line to Pinxton is in the background.

top made it worthwhile.

We were under canvas on the cliff top overlooking a vast stretch of ocean. The field was a sea of mushrooms so we were camping on our own mushroom farm! We all shared in food preparation and the resulting washing of utensils. Time was set aside for Bible study in groups and then the rest of the day was ours. Exploring on the beach was a must but it took some finding as the sand was at the water-line, and rocks and shingle had to be negotiated to get there. There were rock pools deep enough to swim in, and they contained much marine life — crabs, shellfish, molluscs, limpets and seaweed. The smell of the whole area was something to experience and savour. Work and the acid smells of the factory at Derby seemed to be in another world!

It was a strict regime which prepared us well for later years when we ourselves were conscripted into National Service at the age of 18. Initially we were to serve for two years but this was increased to three years owing to the Korean War and other pressures of the period. After three years of military discipline and work experience, in my case in Bomb Disposal teams, we found ourselves back at work in civvy street as civilians! Old contacts were renewed and the century moved on.

Fred Skillington
born 1931

National Service at RAF Watnall

Having finished my National Service training in 1949 as a Ground Wireless Engineer, I was posted to RAF Watnall to be part of a very small team responsible for the maintenance and operation of transmitters for air traffic control.

Shortly after arriving at Watnall I was instructed with others to report on Remembrance Sunday for church parade. Time dulls the memory of some aspects of that day, but I think we were issued with rifles and then marched from the parade ground at Watnall to Greasley Church. The Vicar, Revd Arnold Doxey, naturally insisted that rifles be left outside the church

— presumably guarded by volunteer corporals and sergeants who were smokers! It was somewhat strange to be in the church again on that day, having worshipped there sometimes with my father who frequently attended and who of course was also there on that occasion. Afterwards it was march back to Watnall and hand in the rifles. Then I had time to bike back home to Eastwood for Sunday lunch, before returning to the camp in time for night-shift duty.

The transmitters were always placed some way from the radio operators. In Watnall's case they were in a field off Main Road (now a housing area around Philip Avenue). Having signed the Official Secrets Act — actually it was only minutes before being demobbed that they realised I had not been asked (or was it ordered?) to do so — I must be a little cautious as to what I can report.

Eastwood Urban District.

Civil Defence Sunday,
24th NOVEMBER, 1940.

At the Invitation of the Eastwood Urban District Council, the following Services will

PARADE

No. 1 PLATOON, "B" CO., 4th BATT. NOTTINGHAM CITY AND DISTRICT GROUP, HOME GUARD.

EASTWOOD SECTION OF NOTTS. SPECIAL CONSTABULARY.

EASTWOOD FIRE BRIGADE and AUXILIARY FIRE SERVICE.

EASTWOOD AIR RAID PRECAUTIONS PERSONNEL, comprising Works, Medical, and Wardens' Services.

All under the direction of Capt. C. Potts, Commanding Officer of "B" Co., No. 4 Batt. Nottingham City and District Group, Home Guard.

The Procession will leave leave the THREE TUNS INN SQUARE at 10.15 a.m., and proceed via Walker Street, Nottingham Road, to Victoria Street.

DIVINE SERVICE
11 a.m.
VICTORIA STREET METHODIST CHURCH,

The problem for our country at that time was the Berlin air-lift. As the Russians had blocked off Berlin from the rest of Germany, air was the only way to supply all that the city needed to survive. Air Traffic Control at Watnall was very involved in part of the action. Russia was jamming our transmissions, i.e. making it difficult to get information clearly in our sector. In great secrecy we changed frequency to stop jamming. However it was only a few days before they found our new wavelength and were able to jam the transmissions once more. I wonder how they found out so soon, or was it — as so often was said at the time — 'did we have Reds under the beds?'

Thank goodness things in Berlin were resolved and common sense prevailed eventually. Had that not been so, there may have been even more names on the memorial in Greasley Church to be commemorated on Remembrance Sunday.

David Machin
born 1929

A Century Remembered

My First Six Weeks of National Service

After serving six years' apprenticeship with J W Bygrave, builders and undertakers of Nottingham Road, Hill Top, I was called up to do my National Service. After passing my medical A1, I was ordered to report to the Army Catering Corps training centre at Ramilles Barracks, Aldershot on March 19th 1959. My train journey started from Langley Mill station, and on arrival at Aldershot we were met by an army truck and taken to the barracks. There we were marched to the Company stores and given a kit bag into which, as we moved along, an array of clothes was thrown. What a shock to the system — I shall never forget it! We were split into squads and marched into our barrack room where we were confronted by a bellowing sergeant and corporal. Being the youngest in a family of eight, I was used to being told what to do by the rest of the family, also at work where I was again the youngest, but never in the manner to which I was to become accustomed. To have someone bellowing at you with his face no more than six inches from yours was unbelievable!

From the end of the Second World War until 1963 more than two and a half million young men were conscripted for two years' National Service in the armed forces. Kenneth Lord (2nd from right) served from 1959 to 1961.

In the next few days we were marched to the barber, the tailor, the church and of course the parade ground where drill practice seemed to go on forever. There was a morning break when an urn of tea was brought out to the side of the parade ground, and we had a mug of tea and a hard-tack biscuit. Those biscuits lived up to their name as one survived being mailed home to Eastwood without breaking! For the first six weeks we were confined to camp with no leave, and most evenings were spent cleaning kit or 'bulling' boots. No matter how hard we tried, the result was never good enough for good old Sergeant Johnson.

We were paid £1 4s 6d a week, and with what little cash we had to spare we went to the camp's NAAFI for a beer or mug of tea. Sundays were taken up with church parade in the morning, cleaning in the afternoon, and another religious meeting on camp. After six weeks — the longest time I had ever been away from home on my own — we had a passing-out parade which was nerve-racking but satisfying when it had gone without a hitch. We were given a 72-hour pass and I made my way home to Eastwood via several trains and missed stops. On this particular leave we were supposed to take all of our kit home, but I left mine in a left-luggage locker at Waterloo station and collected it on my way back to camp!

Kenneth Lord
born 1938

Chapter Seven

The First World War 1914 - 1918

Wartime Life on the Home Front

The First World War enforced many changes in our school life at Beauvale. At first there was a great emphasis on patriotism with military style drill. As events grew more serious school allotments were begun, the girls took up nursing and first aid, and we spent many days helping local farmers with the harvest, feeding livestock and potato picking. We collected tons of blackberries, apples, waste paper, bottles, and tin cans. We also sought out acorns and nut shells which would be ground into tiny fragments to make imitation 'fruit pips' put into substitute turnip jam for the troops — it's a fact!

I can remember hearing the 'Big Bang' which shattered some of the school windows in July 1918. That was the explosion which killed 134 workers at the National Shell Filling Factory at Chilwell. I also remember a local war hero, Sergeant Hemstock from Cross Street, being cheered by the assembled pupils as he told us how he won the Military Medal.

This jingoism simmered down as the casualties mounted and the food queues grew longer. One of my sisters became a tram driver; another was a successful commercial traveller for Baxendales of Nottingham; two others worked in arms factories until bad conditions caused a breakdown in their health and both had a spell in Nottingham General Hospital, where one stayed on as a nurse.

Rationing caused by the German submarine menace became really desperate. We spent many hours in long food queues for tiny amounts of fats. *Eat Less Bread* posters were everywhere. There was no sugar. The Cross family ate nettles and turnip tops, and drank gallons of cabbage water when tea was unobtainable. Beer was also rationed in many pubs.

Percy Cross
born 1906

The beginning of the World War in 1914 brought a drastic change in our way of life. I remember having to wait outside the butcher's shop in order to obtain a portion of whatever it was he had to sell that day. If you were lucky you managed to get something; if not, you just went without. The 'pea-soup kitchen' on Church Walk came into being, and here children could get a bowl of soup which, along with a slice of dry bread, constituted our dinner for that day.

The war years created a different atmosphere locally as many of the older boys were called up into the forces, while the miners were given armbands to wear to show that they were in a reserved occupation. It was also very hard and frustrating for mothers to cater for their families, what with the rationing and shortage of foodstuffs. These were trying times indeed. A miner's wage was not very large, but they made the best of things and always had a cheery word for all.

Kenneth Poynter
born 1904

The Zeppelin Raid

I remember very well one particular night, a rather dark one, in 1916. I had been sent by my mother with a message to Mrs Welcher at the chip shop on Mansfield Road, and in return I was to be given a bag of chips. I was on my way back home again, with my bag of chips, along Nottingham Road and was near Albert Street when suddenly every street lamp went out. To my sorrow up in the air went my precious bag of chips, along with my evening's enjoyment!

Shortly after this the local pit whistles and blowers started to sound, which meant that a Zeppelin air raid was about to take place. The Zeppelin came over Eastwood and dropped its bombs very close to the railway viaducts down Awsworth Lane. The pilot was probably trying to find the ironworks at Bennerley. My father had gone to the Three Tuns that night and as soon as he heard the explosions he came home. On coming down Queen Street he saw in the moonlit sky the Zeppelin heading towards Ilkeston. He rushed into the house to fetch out my mother and me (we had been in the pantry, under the stairs, shivering!) just in time to see the Zeppelin before it disappeared into the night sky.

The next morning when I arrived at school it was all the talk that Ilkeston had been badly hit by bombs. However our teacher Mr Coffey, in order to gain further information, cycled over to Ilkeston and brought back the news that the town had not suffered any damage at all.

Kenneth Poynter

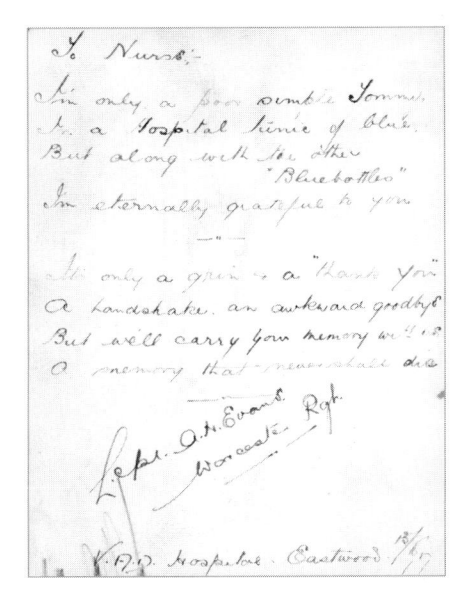

A page from the autograph album belonging to Annie Mellors, a nurse at the Eastwood VAD Hospital for convalescent soldiers on Church Street during the First World War.

I was in the Empire Cinema when the Zeppelin was approaching Eastwood. Mr Fulwood, the plumber's son, then a teenager, was sent to carry me home on his back. Everywhere was in darkness, except for one chink of light from Hawksworth's chip shop window. I can see that chink of light even now. When I got home we went up to our top room on the third floor. We could hear the humming of the engine as the Zeppelin passed right over Eastwood, and with binoculars could see the undercarriage and the men working in it — it was that near. In my mind's eye I can still see it now, like a big cigar and that lighted undercarriage.

Dr Forbes' old house on Church Street was used as a Red Cross convalescent hospital for wounded soldiers from all parts of Britain and other countries. They wore a blue uniform and soon became friendly with the local people. The nurses were members of the VAD, the Voluntary Aid Detachment, and my mother used to go and help there. (The building later became the Lads' Club.)

Winifred Stoakes
born 1909

Far worse than the war, in its death toll, was the great and terrible flu epidemic of 1918, brought on principally by malnutrition. It spread across Europe, killing some 20 million people, and reached England in the autumn. Schools closed for several weeks. A cough or a sneeze caused panic.

In Britain some families lost two or three of their number but the Cross family came through it unscathed. We all wore flannel neckbands and camphor discs. Smarting chest rubs with horse liniment were a nightly operation, and frequent scalding hot drinks of yarrow, wormwood and wood betony all helped to charm the dreaded scourge away — and we survived!

November rains helped to wash the flu away and with them came the Armistice, on the eleventh hour of the eleventh day of the eleventh month. There was no great jubilation however. The loss of fathers, sons and brothers was too poignant for that. All I remember was a solemn service in the square at Hill Top which stopped all traffic, and the lifting of the blackout. Our peace celebrations came in the summer of 1919 with a carnival procession and sports in the field across from Beauvale School which inaugurated it as the new recreation ground.

Percy Cross

The Second World War 1939 - 1945

I remember the day that the Second World War broke out, September 3rd 1939. The Wakes people had come to see us (the Wakes fair was held across the road from our house where Walker Street School now stands), and we were in the living room listening to the wireless. We stood and listened to Mr Chamberlain. The older ones had tears in their eyes; they remembered the First World War which had ended only 21 years before, the worst carnage of a century, a generation wiped out. My own father fought at Ypres.

Every year a service of remembrance was held on the roundabouts at the other Wakes site, on what is now Coronation Park. We went that afternoon, but suddenly the air raid siren sounded and we ran like blazes. I lost my shoe but went back for it. Arriving home in Walker Street we sat in the cellar, but the all-clear sounded shortly afterwards. We were all very scared.

*Enid Goodband
born 1924*

Air Raid Precautions

As a result of increasing international tension the Government decided in 1938 that all children should be issued with gas masks. I remember the evening we received our gas masks at a special distribution held at Beauvale School. As a family we had been looking forward for some time to a visit from our distant New Zealand cousins who were visiting their British relatives. They arrived in time for tea and gave me a box made out of Derbyshire wood which had been taken to New Zealand some years previously. After tea we were taken in their hire car to collect our gas masks. Three sizes were available with a special one for babies. We returned home hoping we would never be required to wear them in a gas attack.

Later that evening we took our cousins to visit my aunt but received an unpleasant surprise on our return. Being unfamiliar with our gas system they had a problem with our bathroom gas mantle, and a strong smell of gas was noticeable on our return. Father had the unexpected opportunity to use his newly acquired gas mask! Our cousins, who had intended staying for several days, decided to leave the following morning. They hurried back to London to book the first available passage home.

Throughout the war we received food parcels from New Zealand at Christmas and were able to thank our younger cousin when she revisited us after the war. We took our gas masks to school and in the early years of the war had to wear them for a short time each afternoon. Thankfully they were never required in an emergency.

Don Chambers
born 1930

Eastwood U.D. Council

Gas Masks

Is Your Gas Mask in Good Repair and fit for **IMMEDIATE USE?**

Consult your Warden NOW

Free Repairs of Gas Masks will Cease at the End of February.

1944 notice

We queued at the British School on Albert Street for our gas masks. We were so afraid of the Germans dropping gas bombs that we carried the masks everywhere. The square cardboard box over your shoulder became a familiar sight. I remember the black-out: black curtains at the windows of houses, there were no street lights, and the buses had dimmed lights and their windows half-painted in green.

> **EASTWOOD URBAN DISTRICT COUNCIL.**
>
> **AIR RAID PRECAUTIONS.**
>
> In connection with the issue of **BABIES' PROTECTIVE HELMETS** and **EXTRA SMALL RESPIRATORS FOR CHILDREN UNDER FOUR YEARS OF AGE**, the Air-Raid Wardens are now visiting residents in the town in order to compile a register of all children under four years of age. Any parents of such children who have not been visited by Saturday evening should immediately get into touch with an Air Raid Warden in order that their children may be registered.
>
> **Neglect to register may result in protection not being available.**
>
> In this connection attention is once more drawn to the need for Wardens. Four part-time unpaid Wardens are needed in the Mansfield Road Sector referred to above, and it is hoped that residents will now get together and find four suitable persons who will undertake the work.
>
> There are still a number of vacancies for Wardens in other parts of the town, and any number of Reserves can also be enrolled. These Reserves will be trained and held in readiness to fill vacancies as they arise.
>
> A. G. WHEELER,
> A.R.P. Sub-Controller.
>
> Eastwood,
> October 12th, 1939.

Enid Goodband

At Beauvale School we had regular fire drills and air raid practices. We carried our gas masks at all times and were allotted billets near the school to which in an emergency we were to run for safety. Many of the houses at the top of Mill Road and on Beauvale would be sent up to a dozen children, and we were sent back to school about ten minutes later.

Evelyn Draper (née Skillington)
born 1934

I was a fire-watcher and, helmet on head, I along with another girl patrolled Dovecote Road as far as the Miners Welfare and back again. When I was working at a factory in Hucknall we often had to stay at night. There was a bed provided, and two of us used to take it in turns to fire-watch at the factory.

Mary Bend
born 1918

When the Second World War started my father became an air raid warden. We had been issued with gas masks, and I remember the first air raid warning siren sounding. My mother took my brother and me to sit under the stairs with our gas masks on and feeling very frightened, until Dad came home to tell us that it had been a false alarm.

Leila Keam
born 1930

On moonlit nights Moorgreen Reservoir was useful to enemy bomber pilots when targetting Hucknall aerodrome.

During the war Moorgreen Reservoir was used as a bombing range. German bomber planes used it as a guide to pinpoint Hucknall Aerodrome especially on moonlit nights when the water glistened like a beacon. The searchlight situated at Felley Mill would try to locate the planes, sweeping the sky with its circle of light.

Maurice Holmes
born 1933

Owing to the proximity of Hucknall Aerodrome and the linked underground operations room at Watnall, barrage balloons and searchlights could be seen in the night sky, and I shall never forget the droning sound from the engines of the aircraft leaving at dusk and returning at dawn. Sometimes a plane would limp back damaged or unable to reach the airfield at Hucknall. I remember following the crowds to Watnall Hill where bits of plane were hanging from the trees, and on to the fields where the wreckage was strewn and kids would pick up fragments as trophies. All factory buildings and the barracks at Watnall Camp were painted with camouflage (khaki and green). Kerbstones, steps and some house and factory bricks were painted white to show the way in the dark.

Evelyn Draper

I can remember sitting at the sewing machine for hours making yards and yards of blackout curtains to cover every window.

Winifred Stoakes

At Walker Street School in the early 1940s there was a real danger of enemy aircraft dropping bombs on us, so it was arranged that if the air raid siren (which was on the police station) sounded we were to run out of school to our billets. Arrangements had been made with local people to give us shelter until the all-clear sounded and then send us back to school. We were given two addresses in case one person was not at home, and with two other boys I was to go either to a house in Grosvenor Road or to Wood Street. The lady at Wood Street had a yapping Pekingese dog and I was afraid of it, so we went to the other house. Luckily we only went when we had two practice runs and one real alert.

Fred Skillington

The second time that I heard the air raid sirens was when I was at the Eastwood Wakes with four girls from work. All the lights went out and everything just stopped. We could hear the drone of the planes but could not see them. It was rather frightening for us all as we were two miles from home. There were buses coming from Nottingham all in darkness, and the conductors told us to get on if we were going as far as the Midland General garage. We were not charged for that ride — I think everybody just wanted to get home.

Betty Richardson
born 1922

EASTWOOD U.D. COUNCIL.

Air Raid Wardens

The duty of the Air Raid Wardens is to advise and help the general public in matters relating to Air Raid Precautions, and in time of danger the Wardens will be at hand to render assistance where required, but primarily in the neighbourhood in which they live.

EASTWOOD HAS NOT YET SUFFICIENT TRAINED WARDENS TO COVER EVERY STREET. More Wardens are urgently needed for the streets named below:—

Lower Derby Road, from Bailey Grove.
Western portion of South Street, and Bailey Grove.
Brookhill Leys Road, Bridge Terrace, and Newmanleys.
Walker Street, Three Tuns Road, and Percy Street.
Mill Road, Lower Beauvale, and The Breach.
Princes Street and Albert Street.
Victoria Street, Scargill Street, and Wellington Street.
Mansfield Road, from Market to Boundary.

Men over 30 and Women over 25 years of age living in or near the streets named above are urgently requested to enrol as part-time Wardens without pay.

Wardens are also needed in other parts of the town to bring the numbers up to establishment and to form the nucleus of a reserve.

Full training will be provided.

Application should be made at the Council Offices any evening, where further details may be obtained and recruits enrolled.

1939 advertisement

My father was an air raid warden, and at the first sound of the siren he would leave the house and patrol the area, making sure all lights were 'blacked out' and checking on the air raid shelters. Mother brought us children downstairs and we were bedded down under stairs or table. (The nearest shelter was at the bottom of Mill Road, a dark dank corrugated shed covered by sandbags.) No lights must show lest the enemy planes should be guided to the populated areas. We drew the blackout curtains or blinds over the existing curtains, and even hand-torches had to be taped over so that the beam fell only on the ground, similarly our bike lamps.

Sticky brown paper criss-crossed all window panes, especially at Beauvale School, in case of flying glass during an air raid. Luckily none came but a stray bomb was unearthed in Moorgreen Pit yard which found its way to our back garden. There it was placed in a fire-bucket and contemplated by father and his fellow wardens who deemed it to be just a 'dud.' As my father was custodian of the stirrup pump, fire practices were held in our garden on Mill Road.

Evelyn Draper

Air Raid Wardens' Fire Practice 1941 - 1942

'Stirrup pump's come, 'Erbert,' said Reg, when Dad called to give him some veg.
'Stirrup pump's just like I said; I'll just goo an gerrit from t' shed.'

A practice night then was arranged — at our house — then it was changed.
'We can't light a fire at night,' Dad said, 'Jerry might see it, and bomb us instead.'

So an afternoon practice was fixed, with a fire encircled by bricks.
Cardboard box and firewood — it was ever so good! — and the pump in a bucket it stood.

The fire was lit in due course, and smouldered away with no force,
So my Dad fetched a tin which contained paraffin, and

A Century Remembered

the fire was away like a horse.

The water was forced down the hose, but directed all over Dad's toes.
'Ovver theer,' he soon said, with a look killed them dead, 'I'm not on fire, tha knows!'

The fire was out in a jiff; the smoke was something to whiff.
'Owd on sorry,' came a call.
'Gizz a match,' I recall, 'Re-light the bugger and quick.'

A 1940 invitation

The fire, re-kindled, did blaze and its warmth us kids did amaze.
Dad said, 'Now all owd on, don't put watter on, or there's nowt ta purrout, lerrit bon.'

And so the practice went on; to us watching kids it was fun.
But the films that we saw, when they showed the real war, taught us things that are still going on.

Reg Plant was the leader of the local air raid wardens, including Herbert Skillington. There were some twenty men in the ARP team around the district.

Fred Skillington

The area surrounding Eastwood and Greasley received its share of bombs mostly jettisoned while the German bombers were being chased by our fighters. One night a stick of bombs was dropped in a line across the area but failed to explode. One hit Alandene Avenue, Watnall with fatal results. It struck the chimney stack and the falling masonry killed a young engaged couple at number 9. Another night a 10 lb bomb fell through the roof of a house on Cliff Boulevard and into the foundations without exploding. On this occasion the occupants survived.

The Luftwaffe over Eastwood

One night German bombers came over on a raid, their presumed target being either Bennerley Viaduct, Bennerley Ironworks or the Pinxton branch line which went over the Giltbrook Viaduct ('40 Bridges.') If the latter was the target the two 500 lb bombs missed it by only a few yards, the only damage being the shattering of all the window panes in the Digby Sidings signal box. One of the bomb's tail fins was found almost intact.

Ken Marsland

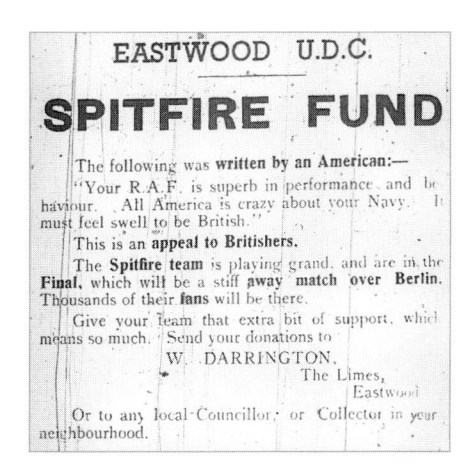

A patriotic appeal, October 1940

It was 2.30 p.m. on Wednesday November 13th 1940 when the siren on Eastwood Police Station sounded and selected pupils from Walker Street School were sent to surrounding safe houses, thus reducing casualties should the school be attacked. The less fortunate simply had to lie under their desks. The Battle of Britain was over, the German Blitz was in its opening stages, and the Midlands was experiencing a concentrated bombing campaign. High explosive and incendiary devices wreaked havoc on the cities of Nottingham, Derby and Sheffield whose factories were contributing a vital service to the war effort.

On November 13th the Luftwaffe were attacking the Stanton & Staveley forge, then situated at Jacksdale, which was heavily employed in making tank tracks and turrets. A Heinkel He111 bomber successfully dropped two bombs onto the plating section and caused considerable damage before coming under fire from the Nottingham and Derby anti-aircraft batteries, forcing the pilot to flee. As he flew south-west in a large circle towards Eastwood, a further bomb dropped into Codnor Reservoir killing a multitude of fish and bringing their bodies to the surface. Every cat around converged for the unexpected treat!

Minutes later in Eastwood children were still straggling back to their classrooms when the bomber and two Spitfires flashed at low level over the school roof. Fighters from 504 (County of Nottingham)

A Century Remembered

Squadron had joined the pursuit and Watnall's anti-aircraft battery also opened fire, showering the area with shrapnel. The Headmaster, Mr A H Scott, frantically shouted to the dumbstruck pupils in the playground to take cover.

As the aircraft approached Baker Road in Giltbrook the final bombs were jettisoned. This was common practice if there was a danger of crashing, or to attempt to gain height and speed quickly, thus minimising the risk of being shot down. The first bomb fell into the garden of number 45, the property of Mrs Rose Stimpson, making a large crater and blowing out windows, while the second landed in the adjacent garden owned by Mrs Fowler. This promptly caused the first crater to be refilled with soil from the second, giving rise to the belief that only one bomb had exploded. Owing to recent rain the earth was sodden and most of the force of the explosion was diffused.

Mrs Chambers had a narrow escape. She had just opened her windows to clean them, and this allowed the shock wave to blow harmlessly through the opening. Less fortunate was the local butcher, Albert Ball, whose van was badly damaged by flying debris as he talked to Mrs Dorothy Walden at the gate of number 49. The full force of the shock wave threw her to the floor. Pupils at Gilthill Primary School saw the aircraft seconds after hearing the explosions, their headmaster demanding — to no avail — that they seek shelter in the bicycle sheds. Later, when the hometime bell sounded the children hurried away to pick up the shrapnel!

The only fatalities were a complete brood of hens owned by a neighbour of Mrs Fowler, but if the bombs had landed mere yards on either side it would certainly have been a grimmer story. In the aftermath the whole area was covered up to the ankles in mud and debris while a few of the residents had to be rehoused. Newspapers the next day confirmed that three German aircraft had been active in the region before being chased off, one crashing in flames off the east coast. By the end of the bombing campaign the Eastwood area had undergone 168 air-raid alerts, with

A Century Remembered

no casualties caused by enemy action. The only casualties occurred as a result of the blackout.

Carl Richards with assistance from Don Chambers, Fred Chambers, Peter Calloway, Les Holdsworth, Mrs E Leary, Patricia Purdy and Mrs V J Wright.

One of the casualties was a crop of potatoes the householder was growing for the war effort. It is said that he remarked, 'Jerry might have waited 'til me taters were ready for picking!'

Ken Marsland

The War Effort

Various events were held to raise funds for the 'war effort.' During Warships Week the people of Eastwood, Greasley and Kimberley aimed to collect £210,000 to adopt the destroyer HMS Kimberley, and the intention of War Weapons Week in May 1941 was to raise £150,000 to pay for 30 aircraft. Everyone was encouraged to keep chickens, pigs and rabbits for the table and to grow their own garden produce, urged on by poster slogans such as *Dig For Victory*.

Ken Marsland

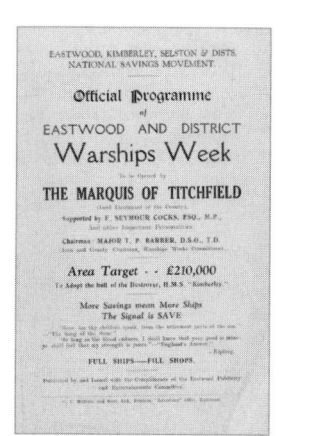

February 1942

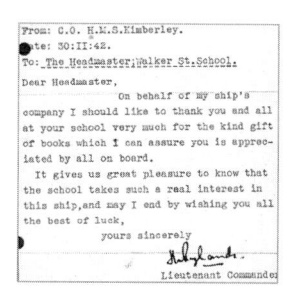

The destroyer HMS Kimberley was 'adopted' by Walker Street and other schools and organisations.

Page 105

A Century Remembered

When I was at Walker Street School we were sent out potato picking. I remember going to a large field near the Horse and Groom at Moorgreen and in the early frosty foggy morning, waiting for the tractor to start spinning out the rows of potatoes from the red sandy soil. We took with us from home a large bucket, a packet of sandwiches, and a drink in a bottle. We felt like farm workers who had left school, but after a while school seemed the easier option. Many sacks were filled, and we took home what we could carry in potatoes. The project lasted until the harvest was in, and then it was back to the 'pen and ink factory' as some described it. Pay was distributed at school but it couldn't have been much or I would have remembered!

Fred Skillington

During the war and for some time afterwards petrol was rationed, which left the roads fairly clear of traffic. We used to walk our cattle from Greasley Castle Farm through Eastwood to grazing land at Langley Mill. Like all farmers I was ordered by the government to plough up some of this grazing land in order to grow wheat for the needs of the country. The army helped us to transport the wheat

The Moorgreen Show in 1951 was held on the Eastwood Hall Park on Mansfield Road. During the war cattle grazed here, on what are now the grounds of the Comprehensive School. (On the right are the houses on Princes Street.)

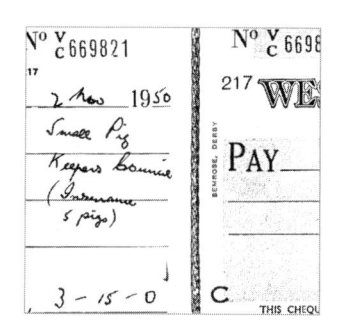

A stub from a Birnam Products Ltd cheque book. During the war (and until 1952) pigs were kept at the New Eastwood factory to help the war effort.

A 1942 appeal to help the war effort

from Langley Mill to Greasley. The cattle also grazed on the Eastwood Hall Park, where the Comprehensive School now stands. From 1950 to 1956 the Moorgreen Show was held on this land. I have seen many changes since 1908 and I am still farming in the year 2000.

James Noon
born 1908

For a long time the Birnam's factory at New Eastwood used to keep a pig — in fact until about 1952. It was kept on some land up the back lane where the field dropped away. In those days you were not allowed to throw away 'swill' (peelings etc.); you had to keep it to be collected from your home like the rubbish. The women at the factory used to bring their swill to work to feed the pig, and there were also leftovers from the canteen. The pig was usually fed up for about two years and then it was killed. There used to be a raffle among the women for four prizes, the four quarters of the pig. They liked the idea of all that pork, but sometimes there were a few tears as well because they had been feeding the pig for so long.

Keith Brindley
born 1936

The school railings at Beauvale were removed to be melted down to be used for weapons, as were burnt-out kettles and pans which were collected, and the dustmen had a trailer for waste paper. Everything was geared to the 'war effort' and much emphasis was put on this at school, especially National Savings collections —usually penny savings stamps. Pig swill bins were placed at the end of every street for food waste. There were posters telling us to *Dig For Victory* with Potato Pete, and so our front lawn gave way to a cabbage patch. We were urged to grow our own food and eke out the meagre rations. We had to *Beware Of The Squander Bug* and *Make Do And Mend* as clothing coupons were scarce. Old faded clothes were turned inside out to make other garments, and shirt collars were turned.

Evelyn Draper

A Century Remembered

'Keep Smiling Through'...
Life Goes On

My wedding was arranged for Easter Saturday, April 12th 1941, and I had decided to wear the lace dress which had been made for me as the Eastwood Carnival Queen in 1939. Because of the rationing, friends and relations saved sugar and fruit and all the ingredients for my wedding cake which Jim Bolton, the baker at Bricknell & Williamson's, made specially for me.

The Eastwood Miners Welfare had been booked for the reception as it was near to St. Mary's Church and the guests would not have far to walk. The organ and choir were also booked, but we were not allowed to have the church bells because they were to be rung only in the event of an enemy invasion. The invitations had been printed at Brittain's, the catering arranged and the drinks and glasses ordered. The local Fire Service had formed the NFS Band and they were going to play the music for dancing in the evening.

So all the preparations were going smoothly until Albert Leivers called at our house to tell us that we would not be able to have the reception at the Welfare as it had been requisitioned for the WAAFs to be billeted there. Instead we were offered the Colliery Institute (now Durban House), and Mr Leivers took the invitations away and paid for them to be altered. Fortunately none had been sent out!

Ivy Attenborough
born 1921

For her marriage to Jim Layton in 1941 Ivy Williamson wore the dress which had been made for her as the 1939 Eastwood Carnival Queen.

BRICKNELL & WILLIAMSON

High-Class
Bakers and Confectioners

Weddings and Parties Catered for.
Trifles and Cream Pastries—a Speciality.

Try our Golden Coburgs.

MANSFIELD ROAD,
EASTWOOD.

1935 advertisement for the firm which made Ivy's wedding cake.

WARNING!

Curtailment of Bus Services

IT IS NECESSARY TO REDUCE FUEL AND TYRE USAGE.

ON AND AFTER SUNDAY, 22nd NOV. The Bus and Trolley Bus Services of the undermentioned Companies will be Curtailed as under:

ORDINARY SUNDAY SERVICES before 1 p.m. will be DISCONTINUED.

EVENING SERVICES DAILY will Cease EARLIER

Except for Special Journeys to carry Essential Workers to and from Work.

The Remaining Services Cannot be Strengthened To Provide Additional Accommodation on Existing Times.

Leaflets giving Details of Ordinary Service Cuts can be obtained from the Offices of:

MIDLAND GENERAL OMNIBUS Co., Ltd.

NOTTS. & DERBY TRACTION CO.

MUST YOU MAKE THAT JOURNEY?

1942 notice

As the young men were called up into the forces, women took over their jobs. I always admired the 'clippies' on the buses, always good-hearted and with plenty of banter — 'Move along there!' The buses were packed to the brim as petrol was rationed and there were very few cars.

Enid Goodband

The 1st Eastwood Guide Company continued through the war years, meeting in the old Girls' School on Church Walk. The Guides were involved in the 'Holidays At Home' scheme, also with the war effort and at its conclusion, with the VE Day celebrations.

Eileen Harvey

The 1st Eastwood Brownies continued to meet during the war, and enjoyed snowballing in the winter of 1939–40.

The 1st Eastwood Brownies pack held its meetings throughout the war, although Saturday afternoons replaced winter evenings to avoid the blackout. The log book for August 29th 1940 records 'short meeting — air raid warning.' Nevertheless a yearly visit to the pantomime at the Theatre Royal was a must, travelling by train. 'January 27th 1940 — terrible day, snow very thick and still snowing. Brownies met in the market for bus to Kimberley, catching the 12.50 p.m. train to Nottingham for the pantomime Mother Goose ... arrived back at Eastwood at 6.30 p.m., still snowing very fast.' 1940 was a famously severe winter but the Brownies had wonderful fun snowballing etc.

Leila Keam

We were young then and took everything in our stride. We only had half a crown pocket money and it had to last a long time. On Friday nights after the 'pictures' we followed, like the Bisto kids, the delicious smell coming from George Hawksworth's chip shop next to the Eastwood Empire. Those lovely golden steak and kidney pies, the rich gravy simmering in a massive pan, and golden chips. Ambrosia!

On Saturdays we danced to Chick Riley and his Hot Spots at the Eastwood Miners Welfare, doing the hokey-cokey, the Lambeth Walk and — my favourite — a slow foxtrot. The Vicar of Greasley organised a dance at the Church Hall. There was a Royal Artillery camp on New Road at Moorgreen, and their cook made the buffet — sandwiches and mock chocolate éclairs, a feast. We danced all night; the hall was packed and there was no shortage of partners — the Army, the RAF and WAAFs from Watnall, and Polish airmen. After the dance we went home in the black-out on our bikes, pedalling like blazes until we reached Newthorpe Main Street and saw some houses.

As I was working in Nottingham I used to go to a little dancing class in Bridlesmith Gate to learn the latest steps. We danced to Victor Sylvester records all evening. We caught the last bus home but were never afraid. Men in those days respected women and invariably would stand and offer a seat on buses and trains. Although we only had about three dresses for dances, we would make them look different each time by pinning on a brooch or flower. We dressed up as much as we could in spite of everything being on clothing coupons. We always bought a little hat to match our one and only suit, high heels and silk stockings (making your one pair last for months). We tried to look nice when the boys came home on leave.

Enid Goodband

The Brownies on an outing to Beauvale Priory in June 1940.

BLACK-OUT TIMES.

	p.m.	a.m.
Fri... July 30th	10.49 to	5.34
Sat., July 31st	10.47 to	5.35
Sun., Aug. 1st	10.45 to	5.36
Mon., Aug. 2nd	10.43 to	5.38
Tues., Aug. 3rd	10.41 to	5.39
Wed., Aug. 4th	10.39 to	5.41
Thurs., Aug. 5th	10.37 to	5.43
Fri., Aug. 6th	10.35 to	5.45

'Double Summer Time' was in force from April to October throughout the war.

A Century Remembered

Pupils at Beauvale School performing Soldier Soldier in the 1940s. Standing on the chairs (l to r) are Pat Oates, Ian Leverton and Norma Turner. Other children include Janice Clarke, Barry Clay, Janet Body, Glenys Wheat, Nigel Stacey and Jean Leverton.

Memories of Beauvale School during the early years of the 1939-45 war are still very fresh in my mind. Behind windows criss-crossed with paper tape we carried on with our lessons as usual. Mr Mollart was our headmaster, and as a teacher was exceptional. In one lesson we had to tell short stories or jokes, and when it was my turn I had to dig deep to remember one. We were all familiar with the names of the German leaders of the war and knew that Rudolf Hess, Hitler's second-in-command, had flown to Scotland and been arrested. Also I remembered that in our comics (*Dandy* or *Beano*) the jokes were printed at the top of the pages, and one came to my rescue: 'Why are there only 25 letters in the German alphabet?' Answer: 'Because S is missing!' Everyone groaned, but it got me off the hook!

Fred Skillington

Every night we sat and wrote to our loved ones after listening to the news. We knew that something was happening — troops marching to the station, tanks lining up at the ports — and at last D-Day. We went to a service at Greasley Church and prayed, 'Oh God, let them be safe.'

Enid Goodband

My friend's father was in the Home Guard as well as working at the pit. We spent our evenings helping to make pictures from the silver paper on cigarette packets and chocolate wrappers, or winding raffia around cardboard milk-tops to make baskets which were sold locally, or clipping up old clothing to make rug bits which were pegged into washed sack bags and used as hearth rugs. I remember letters arriving from our brothers serving in the forces overseas. Whole passages had been blocked out or cut to resemble doilies, where the censors had been at work, and consequently we did not know where the boys were stationed.

Evelyn Draper

Rationing! How ever did our mothers manage to make us a square meal? 2 oz of butter, 2 oz lard, 2 oz margarine, 8 oz sugar, 2 oz tea, and an egg if you could get one.

Enid Goodband

Food Rationing

In the schoolrooms behind the (now demolished) Congregational Church on Albert Street the British Restaurant served excellent plain food, and at the top of Mansfield Road there was the Food Office where ration books were allocated. Shortages were the norm, and our interest was centred on the 'D' and 'E' sweet coupons, the 'E' being worth most.

Evelyn Draper

The food rationing was horrible, but I was lucky in that my husband was stationed in the Orkneys and living in a farmhouse. Thus he was able to send home every week a pound of butter, packed in a wooden cartridge case. For years long after the war was over Mrs Hay used to send us a Christmas turkey all the way from the Orkneys.

We were quite friendly with Mr Glover the pork butcher, and when I used to go into the shop with my ration books he would say, 'What do you want this week, Winnie?' I replied, 'I'll just have the same as you're taking home,' and he would laugh. I never knew what was coming, but Mr Glover's son used to bring it to the house in a cloth-covered basket on his arm and say, 'Father's sent you this.' I took it in, no matter what it was.

Winifred Stoakes

When bananas returned to the shops after the war, it was the first time that many children had seen them. The news soon spread: 'There's bananas at Gregory's!' Very soon there was a queue of people, ration books in hand, outside the shop on Nottingham Road, past the entry and across the front of Boots (which at that time was near Barclays Bank). When we finally reached the counter Ben took the ration book, dipped an indelible pencil into half a rotten orange, marked an X in the 'Specials' square, and then allowed Maud — or was it Sally? — to serve the bananas. Not only was it the first time I'd seen bananas, it was the first and last time I saw a purple orange!

Mick Parkes
born 1939

Evacuees

Evacuees left the big cities in their droves, carrying their gas mask and a few possessions in attaché cases and carrier bags, including a favourite toy. On the lapel of their coat was a label showing their name. On reaching their safe destination they were met at the station and taken to selected homes of people who had room to accept them (this was compulsory). The children were a pitiful sight, fearful of what to expect in their new environment, and many of them cried themselves to sleep for nights on end.

Ken Marsland

As we had two brothers serving in the Army, and consequently a spare bedroom, our parents were allocated some evacuees — the Scoble family from Sidcup in Kent. Despite the overcrowding we got on well but it was with some relief that they decided to return home during the hop picking season and they never returned.

Evelyn Draper

After the Blitz of 1940–41 a period of relative calm existed in Southern England. For the next three years or so schools re-opened, children who had been evacuated returned home, and people led reasonably normal lives in what were abnormal times. This 'peace' was shattered during the summer of 1944 when the V1 and then V2 rockets began to threaten the civilian population. The plans to evacuate children were reinstated, and many children from what is now the London Borough of Merton where I lived were dispatched to the Nottingham area.

I can remember seeing the older children leave. It was a beautiful summer morning and buses had been drawn up into the school playground for the occasion. I returned home with my mother but my older brother, who was 12, left with the other evacuees on what seemed to be more of an adventure holiday than a war evacuation. Not long after, my mother began to receive not very happy letters from my brother and as there were only two of us at home then, my father being away in the Army, she decided that we would leave London as well.

By chance we had a distant relative, Mrs George, living at 98 Church Street, Eastwood, and as she was a widow with a son of my age, she kindly agreed to take us in. There were also two Bevin Boys who worked at a local colliery lodging there. Mrs George worked long hours in a factory, and my mother did the cooking and housekeeping for all of us. (My brother had joined us as well.)

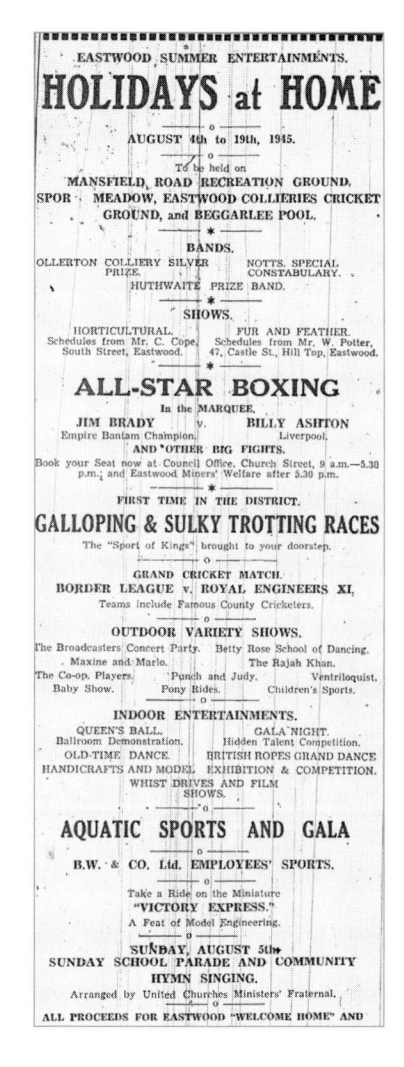

I can vividly remember arriving at Nottingham Victoria Station and being directed to a blue trolley bus which took us to Eastwood. A local lady helped us with the cases and accompanied us to the door of number 98. From then on life was far happier than it had been for a few years. I had to attend the junior school just behind the church and I recall being teased because of my London accent! However I too was soon saying things like 'in 'ouse' and not 'indoors.' This backfired on me when I returned home because by then I had begun to sound very 'Midlands' which sounded odd in Wimbledon.

Most of my memories are very happy. We spent lots of time playing near the Cut at the bottom of Church Street and in the farm fields which were opposite number 98 at that time. We also enjoyed sliding down slag heaps which were plentiful then. As there were no men in the household we had little discipline, which for young boys meant unrestricted fun for most of the time. For a special treat we would be taken to one of the two Eastwood cinemas, or into Nottingham for a special occasion. We returned home in the spring of 1945, but I have always retained fond memories of our evacuation. The people were kind to us, and despite the fact that there was a war on which meant food shortages and hardly any sweets etc., we had a happy childhood.

John Wright

VE Day

At the end of the war came VE Day and VJ Day and almost everybody had a street party. Ours was on the cul-de-sac where we lived on Mill Road, and huge tables were placed end to end along its whole length. The houses were decked with Union Jacks and a piano was brought out for community singing. We finally got street lamps again and we were able to play outdoors and visit areas previously out-of-bounds, especially around Watnall. A hostel on Derby Road which had housed prisoners of war and displaced persons became home to refugees and ex-servicemen, mostly from Poland and the Ukraine. These young men worked in the pits and factories, and many married local girls. The old 'married quarters' situated between Hucknall and Watnall and at Crowhill on New Road, as well as any abandoned buildings, became home to squatters, and equipment or anything left from the war was widely utilised.

Evelyn Draper

A Century Remembered

The Candid Camera: a tale of VE Day

In 1995 as the 50th anniversary celebrations of VE Day loomed ahead, I tried to recall the actual day in 1945 so I quickly thumbed through the family photograph album to revive the memory. Sadly I no longer have it today but there it was then — the original 'snapshot' in black and white, although rather creased and looking worse for wear. 'A photo cannot lie,' someone once said, and there was the 'tell-all' picture to prove the point!

Although my twin brother Ian and I were only three and a half years old on May 8th 1945, memories of the festive occasion flooded into my mind. Every household had been busy preparing for the grand occasion. Union Jacks trapped by sash cord windows hung triumphantly from the upstairs of the terraced houses of Newthorpe Common, and coloured bunting erected across the entrance to Skinners Field fluttered in the breeze. The afternoon's activities would consist of sports and games and a picnic tea for the children. My father, who was tall and strong and considered 'athletic,' organised the sporting events and proudly guarded the hard leather cricket ball which did not bounce when dropped.

VE Day dawned, and excitement mounted among the residents as they were shepherded through the open gate into the front field of Daisy Farm. Normally this was a no-go area for us children, so we felt privileged to be allowed to roam freely within the confines of the hedgerows. Everyone was carefree and happy; the war was over and the relief from tension could be felt. Certainly this would be a day to remember, never to be repeated, when the whole population of Newthorpe Common united in one cause to share their joy, give thanks, and just be free to have fun and picnic in the farmer's field. Today, when I gaze upon the same area, I recall the importance of that day, as the farmhouse, fields, duck pond and cowsheds have now disappeared and a housing estate has replaced the country scene. Over the years the original residents and their descendants have scattered, taking their memories with them.

On that day in 1945 the weather, being fine, presented an ideal setting for sporting activities. Children, grouped into teams according to age, ran three-legged or flat and sack races, while others skipped merrily through a rope. My sister Marion proudly carried home a prize for winning the skipping event. A tug-of-war for grown-ups proved to be a riotous affair and ended with everyone keeling over and sitting on each other, shrieking with abandoned laughter. The cricket match was a rather 'gentlemanly' game as the men played the women, with the proviso that the men bowled and batted left-handed to give the ladies a fair advantage. Later the ladies carried away the trophy!

'Time for tea,' yelled the MC, and the children ran towards the long line of trestles which stretched from the New Inn to the bottom of Grey Street. These rough but adequate tables had been borrowed from pub and chapel and were disguised with table cloths of various colours. Potted meat sandwiches, jellies and jam tarts graced the tables and attracted much attention. No-one knew how so much food could have been provided but mothers, grandmothers and aunties had scrimped and scraped from their ration books to donate the goodies.

It was after the children eagerly scrambled into their seats that the camera 'snapped' the picture for posterity. Each child, with pious dignity, neatly folded hands together and closed eyes to say their prayers — except one little boy, my brother Ian, who was caught on camera happily tucking into a jam tart! Yes, 'be sure your sin will find you out,' as Ian discovered when my mother gazed upon that photograph for the first time.

Jean Duckworth
born 1941

At long last they were coming home, our sweethearts and husbands we had not seen for years. Everybody went mad. I rushed around getting everyone's clothing coupons to buy material for my wedding dress. My sister-in-law made the little bridesmaids' dresses. We saved our rations and managed to get a ham to boil for the reception for which I had booked the Co-op Hall. I was relying on my husband-to-be to bring some tinned fruit from Australia (he was serving in the Pacific Fleet).

The big day arrived and the August weather was perfect. Walking up the aisle at Eastwood Church I was in a dream! Among the wedding presents we received seven water sets, and someone had spent their precious coupons on a pair of sheets in spite of everything being on short supply. My husband only had four days' leave and then had to return to Portsmouth. The time went so fast.

Enid Bailey and Jesse Goodband on their wedding day in 1946

We lived with our parents until we found a house of our own. We were encouraged to *Make Do And Mend*. My generation is still very careful, reluctant to throw things away, and I get angry when I see food wasted. In that sense the war was a good lesson for us, but I wonder how this generation — the 'throw-away society' — would cope? The spirit of comradeship was at its best, everyone helping each other, and it will never be the same again.

Enid Goodband

Chapter Eight

Mansfield Road Shops and Businesses 1936

Shops and Businesses

Bricknell & Williamson, provision dealers
Britannic Assurance Co. Ltd
William Burrows, shopkeeper
Elizabeth Carlin, shopkeeper
Thomas Chambers, butcher
Frederick Chrich, joiner
Percy Clark, newsagent
Ethel Cope, grocer
Eastwood Miners' Welfare Centre
(secretary, Albert Leivers)
William H Gregory, shopkeeper
Kenneth Horton, solicitor
Fred Jones, beer retailer
A Myers, plumber
James Nelson, cabinet maker
Thomas Beresford Nix, Registrar of births and deaths
Ethel Nix, Deputy Registrar
Frank Nix, plumber
William Shepherd, outfitter
William Travers, confectioner
Alvah Webster, fried fish dealer
Percy Wesson, hairdresser
William Worthington, boot repairer

Kelly's Directory of Nottinghamshire 1936

My mother was the caretaker/cleaner at the first Trustee Savings Bank in Eastwood, a tiny shop at the corner of Mansfield Road and the market place. As there was no running water on the premises, she had to take a hot water bottle from home to wash the door step! She would go across the road to Mrs Clark, the newsagent, to fill a kettle for tea.

Rose Keech
born 1919

I lived with my family in Langley Mill until I was almost ten years old. When I was born, my father combined being an electrician at Moorgreen Colliery with being the manager of the Rex Cinema near the Sun Inn. After the war, he bought a watchmakers and jewellery shop on Mansfield Road and then shortly after moved to a shop opposite the

Wellington Inn. He worked there continuously until his death.

The Rt. Hon. Kenneth Clarke, QC, MP
born 1940

Thursday, when the groceries were delivered, was a happy day. My mother would give me sixpence and with that I could buy threepence worth of pie meat; the grocer gave me six cracked eggs for twopence, and the remaining penny was spent on 'specked' apples. With these items and the delivered provisions, my mother made an apple dumpling, apple pasties, an egg custard, a cut-and-come-again cake, and a big meat and potato pie.

I loved shopping, and all the shopkeepers knew me and helped, knowing that our poverty was only caused through illness. During the week, while the money lasted, I visited the pork butchers for savoury ducks with gravy and my mother always told me to bring some pork dripping 'with black in it!' Friday was a favourite day: I collected ninepence for errands I'd done that week and Bricknell's on Mansfield Road had usually saved a ham bone for me. There was usually about a pound of best boiled ham, and also included would be a bag of yesterday's cakes, still beautifully fresh. Then after tea came the weekly trip to the market.

Alice Geeson
born 1912

The market was held on Fridays in front of the Sun Inn and extended into the yard at the back. Although small, it was always lively and stayed open until about 9 p.m.

Constance Barrett
born 1924

1955 advertisement. Clarke's first shop in Eastwood was on Mansfield Road, next the Miners Arms.

The Market Place

A Century Remembered

Of the stalls at Eastwood market I particularly remember 'Mad Harry' who sold pots, and the toffee which was made while you waited.

Mavis Williamson
born 1922

Demolition of Machin & Hartwell's original showroom next to the Sun Inn in 1973 to allow for road widening.

I still have part of the dinner service which I bought from the pot stall on Eastwood market. There was also a penny stall which sold boot laces and black lead. My brother worked as a master baker at Bricknell and Williamson's. I also remember when cattle were driven from Nottingham to the butcher's yard at the end of Eastwood to be slaughtered.

Sybil Griffin
born 1905

Nearly every street corner had a shop on it, often open from early morning until 10 o'clock at night. As a child I lived at Kimberley in the area known as Jubilee Bottoms. The local shopkeepers included a haberdasher, Mrs Hatton, who also had a stall on Eastwood market in front of the Sun Inn on Friday nights for 30 years between the wars and beyond. I remember that hers was the only stall left on the market when the other traders had closed for the night; she stood there all alone.

Every Friday the traders ran a 'Spot the Ace of Spades' competition. A different shop each week would hide a card in their window display, and the first person to spot it could claim the prize which I think was a pound note. The Nottingham newspapers ran similar competitions: the *Evening Post* had a man called Knocker Post, the *Evening News* had Final Freddie, who would knock on doors and if the lucky householder could produce the appropriate newspaper he would be rewarded with a ten shilling note.

Ken Marsland
born 1924

1   Sun Inn, (Landlord, Sam Wood)
5   Frank Brown, wireless engineer
7   Barclays Bank, (Manager, C.W. Harper)
9   Machin & Hartwell, ironmongers
11 Gregory's, fishmongers
13 Boots The Chemists
15 Alfred Piper, confectioner
17 Mary Mather, ladies hairdresser
19 Joseph Burton & Sons Ltd, grocers
21 George Cornelius Sanders, outfitter
23 G C Brittain & Sons, booksellers, printers
      The Eastwood & Kimberley Advertiser
25 Bernard Johnson, confectioner
27 Westminster Bank, (Manager, W.Ground)

Kelly's Directory of Nottinghamshire 1936

Nottingham Road Shops and Businesses in 1936 - from Mansfield Road to Victoria Street

The business was founded in 1922 as a partnership between my father Mr Aubrey E Machin and Mr Arthur Hartwell, trading as ironmongers at 3 (later re-numbered 9) Nottingham Road, Eastwood, next to Barclays Bank, and serving an area of approximately six miles radius. The first year's trading produced a profit of just over £51 on sales of £1777. That profit was shared by each partner and re-invested in the company. The annual wages for both partners totalled £221 12s 6d. Mr Machin lived above the shop with his mother Mrs Annie Machin until his marriage to Miss Elsie Slater when they moved to Ratcliffe Street to live.

From early on in the company's history goods were delivered to customers, at first by motorcycle. As business increased, a showroom for selling 'Yorkist' cooking ranges and tile fireplaces with wood mantels was opened from premises next to the Sun Inn.

Machin and Hartwell - 1922 - 1997

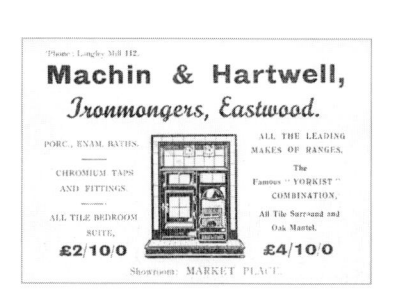

1935 advertisement

A Century Remembered

Nottingham Road in the 1950s. Machin & Hartwell's original shop next to Barclays Bank is on the left. The spire is that of the Congregational Church at the corner of Albert Street.

This showroom was rented from Mr and Mrs Taylor who lived above (Mr Taylor was a retired sea captain). Further storage was later rented from the Eastwood Lads Club on Church Street, using the old stables and carriage storage areas. The rent monies helped towards the running of the Club.

As other buildings at the side of the showroom on Mansfield Road became vacant they were taken to display boilers, all-night-burning fires, and bathroom suites. Further storage for fireplaces and tiles was taken using the old fire station on Derby Road, opposite the Sun Inn. On the death of Mr Hartwell the company was incorporated on January 4th 1950 as Machin & Hartwell Ltd. In 1952 a branch shop was opened at Church Square, Heanor.

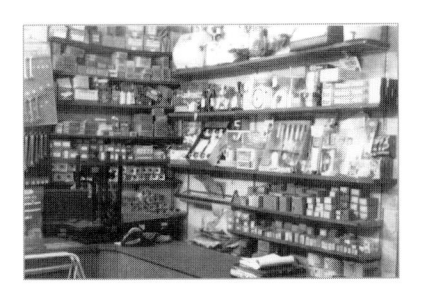

Machin & Hartwell's sales counter in the original shop, c.1962.

July 1964 saw the move from the first Eastwood shop at number 3 across the road to 28 - 30 Nottingham Road, a much larger establishment which had previously been the Co-op butchery and the menswear sales area. The upstairs had been used as a meeting place for the Women's Co-operative Guild, of which D.H.Lawrence's mother Lydia was a member. Shortly after we moved into the new shop a road widening scheme was announced for the crossroads. This caused problems for the company as it would require the demolition of the showrooms next to the Sun Inn, the old fire station on Derby Road and the loss of the large storage areas at the Lads Club. As a precautionary measure, although it was not ideal, the old chapel at the corner of Chewton Street and Nottingham Road at Hill Top was bought from the church authorities as a possible showroom and storage facility.

William Roache (Ken Barlow in Coronation Street) on a promotional visit to the shop at 28–30 Nottingham Road in 1981.

Soon after buying that building we obtained the main Flymo distribution agency to supply mowers, parts, service and training for sub-agents throughout Nottinghamshire, Derbyshire and part of Leicestershire. Later, also via Flymo, an agency for the Toro range of mowers for professional grass cutting of large areas such as cricket fields, golf courses and

Page 123

airfields was added along with its large range of parts and service. The space required for all these operations, together with another agency for Selkirk metal chimneys, took up all the old chapel site. The problem of re-siting the showroom and warehousing was eventually solved in 1973 when we obtained the whole of the site on the corner of Church Street and Derby Road. This included the Lads Club buildings, the old fire station and Skelton's Chemists building.

The new showroom on the corner opened on July 28th 1973, and the old showrooms between the Sun Inn and the Miners Arms were demolished shortly afterwards. The opening of our new sales area was performed by 'Humphrey,' a camel from Hucknall Zoo. He paraded through the streets of Eastwood from Hill Top to Derby Road, draped in a red and white cloth over his back and front to advertise the event. Unfortunately red and white were his least favourite colours and he objected to being so draped. He had to be pacified with lots of apples — and soon the drapes were red, white and brown!

Messrs Flymo, through a sub-company, bought Machin & Hartwell's mower department in 1982. The rest of the company was closed in 1997, just over 75 years after it started.

David Machin
born 1929

David Machin making friends with Humphrey who 'opened' Machin & Hartwell's new showroom at the corner of Church Street and Derby Road in July 1973.

During the First World War my father's family the Gregorys set up in business as florists, greengrocers and fishmongers at 5 (later re-numbered 11) Nottingham Road, opposite the shoe shop and post office belonging to W E Hopkin, D H Lawrence's friend and mentor, with whom they became very friendly.

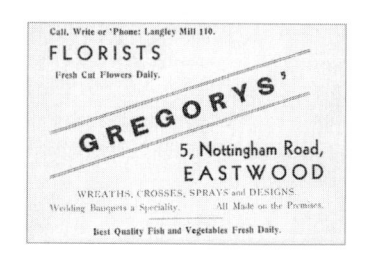

Leila Keam
born 1930

1935 advertisement.

A Century Remembered

Piper's (at no.15) bakery and main shop was at Langley Mill. The younger Piper brother, Alf, ran the Eastwood shop and there was a small restaurant.

Constance Barrett

Brittain's Shop and the Advertiser at 23 Nottingham Road

Winifred Brittain standing in the doorway of the family shop at 23 Nottingham Road in 1930.

In 1874 at the age of 21 my grandfather George Casswell Brittain came from Spalding to Ripley with his new wife Elizabeth and with £100 in his pocket. A printer by trade, he used the money to buy a small printing and stationery business which eventually grew to become G.C. Brittain & Sons Ltd. Their five sons as they came of age all went into various parts of the business.

My grandfather's first newspaper, the *Ripley & Heanor News*, appeared in 1889 and five years later the first edition of the *Eastwood & Kimberley Advertiser* was published on November 30th 1894. The company's first premises in Eastwood was a little shop on Mansfield Road, next to the Miners Arms. My father, Ernest Albert Brittain, then recently married, moved to Eastwood and became editor of the *Advertiser* in 1898, a position he held for nearly sixty years until his retirement in 1957.

As the business expanded they moved to 11 Nottingham Road, then further expansion necessitated another move along the road to number 23 (where the *Advertiser* office still is today). Here I was born, and we lived above and behind the shop until 1921 when we bought a house on Percy Street, and all the living accommodation was then taken into the shop.

In the early days the shop had toys, sports goods, stationery and, of course, the *Advertiser* office. We used to have a few fancy goods but my father was never interested in that. Although I was interested in the shop I had nothing to do with the running of it until I was 50. My parents had never enjoyed the best of health, and as an only child I looked after them and more or less ran the home from the age of 12, even after I was married.

Following the death of my father and other directors I was invited in 1960 to join the board, and was given a free hand to modernise the three shops (at Eastwood, Belper and Ripley). I wanted to bring them up-to-date from their antiquated state, as nothing had been done with them for years. I started with the Eastwood shop, changed the frontage and installed new fittings. I set out to buy high quality merchandise such as good china etc. The shops did very well because there was nowhere between Derby and Nottingham where you could buy Wedgwood, Doulton and the others, although I had a struggle to persuade Wedgwood to sell to me.

Although we could do small printing jobs such as posters, tickets and pamphlets at the Eastwood shop, the *Advertiser* was always printed at Ripley. Every week my father wrote up all the copy at the Eastwood office. He worked very hard and was out nearly every evening reporting meetings and other events which then had to be written up. He also edited the reports from local correspondents. All the copy had to be at Ripley by Wednesday night or Thursday to be printed. Originally of course the type was all set by hand, then we got Linotype machines, and eventually modern machines where the paper went in from a roll at one end and came out at the other end printed, folded and counted. We marvelled at this new technology!

I remember in the early days the newly printed papers came from Ripley in a pony and trap. An office boy carried them into the shop where they were sorted ready for the dozen or so young boys who came to deliver them throughout the area after school. There were not many newsagents then, and most copies were delivered direct. The boys were paid for each dozen; some delivered as many as ten dozen copies.

Winifred Stoakes (née Brittain)
born 1909

A Century Remembered

Nottingham Road Shops and Businesses in 1936 - from Victoria Street to King Street

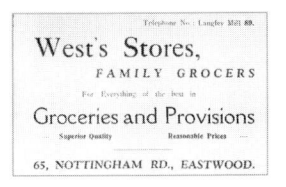

29 Clifford Motories, motor car agents
31 Samuel Brown, confectioner
33 Bertram W Granger, draper
35 Sketchley Dye Works, (receiving office)
37 George Clift, boot dealer
39 John H Naylor, paperhanger
41 Henry Thomas Haynes, draper
43 Grace Edwards, fruiterer
45 William Allcock, shoe maker
49 George Henry Hopkin, newsagent
51 Elizabeth Upton, draper
53 Midland Bank, (Manager, Percy Towlson)
61 Carmi Hillman Turner, china dealer
63 Lily Hartwell, ladies' outfitter
65 West's Stores, grocers
75 Henry Robinson, wholesale confectioner
79 John T Nightingale, wallpaper dealer
85 Reuben Knighton, greengrocer
87 Samuel A Perry, tobacconist
89 Gertrude Coe, milliner
91 William Clarke, gowns
95 Linwood Music Publishing Co. Ltd
97 Holbrook & Co., monumental masons
99 George Hawksworth, fried fish dealer
   Empire Cinema, (Proprietor :F G Stubbs)
   Wellington Inn, (Landlord : Fred Barratt)

Kelly's Directory of Nottinghamshire 1936

West's Stores,
FAMILY GROCERS
For Everything of the best in
Groceries and Provisions
Superior Quality   Reasonable Prices
65, NOTTINGHAM RD., EASTWOOD.

1935 advertisement

Nottingham Road in the 1920s, with Albert Street on the right. Note the tram lines and wires.

Grangers (at no.33) had quite a few shops. In Eastwood it was always known as the 'trimming' shop as it sold little things like laces and ribbons. The Sketchley shop (no.35) was I think one of the first outside the larger towns. I remember they employed a delivery boy, and I vividly recall his bike with a basket in front of the handlebars, and the firm's name emblazoned on a plate down the side of the crossbar. Miss Hartwell (no.63) the dressmaker whose shop was opposite Alexandra Street, was the sister of Arthur Hartwell (of Machin & Hartwell). District Nurse Padgett lived on the corner of Wellington Street (where there was also a maternity nursing home), in the house formerly belonging to Mr Cockburn the vet. Between Wellington Street and Wood Street to the side of Whitelock's house, The Hollies, stood Cherry Tree Cottages. The Carlins lived in one, and the Stones in the other. We used to go there for sewing machine needles, and it eventually became the first office of the Halifax in Eastwood.

Constance Barrett

Allcocks (at no.45) repaired not only boots and shoes, but also furniture. I was friendly with their daughter Betty and often went to the shop. I remember watching fascinated the man who did the shoe repairs as he kept in his mouth dozens of nails which he took out one by one and hammered all round the shoes. Until well after the First World War it was the last shop in that row before Albert Street. From her kitchen window (at that time all shopkeepers lived behind their premises), Mrs Allcock looked out towards the Congregational Church. The Midland Bank was then on Church Street (now the Conservative Club). I recall that during the war two tanks were placed on display on the corner of Albert Street and we went to buy savings certificates which were stamped with a special tank design. It was wonderful — we actually went inside the tank to buy the certificates.

Winifred Stoakes

When I came to Eastwood as Librarian in November 1967 the library was at 47 Nottingham Road and had been there since the 1940s, having moved from Church Street, I believe. The adult library was housed in three small interconnected rooms downstairs. The middle and rear rooms were heated in winter by coal stoves, and I remember some of the older residents would walk up in their carpet slippers from Scargill Street and neighbouring roads to sit by the fire and read a magazine — and they also taught me much about local history!

The shops opposite Alexandra Street c.1900, including West's the grocers.

1935 advertisement

Eastwood Library

A Century Remembered

West's grocers delivery cart outside 72 Nottingham Road (the shop which became Barrett's in 1935).

The children's library was situated above the neighbouring shop (no.45) and was reached by a steep flight of stairs from the shared passageway. Also on the first floor was the original bathroom (I think it must have been the only library in the county with a bath, although the caretaker stored coal in it) and the staff room which was heated by an open coal fire — ah, memories of the toasting-fork for lunchtime beans on toast! We entertained the late Brian Johnston there when he came to Eastwood to record *Down Your Way* in 1972. On the very top floor was a warren of store rooms.

When the shoe shop at number 45 became vacant we moved the children's library downstairs which of course made it much more visible and safely accessible. Eventually the long-awaited purpose-built library on Wellington Place opened in June 1975, with all its much improved and expanded facilities, and 45 - 47 Nottingham Road and the rooms above became home to various businesses.

Michael Bennett

Clifford Motories 1907 - 1982

Clifford Motories was founded in 1907 at 29 Nottingham Road on the corner of Victoria Street, opposite the bank. The shop was opened by my grandfather Arthur Clifford who was married to Susannah Carlin. They had nine children, three boys and six girls. In the early days the shop sold bicycles, records and gramophones, and later motorcycles, accumulators and batteries.

Arthur was one of the first men in Eastwood to own and drive a car. During the Second World War the engineering side of the business was commissioned by Rolls Royce to make parts for aeroplanes, turning out work which was of 1A quality, the highest standard possible.

Arthur died in 1956 but not before he had bought

A Century Remembered

bigger premises at Essex Street behind 164 Nottingham Road, at the other end of Eastwood. Arthur's three sons — Wilfred, Bernard and William — continued to run Clifford Motories, selling and servicing motorcycles and cars until December 1982 when Bernard died and the business was sold. Wilfred died in 1994, and the remaining members of Arthur's family are William ('Bill'), Mabel and Joan.

Fay Hickinbotham (née Clifford)

166 Hector Cockburn, veterinary surgeon
164 Ronald Mervill, fried fish dealer
154 Public Assistance Department
     (Relieving Officer, G H Long)
152 Henry Towle, boot repairer
150 Elisha Hopkin, house agent
148 Fred Hopkin, plumber
144 Alex Flett, tailor
142 Joseph Christian, shopkeeper
138 Frank Wright, shopkeeper
136 William Parker, greengrocer
132 Herbert Greenhalgh,
     cycle repairer
130 George E Gascoyne, dairyman
128 James Brown, printer
126 Elizabeth Hollymould,
     shopkeeper
124 James Gregory, confectioner
122 Gertrude M Platts, newsagent
118 Clarke's Army Stores, clothiers
     Langley Mill & Aldercar
     Co-op. Society
100 James Chambers & Co. Ltd, wholesale chemists
98   William Rowley, greengrocer
96   Sarah Ann Noon, shopkeeper
94   Gwendoline, ladies' hairdresser
92   John Booth, hardware dealer
88   Dorothy Bradley, draper
86   Thomas Austin Blowers, auctioneers
     Royal Billiard Saloon (Prop.E.Hutchinson)

Kelly's Directory of Nottinghamshire 1936

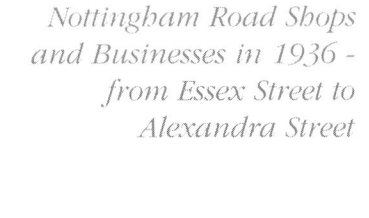

> Get your new
> **Austin, Morris, Hillman and Standard Cars**
> From
> **Clifford Motories,**
> Nottingham Road,
> EASTWOOD.
> *Always a Good Selection of Nearly New Guaranteed Cars in Stock. Terms and Exchanges.*

1935 advertisement

Nottingham Road Shops and Businesses in 1936 - from Essex Street to Alexandra Street

Construction work on the new Co-op store. A row of cottages had stood between the original store and Clarke's.

Page 130

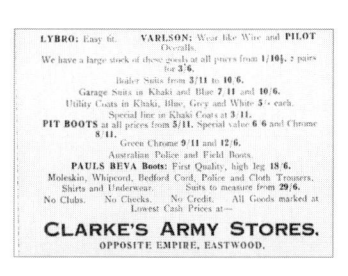

As well as having the shop (at no.144) Mr Flett went around the streets, hawking whatever he was selling at the time.

Winifred Stoakes

One of our favourite treats was ice cream from Wrights (at no. 138), opposite the Wellington Inn. It was hand churned, and we frequently had to watch and wait for it being made — it was quite delicious. Chips from Mervills (no. 164) were also a treat.

Leila Keam

John 'Jakey' Booth (at no.92) was quite a character. His shop sold everything from a bucket to a wine glass.

Constance Barrett

As well as running his general store Jakey Booth worked as a postman. Postcards were then very popular and of course the messages could be read very easily. Often his customers would meet him at the door before he had time to put the post through the letter-box, and before handing over any postcards he would impart the news that 'your sister is a lot better' etc! He was also clever at making up ditties such as :
*I've just glanced at your postcard dear,
It's some kind of a sonnet.
I wish they'd write more clearly though,
I can't make out what's on it!*

George Hardy

1935 advertisement

'Jakey' Booth's shop

1935 Advertisement

Mrs Booth (6th from right) with friends on an outing

Jakey Booth in 1935

Mr Chambers (at no.100) was the first port of call for remedies to cure minor ailments. At the back of the shop Chambers manufactured their own special medicines for rashes, coughs, indigestion etc.

Winifred Stoakes

> Children who are excited are often ill the next day.
>
> **MOTHERS !**
> Give your Children
> **CHAMBER'S**
> **Special Stomach Powders**
>
> after the day's excitement and they will get up in the morning happy and well.

Advertisement for one of the many home remedies available from Chambers chemist shop at 100 Nottingham Road.

The Langley Mill & Aldercar Co-operative Society was founded in 1875. At the time that I started work with the Society in 1940, it controlled from the offices at Langley Mill the following departments in its trading area which included Eastwood: twenty Grocery shops, nine Butchery, seven Drapery, three Furniture, three Boot and Shoe, three Green Fruit, three Confectionery, and three Chemist shops; also a Gents' Hairdressers, a Ladies' Hairdressers, three Gents' Tailoring, and a Paint and Decorating department.

Weekly grocery orders were collected from members' homes. The goods were assembled at grocery stores and delivered at no extra cost later in the week by

The Langley Mill & Aldercar Co-operative Society Ltd 1875 – 1968

A bread delivery van on Church Street in 1922, one of the many used by the LMA Co-op to deliver goods to its members throughout the area.

horse and cart, and to outlying districts by motor transport. Bread and confectionery were produced at the Eastwood bakery and distributed to all shops and outlets in the area, and again by horse-drawn cart to members' homes.

The dairy on Derby Road bottled all its own milk. Again local delivery was by horse-drawn floats and by motor further afield. The Society delivered milk to schools. The milkmen also collected and returned boot and shoe repairs which were done at Langley Mill. The butchery yard on Cromford Road at Langley Mill produced most of its merchandise including sausages, pies, black pudding, polony, boiled ham and pressed tongue etc. During the 1930s and later, the slaughtering of animals was carried out weekly by the Co-op's own butchery staff. Several butchery vans provided a service to members in all areas; the green fruit department used horse-drawn carts.

Coal was delivered to members' homes from the wharf at Aldercar. A Funeral Furnishing department operated from the Langley Mill Co-op yard ('funeral homes' were unknown in those days). The Society also ran a Penny Bank for children who would take their savings regularly each week. The maximum that could be banked was ten shillings.

The LMA, the Ripley and the Selston Co-operative Societies merged in 1968 to become NEMCO, which in turn merged in 1981 with the Derby & Burton Society to become the North-East Midlands Co-op Society. In 1985 another merger took place, this time with the Birmingham Society, to form the Central Midlands Co-op Society. Finally in 1995 the CMCS merged with the Leicester Society, and became known as the Midlands Co-operative Society with its headquarters at Lichfield.

Eddie Hicking
born 1925

The Co-op Shops Recalled

I recall with some regret the demise of the Langley Mill & Aldercar Co-operative Society, because for many years this Society was Eastwood. Its shops supplied every need in those distant days, from clothing, shoes, food, medicines, eye tests, hairdressing, electrical goods, insurance and banking, plus the much needed quarterly dividend. This was paid on purchases made during the previous quarter. Every Co-op shop and Co-op milkman issued a check, recording the cost of all purchases, and we carefully saved these checks at home until the time came to add up the lot, to find out how much shopping had been done and, more importantly, how much dividend to anticipate. Times were hard for the working class families in those days, and the dividend payout was a real bonus. The head office at Cromford Road, Langley Mill kept records of all business done throughout its area.

The Co-op shops in Eastwood promised top quality, and those employed by the stores considered themselves fortunate. There were very few empty premises in those days, and the folks who served in the shops were like friends, always ready to oblige. I especially remember the shoe department which was under the same roof as the tailoring department. Walking past the long shiny counters where Arthur Harwood and Ted Swaby could be seen unfurling great rolls of cloth from which men's suits would be made, I became aware of the tantalising smell of new leather shoes, all temptingly displayed. A Mrs Flintoff was in charge here for many years and her aim was to please every customer.

There were two Co-op butchers in Eastwood (one next to the tailoring department) where I shopped every Saturday for my mother. Here a well-known character called Bill reigned supreme. He knew everyone and would always open the conversation with, 'Nar, my duck, what does your Mam want this morning?' Bill

Crowds gather for the opening of the store by the actor Peter Adamson (Len Fairclough in Coronation Street) on 30 March 1963. The furnishing, hardware, drapery, men's outfitting, footwear and babywear departments were brought together under one roof on the ground floor, and women's fashions were on the first floor. The adjoining self-service grocery store had opened in August 1960

was a most friendly chap, with a string of comical remarks which would brighten the dullest day.

I also remember with affection the grocery department where white-overalled men, young and not so young, cheerfully supplied all our grocery needs. There was always a buzz of activity here as huge containers of dried fruits and sugar were weighed, bagged and neatly stacked ready for sale. I can visualise those familiar stacks of deep blue bags so easily. Also behind the high counter there were sounds of the butter patters, as chunks of butter from a big block were shaped and packed attractively, ready for the customers. This task with the butter was a skilled one, and only the more experienced assistants were seen to do it. Altogether this department was very efficiently run, again most cheerfully. At this time all customers who wished to do so would order their basic grocery needs early in the week, and these would be delivered towards the weekend. I remember the Co-op supplied a special order book which would be collected from each house. Such a service in those days was taken for granted. Again this regular caller became a friend, much appreciated by those living alone.

The Co-op had two butcher's shops on Nottingham Road. This one was at 28–30, the premises later acquired by Machin & Hartwell.

The system for dealing with cash in the stores always fascinated me. There was an overhead cable on which were suspended round containers, designed to take the cash from every sale up to a tiny room in the corner of the store. Here the cashier removed the money for the purchase, and where necessary put change in the container which was sent on the cable to the counter below. It was a simple system, which worked well enough and also provided entertainment for all the children who went shopping!

The Co-op drapery department was also very prominent in Eastwood. The rather large windows, displaying attractively arranged goods, curved from the pavement to the centre doorway. This provided a covered area from which to study the goods in the windows. In the middle of this spacious entrance was a separate glass cabinet showing choice items of ladies' wear.

The greengrocery department and the furniture and hardware stores were very popular, run by skilled experienced managers. In those days a manager would be employed until his retirement and was usually a local man, known by everyone. The confectionery store was always very busy, and the two hairdressing departments flourished with regular customers. The chemist shop provided all customers' needs and also offered eye testing every month when a visiting optician came to Eastwood. There was a well-stocked electrical store too, which was an asset. Yes, the Langley Mill & Aldercar Co-operative Society provided all our needs. It's a pity that things had to change, but that's life!

Doris Reeve
born 1921

80   Horace W Merry, decorator
78   Charles Barrett, saddler
76   George Gavin Sloane, dentist
74   George Carlin, painter
72   Evelyn C Barrett, outfitter
66   John Bennett, baker
64   T A Wrightson, corn dealer
62   Sidney W Stiles, boot maker
60   Winn & Brown, clothiers
58   Eric Steeples, butcher
56   Frank W. Harris, printer
54   Enoch Smith, hairdresser
52   Ellen Evans, draper
50   Henry Wyld, wine and spirit merchant
48   Sarah Smedley, baker
46   William Arthur Lynam, jeweller
44   Reginald Webb, fruiterer
42   Meadow Dairy Co. Ltd.
38   Horace Bennett, furniture dealer
36   William Sleath & Sons, watch makers
34   S Hilton & Sons Ltd, boot makers
32   Hunters The Teamen Ltd, tea merchants

Nottingham Road Shops and Businesses in 1936 - from Alexandra Street to Church Street

PORK PIES, SAUSAGE, POTTED BEEF A SPECIALITY.

ENGLISH MEAT ONLY.

Eric Steeples

HIGH-CLASS

Beef and Pork Butcher
58, Nottingham Rd.
EASTWOOD

Orders Called For and Delivered Daily.

1935 advertisement

A Century Remembered

Langley Mill & Aldercar Co-op Society
26   F Glover & Sons Ltd, butchers
24   Hopkin & Son, shoe makers
20   Lord Nelson PH, (Landlord:Chas.Watson)
4   J Hogg & Son, butchers
2   J H Skelton Ltd, aerated water manufacturers

Kelly's Directory of Nottinghamshire 1936

Barrett's Shops 1919 - 1986

Nottingham Road in the 1950s looking towards Alexandra Street, with the Billiard Saloon on the far corner. On the right is Barrett's shop, with the living accommodation above.

I was born in Eastwood but my parents Charles and Evelyn Barrett came from Lichfield. My father moved to Eastwood in 1919 after being 'demobbed' from the war to take over Mr Hurst's leather and saddlery business at 78 Nottingham Road. Housing was scarce after the war, and at first my mother stayed in Chasetown, Staffordshire while father lodged here and returned home at weekends. However, after my brother was born mother felt that she really should be in Eastwood and when a house became available in Addison Villas she moved, and that's where I was born. Later we moved to Alexandra Street to a house owned by Mrs Pollard who lived next door. By coincidence her husband had also been a saddler. One of my childhood memories is of going into Mrs Pollard's sitting room and seeing a huge propeller! It was never explained, but perhaps Mr Pollard had been in the Royal Flying Corps in the war.

My father had his workshop in the old stables in the yard behind the shop. He made some beautiful things in leather, as well as more practical goods like cash bags for the Co-op, one of his major customers, and miners' knee-pads. He did saddlery repairs for firms over a wide area; I remember the Cannock Chase colliery company in Staffordshire used to bring repairs to him. If anyone wanted to order a saddle, which of

Page 137

A Century Remembered

course was made to measure, I used to go out with him for the measuring and fitting — it was very interesting.

I suppose that in 1919 when my father bought the business it must have been quite a worry to think that he was taking on a dying trade. People were getting more affluent, farms were being mechanised, and cars were becoming more common — so he adapted to the new world by, for example, making fabric hoods for cars. He also used to restring tennis rackets, including work for Tony Pickard, the national coach.

Constance Barrett at her shop in 1985

When I left school I worked for my mother, who had started her wool and drapery business in 1935. Her premises at number 72 were separated from my father's by Mr Carlin's shop and the archway leading into the yard. Mr Sloane the dentist had a surgery above the saddlery, and from 1935 we lived above the wool shop. There were two floors of accommodation including a huge sitting room on the first floor. There were three children by then and we had a very happy life there. The rooms were so big, and at the front we had lovely views over towards Underwood.

The two businesses operated separately until my father finally retired at the age of 80 following ill health. He had hoped to sell the saddlery as a going concern but negotiations fell through, and in the end I agreed to buy from him the stock of small leather goods that I thought I could sell in my wool shop (which I had taken over from my mother at the end of the war). That is how it came about that the left-hand window of my shop at number 72 had leather goods on display. It worked very well, and meant that Father was still able to take an interest because otherwise he would have been quite 'lost.' I used to say that I would take a leaf from my father's book and also retire at 80, but it was not to be and I sold the shop in 1986.

'Skelton's Corner' at the junction of Church Street and Derby Road. The business closed in 1967 and the building was demolished to allow for road widening. The Rex Cinema is in the background.

Constance Barrett

Hunter's Stores

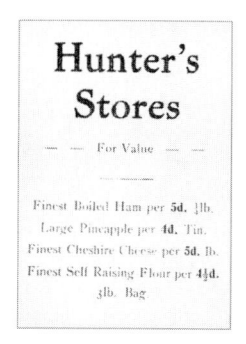

— For Value —

Finest Boiled Ham per 5d. ½lb.
Large Pineapple per 4d. Tin.
Finest Cheshire Cheese per 5d. lb.
Finest Self Raising Flour per 4½d.
3lb. Bag

1935 advertisement

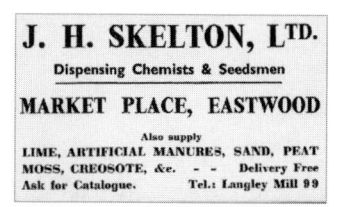

J. H. SKELTON, L^TD.
Dispensing Chemists & Seedsmen
MARKET PLACE, EASTWOOD

Also supply
LIME, ARTIFICIAL MANURES, SAND, PEAT MOSS, CREOSOTE, &c. - - Delivery Free
Ask for Catalogue.   Tel.: Langley Mill 99

1955 advertisement

Church Street Shops and Businesses in 1936

The post office was next to Hopkin's shoe shop. The two shops at the end of the row, on the corner of Church Street, seemed to be always changing hands. Teddy Manners was a terror! I remember he used to ride up Mansfield Road on his motorbike, across the junction and straight in through his ironmonger's shop door. They had three sons, but he always wanted a daughter and he made a tremendous fuss of me.

Winifred Stoakes

For ordinary childhood ailments Skeltons, the old-fashioned chemists on the corner of Church Street and Derby Road, could supply all the remedies. Five Hap'orths (a mixture of five trusty ingredients) was the sure cure for chesty coughs. In fact, many years later my father would regularly get a bottle from there for my own children — they loved it!

Leila Keam

Robert Barber & Sons, solicitors
George Bradley, shopkeeper
Frederick R Chambers, wine & spirit merchant
Charles H Clarke, builder
Conservative Club, (Secretary: Percy Pollard)
Wilson D Fullwood, boot repairer
John Malcolm Glover, grocer
Frederick Marriott, ladies' hairdresser
Benjamin Morris, shopkeeper
George Henry Noon, butcher
Old Wine Vaults PH, (Landlord : John Dalton)
Emma Parnham, shopkeeper
William Walker, farmer
Charles Watts, watch and clock repairer
Wyles Brothers Ltd, boot and shoe dealers

Kelly's Directory of Nottinghamshire 1936

Milk was delivered to houses twice a day from Walker's farm at the bottom of Church Street. The Walker daughters drove the horse-drawn milk cart and measured out the milk in the traditional measuring cans.

Leila Keam

Skelton's cart setting out with a delivery of mineral waters in 1900. The Sun Inn is in the background.

My father Noah Slater began working for the grocery department of the Langley Mill & Aldercar Co-operative Society in 1913. In 1928 he became the first manager of the new Derby Road, Eastwood shop and subsequently managed in turn Newthorpe, New Eastwood, Holbrook Street and Underwood grocery shops until, in 1948, he again became the first manager of a new venture on Church Street, Eastwood which combined a grocery store and a beer, wines and spirits off-licence. He retired in 1959 after 45 years' service with the company. In 1913 the Society had 13 grocery shops with total sales of £137,000; by the time he retired there were 23 shops and one mobile van serving the area, with total sales of nearly £1,750,000.

Melba Nicholson (née Slater)

My parents moved into an empty shop on the corner of Nottingham Road and Dovecote Road at Hill Top and started business. It would be known for many years as 'Cross's Corner.' The shop had originally been the Co-op until new premises were built on the opposite corner. Our shop sold wallpaper, candles, paraffin, pisspots, buckets, shoe leather, nails and all the miners' requisites — lamp oil, lamp hooks, pickshafts and pit chalk.

Percy Cross
born 1906

Shops and Businesses at Hill Top

A Century Remembered

Hill Top Shops in the late 1920s

One corner of Dovecote Road (the Newthorpe side) was completely occupied by the Co-op. The grocery store had a window on Nottingham Road and Dovecote Road; on the other side of the big entry were the butcher's and fish shop. Upstairs was the Co-op bank, and on 'divi' day there was always a long queue. It was all fields and allotments where the houses on Charles Avenue are now.

On the other corner of Dovecote Road (the Eastwood side) Mr Shipley took over the Cross family's hardware store when they moved to Skegness; next door was Fox's wool shop which also sold knitted things; then Alfred Aram the cobbler, and Arthur Gregory the barber. These were all small shops — only the frontages were rented by the shopkeepers, while often other families lived at the back and above. Next to Gregory's was Dorothy Cliff's sweet shop, then Rolling's the draper, and Drayton's who sold and repaired umbrellas. Next came Louis Naylor's fish and chip shop, and Chambers' off-licence. George Cliff kept the post office and also a general store. Next door was George Leivers the butcher; his sister Maud who helped in the shop lived in the adjoining premises. Mellotts kept the greengrocer's, and next to it was a tiny general store kept by George Lowe who also delivered milk.

Nigel Johnson (standing) outside the shop in 1950. With the Man In Space and the Assemblies Of God church the stretch of Nottingham Road opposite between Castle Street and Chewton Street looks quite different today. Originally there were two pubs, the Coach and Horses and the General Havelock, a row of houses and the Mission Church

Then there was a gap in the shops, with a bungalow set back which was occupied by Mr Johnson, blacksmith and farrier. The shops continued with Ball's the chemist, although when I was little it was Clifton's sweet shop, and next door was Thomas Gillott's painter and decorator's business. In the shop next to Johnson's the newsagent, Rowley's sold not only sweets but also churned their own ice cream. We used to take a cup to have it filled with a pennyworth! The end shop was West's the butcher, later Tom Whittamore's. Allcock & Sisson's builder's yard was where Alexandra House is now. A little further along Jesse Clay ran his coal delivery business, and in the large house on the corner of Edward Road lived George Stubbs who built the Eastwood Empire.

On the south side of Nottingham Road, opposite Dovecote Road, the cottages where Phoenix Court now stands were known as Sharley's Row. Chappells kept a grocery shop on the corner of Raglan Street, and on the opposite corner when you went into Miss Horne's shop I can remember the lovely smells that surrounded you from the rice and oatmeal etc. kept in big tubs. Behind the Greasley Castle pub was a yard with several houses; Mr Ward the cobbler was there and Frankie Watts who sold rabbits. King's chip shop was on the corner of Castle Street and Cross Street. Before the Man In Space was built there were two pubs on that site, almost side by side — the Coach and Horses and the General Havelock. Below the Havelock was a row of houses, in one of which Mr Watson the lamplighter lived. We children used to follow him up Dovecote Road as he lit the gas lamps with a long pole.

Mary Bend
born 1918

My mother baked her own bread although there was a baker on Castle Street. On Sundays we could take our joint of meat to the baker for cooking in his oven. He charged sixpence for this. I remember once collecting our joint of rib beef from Leivers the butcher, but when I got home my mother made me take it back because it had a big bone in it. The butcher said, 'Beasts don't grow without bones,' and my mother replied, 'I know, but I don't want them all in my piece!' On Monday mornings on my way to school I left two basins and twopence at the fish shop for a 'mix' to be collected later on my way home.

Florence Smith
born 1918

A Century Remembered

Four-year old Nigel Johnson standing in the doorway of his father's shop at Hill Top in 1922.

O ur fellow shopkeepers at Hill Top in the first two decades of the century included Birkin's where we used to queue for hot pea soup at fourpence a gallon. A jugful was of little use in those days of large families. Miss Brown the newsagent and tobacconist married a Mr Johnson, and here is an interesting story about her. Around 1913 she left her shop door wide open all day long for her customers to serve themselves while she went to her mother's funeral at (I think) Swadlincote. On her return she found herself 'out of pocket' by about four penny newspapers and a few packets of Woodbines. She refused to blame the locals for dishonesty, saying that it must have been strangers passing through who forgot to pay!

Percy Cross

Carnival, 1935.

LET'S HAVE A RECORD.

SNAP IT!

WE DO THE REST.

Our Printing and Developing the Best.
KODAK, SELO FILMS, &c.

We have Exclusive Designs in Traced Goods.
We Specialise in EMBROIDERY, WOOLS, &c.

S. JOHNSON,
HILL TOP,
"Stocks Most Things."

W hen I was young, the Hill Top branch of the Co-op was managed by Mr Cook. Every purchase was rewarded with a ticket which showed the amount spent. The dividend ('divi') was paid out every quarter — an event often referred to as the Hill Top Races! It was a very real help for families to buy basic necessities. Louis Brown the greengrocer saved the rope from orange boxes for children to use as skipping ropes. Mr Smart's general store sold everything from shoe polish to paraffin. Fish, chips and peas at Naylor's cost threepence. The butcher's shop at Hill Top was kept by George Leivers. The pigs were killed behind the shop, and didn't they squeal on killing day — they could be heard for miles. In the shop he sold chitterlings, brawn, tripe, pig's heads, trotters, cheeks and scratchings — oh, and meat for those with money to spend!

Mavis Williamson
born 1922

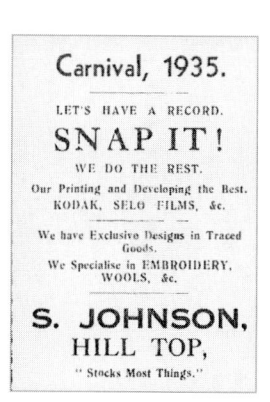

The Saturday Penny

Saturday morning saw lots of youthful activity after breakfast. Young girls were out sweeping, scrubbing, whitening front doorsteps or window cleaning. An army of boys with wheelbarrows, buckets and shovels started out in fierce competition to forage for firewood or collect horse manure. All this worthy occupation was necessary to earn the 'Saturday penny' spending money. Little girls under school age could also earn twopence a week carrying babies in prams to waiting mothers working at collieries, mills or factories so that the babies could get a hurried midday breast-feed.

The purchasing power of the hard-earned penny was considerable. It could be broken down to four farthings, and with a farthing we could spend some time looking in a sweetshop window (Birkin's or Cliff's at Hill Top) and making the big decision — Tiger Nuts, Kali or Locust Beans. Probably you finally chose the four liquorice 'boot laces' and left the shop with a Rockefeller feeling of still having three farthings left in your pocket. Cross's kids had frequent lectures from Mam on the rashness of spending the whole penny all at once, with the warning that Christmas or Hill Top Wakes or that promised day trip to Skeggy were only a few weeks hence. We saved our ha'pennies for these coming delights 'in mother's pocket.'

Percy Cross

Chapter Nine

Getting Around

I remember standing at the door of our shop with my mother and father to watch the first tram come through Eastwood in 1913. Later I went to school at Heanor on the tram but I was never keen on coming down Heanor Hill, and I used to be frightened to death of that awful bend at Basford whenever we went to Nottingham. I could see the driver turning the brake wheel, and I used to chew my nails because I was sure that the tram would come off the tracks! Then I remember the start of bus services, a small bus at first, and we thought it was lovely because it was much quicker than the tram. Later the tram tracks were taken up and overhead wires put up for the trolley buses.

Riding on the open top deck of the 'Ripley Rattler' was a great adventure. The Ripley to Nottingham tram route was the second longest in the UK.

Winifred Stoakes
born 1909

The only family outing that I remember as a child was to take a picnic to the Trent Embankment on Bank Holiday Monday. We always wanted to ride on the open top deck of the tram; it was a rattling good ride, quite an adventure!

Mary Bend
born 1918

1913 brought us the trams. We knew they were there, too. Clang! Clang! they went as they passed the loop outside our home. I dreamed they missed the points and came down our street. I saw this come true twice but they travelled only a couple of yards. It was lovely to ride to Nottingham upstairs on an 'open-air' top deck of the tram when it was fine, but

A Century Remembered

terrible when it was raining and the conductor said, 'Upstairs only!'

When I was married in 1922 I went to live at Langley for two years. During this time a bus company was set up by the two Mr Williamsons of Heanor, and was the origin of the 'blue buses' (later the Midland General Omnibus Co.) to Nottingham. When we lived at Jacksdale we were able to travel on Tansey & Severn's buses on the original Nottingham to Alfreton route, although we also used the train from Jacksdale to visit the market at Eastwood on Fridays.

*Lily Rose
born 1902*

Midland General began operations in 1922. The company expanded considerably between 1929 and 1936 as it acquired many private operators such as Tansey & Severn (on the Alfreton to Nottingham route) and Williamsons (Heanor to Nottingham).

The old tram cars ceased running in 1932 and the first trolley bus service from Eastwood through to Nottingham ran on Goose Fair Thursday October 5th 1933. It was to be a nightmare, particularly for the drivers, on account of a thick fog. Some of the men, especially the inspectors, had no rest or sleep for two or three days. There was keen competition between the various private bus companies, such as Williamsons, Tansey & Severn, Brewin & Hudson, Walters & Leivers etc., whose routes would eventually be taken over by Midland General.

*Kenneth Poynter
born 1904*

I worked for 43 years in various capacities for the Midland General Omnibus Company (MGO) and its successors. It was one of three companies administered from

Trolley buses operated between Eastwood and Nottingham from 1933 to 1953. (The shop next to the bank is the Walk-Round Store, which in 1935 advertised 'wonderful bargains without being asked to buy.')

the head office at the Langley Mill depot. In 1948 the MGO and similar companies were nationalised and later became part of the National Bus Company. In the 1950s the trolley buses were discontinued and replaced with motor buses. The old MGO companies were taken over by Trent in the early 1970s.

*Bernard Pass
born 1915*

When I came to live in Eastwood it was our custom for many years to visit Moorgreen Show. My father took me and my children in the car, but we always made our own way back and at that time there were always special buses laid on to take people home to Eastwood, Heanor and surrounding villages.

*Jean Brinsley
born 1937*

Adventures on the Midland General

In 1945 at the age of 14 I left school and got a job to earn some money. Following in my father's footsteps I found work at British Celanese Ltd at Spondon, on the outskirts of Derby. This entailed a journey of ten miles each way daily. A bus left Hill Top at 6.55 a.m. for Spondon. The fare was sixpence. The bus arrived from Moorgreen Colliery full of night-shift miners who smoked on the lower deck in spite of a NO SMOKING notice. Because of their 'dirty' state the oldest buses were used for the pit-men, and consequently we who had 'clean' jobs had to use old buses with a smoke-laden atmosphere. There was little choice available.

The bus travelled through Langley Mill then made a detour around Langley. The last pick-up spot was Heanor at about 7.10. There followed a revolting, jolting ride of some 20 to 25 minutes through Smalley and turning off through Donkey's Hollow, past Morley Church towards Locko Park and Spondon. Newspapers were read, cigarettes smoked, and conversations covered many subjects.

At Hill Top father talked to his cronies and, being a smoker, travelled on the upper deck. As a non-smoker, and having a choice of empty seats, I opted for the front seat behind the driver and watched his every move. He was in his own little world, separated by a fixed partition. The only access to him was a round hole with a lift-up cover, so that the conductor could speak directly to him if needed. Otherwise he was 'controlled' by one ding of a bell to stop and two dings to go. Some drivers were regulars but some were new, and not being used to the old buses found them hard to drive, with much crashing of gears and lurching stops on suspect brakes.

MGO service C5 to Alfreton waits at the main stop in Eastwood in the 1950s

One of these regulars was a crony of father's named Percy Goddard. 'Eyup Perce,' 'Eyup Herbert,' would go the conversation, and with a nod each resumed his place. Father's advice to me was, 'When you knock off (at 5.25 p.m.) make your heels crack for that bus — it leaves the bus park at twenty to six.' Another agonising smoke-filled ride and another sixpence to return to the joys of Hill Top. There seemed to be no way of avoiding this daily agony except leaving and getting another job, but this alternative never once occurred to me.

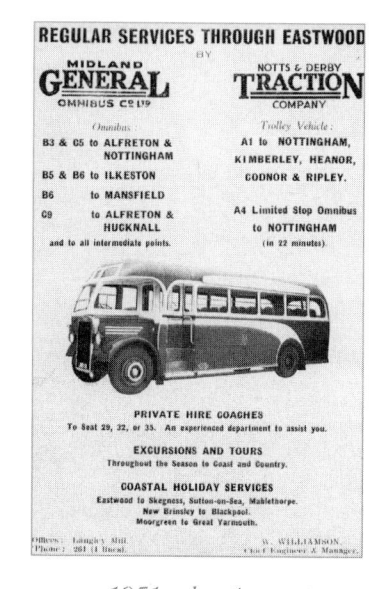

Then I discovered that the workers from the Underwood area used a single-decker service which picked up outside the Blue Kettle Café at Eastwood (opposite the Rex Cinema and the Sun Inn) at 6.50 a.m. There was no detour around Langley, just straight to Heanor and arriving at Spondon at about 7.15 to collect night-shift workers, leaving there again at 7.30. Also it was a service bus (not a 'special'), clean and swift with NO SMOKING enforced. Suddenly the choice was enlarged! Go to Hill Top and

1951 advertisement

Page 148

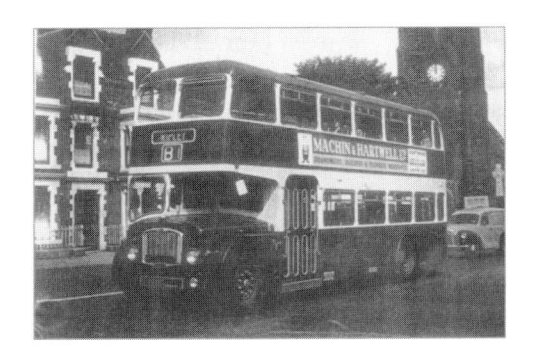

MGO bus at Heanor on the Nottingham to Ripley route, c.1960

catch number 188 or 189, lumbering old buses with all their attendant hazards, or a luxury ride in a single-decker arriving at work 20 minutes earlier with a chance to breakfast in the factory canteen before work started at 7.55.

There were two drawbacks to overcome: the longer distance from home (Mill Road) to the bus stop, and getting up earlier to make the journey in time. The first was solved by cycling to the Eastwood Lads Club on Church Street, leaving the bike round the back of the club and collecting it on return at night; the second by rising earlier! The return bonus was that the Underwood bus left Spondon bus park ten minutes earlier than the other double-deckers, and if I clocked off early in the queue at work and ran all the way (half a mile) to the park I could just make it — heels cracking. Inevitably I sometimes missed the earlier bus and had to wait for the slower one.

In the morning if I missed it I just had to wait. When the later bus came round Skelton's Corner (Church Street) my heart would sink if it was either number 188 or 189, for these 'twin-designed' six-cylinder buses were the worst in the fleet. They needed low gears to negotiate the easiest of gradients, and the climb up Breach Road at Langley, especially in winter snow, was agonising in bottom gear. Another old bus was number 196 which had a better engine, and could actually overtake other buses on the way to work or back.

In summer I again tried to find an alternative way to get to and from work and one day, having missed both the early and late buses, decided to cycle all the way and get to work, albeit late, rather than miss a day. This was not a good idea and was not repeated. So when I was able to obtain a BSA Bantam motorcycle my dreams came true. At last — independence and fresh air. Goodbye to number 188, 189, 196 and luxury single-deckers. Here was bliss; but snow, rain, cold, thunderstorms, winds, breakdowns, backache, colds and fogs all combined to shatter the dream. So the motorcycle was soon out of favour and the prospect of the 188 and 189 loomed again.

Then the factory work was moved to Wigan and we had to find alternative employment. Mine was at P P Paynes factory at Haydn Road, Nottingham but eventually I left there to work as a miner at — guess where? — yes, Moorgreen Pit.

Fred Skillington
born 1931

I remember going to Nottingham in a 'pony and tub' to meet a friend from London. It rained all the way there and back, and except for several stops at pubs to rest the pony it was a miserable day's outing. Eastwood was very lucky to have Leivers' stables. They possessed a 'brake' which held about ten people. Three families once hired this and off we went to Matlock. It was a marvellous day, but not for a cousin of mine who fell out three times! Why this happened we never knew, but I can still picture it happening. We had to climb up three steps to get into the brake. The traffic would be no problem in those days, but it must have been rather a bumpy journey to say the least.

Lily Rose

My grandfather owned one of the first steam cars, and his younger sons were mad keen on cars. However, it was a farce whenever they tried to get up Hartshay Hill because one of them had to get out and push. It was replaced by a petrol car as soon as these became available and we had one of the first in Eastwood. My aunt was the first woman driver in Derbyshire. When she was driving, all the old ladies in their black dresses and bibbed aprons used to come

Carriages and Cars

A Panhard car from Leivers' Garage at Mr Mervill's house on Bridge Terrace. His sister Mrs Wright is on the left. The driver is possibly Billy Beck.

out to watch her and report in wonder, 'We've seen a girl driving a car!' She continued to drive until she was over 80.

Winifred Stoakes

Winifred Brittain, aged three, riding in the family car in 1911

I remember the Revd Peter Caporn, Rector of Eastwood from 1949 to 1965, driving around in a vintage Bullnose Morris, registration number H8.

Mick Brown
born 1941

One of the first cars in Eastwood was owned by the Barber family of Lamb Close, and I recall that the elder brother of Bob Smaller was the chauffeur. By the mid-1920s quite a number of people in the Eastwood area had private cars. A friend of mine, Roy Leivers, owned a garage which had amongst other vehicles a fleet of funeral cars. I had my first driving experience here, for I used to help Roy out sometimes.

A car decorated for a carnival procession

I remember we ran a 'mobile preacher' service! The various preachers in the district used to take turns in visiting outlying chapels to conduct the services. Leivers' garage provided a sort of taxi/chauffeur service for them, and I used to help by driving them to their destinations. I well remember regularly picking up a Mr Argyle from opposite the cricket ground at Langley Mill and taking him to a different chapel each week. The cars were all French Panhards and though a pleasure to drive were somewhat uncomfortable by today's standards. I also helped out by driving at times for Captain Chambers, the founder and leader of the local Boys Brigade.

A number of local tradespeople were beginning to deliver by motor vans at this time, and the Co-op was using motor transport for house-to-house milk deliveries. They also delivered meat by van, on a wholesale basis, to provide stock for their own shops. I have a vivid recollection of a Mr Clements, the then General Manager at the Co-op, visiting the shops (I worked at the Brinsley store) in an old model T Ford in order to check the stock and accounts.

Kenneth Poynter

My grandfather, who founded Clifford Motories in 1907, was one of the first men in Eastwood to own and drive a car. In 1923 my father Wilfred, then aged 16, was asked by Dr Dixon, who lived on Church Street at what is now Eastwood House, if he would chauffeur and look after his car. Wilfred used to drive Dr Dixon and his wife to Skegness, where they had a residence and where they spent weekends when the doctor was not on duty. My father would then return to Eastwood with the car until summoned by Dr Dixon by telegram to fetch him back.

Fay Hickinbotham

A 1933 telegram from Dr Dixon summoning Wilfred Clifford to Skegness

The only two cars I can remember seeing in Eastwood when I was young were Dr Gillespie's with its registration number AL23, and Dr Dixon's 'sit-up-and-beg' tourer.

Lily Whittamore
born 1915

A Century Remembered

An Interlude on Four Wheels

I think it was in 1913, when a passing motor car was still rare enough to bring a crowd running into the street, that a Mr Smith who lived in the row of houses, now demolished, opposite Cross's shop at the corner of Dovecote Road, inherited an automobile from a dead uncle, thus becoming one of Hill Top's first owner-drivers. However, first came the daunting task of driving the vehicle home from Biggleswade, which in those days of non-travel was the back of beyond in 'foreign parts' — 90 miles distant!

Mr Smith recruited a task force for the expedition: himself (driver and mechanic); Alf Watson the publican (captain and baggage-master); and Wag Abbey of New Eastwood (navigator and trailfinder). Wag was chosen because of his experiences in the deserts of Africa in the Boer War. Their combined engineering experience was limited to knowledge of how to pump up a bicycle tyre! The party went by train to Biggleswade and there took possession of a two-seater Daimler, which I think had two cylinders, 6 to 8 horsepower and probably a maximum speed of 12 to 15 mph.

After a one-hour driving lesson and three hours carousing in The Crown, they pulled out of the inn yard at midnight to start the long haul back to Hill Top. The dauntless three were jammed in the two-seater (Alf Watson topped the scales at 18 stones) and tied on the back was 'essential' luggage — two crates of ale, a bottle of Scotch each and, just for emergencies, a bottle of brandy! The car's engine did its gallant best but it constantly ran out of puff, and it was stop-start-stop all the way up the Great North Road to Stilton, and breakfast — 35 miles in about eight hours.

From then on they had to exchange the broad highway of the A1 for narrow cross-country lanes. To lighten the engine's load the captain ordered the stores to be got rid of (by self-consumption), an order enthusiastically carried out. This tack may have improved the engine's performance but concentration on driving and navigation certainly suffered. The mile-by-mile log book from that point showed numerous stops for 're-oiling.' Oddly enough this operation seemed to be carried out to the best advantage in the yard of a

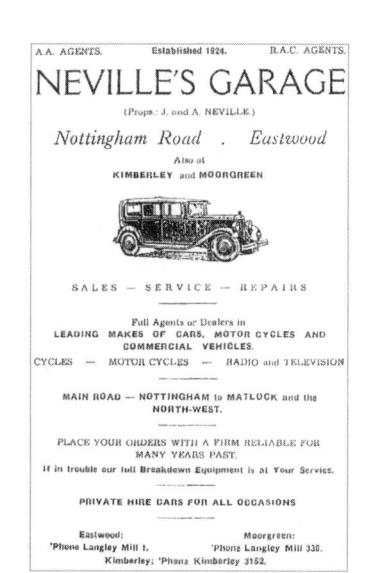

1935 advertisement

public house, and a long list of these pubs where the Daimler and its crew pulled in for further 'lubrication' was recorded. When darkness fell they were still miles from anywhere but happy and singing.

Meanwhile ahead of them the reception committee at Hill Top, i.e. half the population, grew anxious as midnight approached. Bicycle scouts had been sent out ten miles or more to locate the long-overdue vehicle, and police telephones had been requisitioned without success. It was past 2 a.m. when a tired but triumphant chug-chug-chug was heard panting the last mile from Moorgreen, an entirely unexpected direction. The Daimler and its intrepid trio had triumphed!

Percy Cross
born 1906

Canals - The Great Northern Basin

Down the hill from Eastwood's town centre and at the junction of three canals lies the Great Northern Basin. It takes its name from the Great Northern Railway Company who were for some time owners of the Nottingham Canal, one of the three terminating at Langley Mill. The only canal remaining in use today is the Erewash Canal, the first of the three to be built, linking Langley Mill to the River Trent via the Erewash valley through Ilkeston and Long Eaton.

It is perhaps ironic that in the 19th century the local canals carried large quantities of stone to be used in ballasting the railway lines, especially between Birmingham and London. It was the same railways which were instrumental in the demise of freight carrying on the canals. Commercial traffic ended in 1952 when coal from Moorgreen Colliery to Loughborough was transferred to the roads.

In 1968 the Great Northern Basin was derelict and silted up. The Transport Act of that year condemned the Erewash Canal to 'remainder status,' meaning that virtually no money could be spent on it other than that necessary for public health and safety. However, this was the stimulus for the creation of the Erewash Canal Preservation and Development Association which over the years has done sterling service both physically and

Railways

by applying political pressure to help the canal owners, British Waterways, with the support of local authorities, to restore the Erewash Canal to the status of Cruising Waterway. This gives the Great Northern Basin, including a short stretch of the Cromford Canal, a new lease of life for leisure, tourism and recreation and the associated job creation for the people of Eastwood.

Roger Harvey

Because my husband was a signalman, we had free travel on the railways. This was useful when we went on holiday to Skegness where we stayed at a boarding house owned by my friend's mother. Another outing we enjoyed was an evening trip to Sheffield to see my Aunt Daisy who would have a big stew waiting for us! We caught the train at about 5 p.m. and come back at 9.30.

Mary Bend

Eastwood and Langley Mill Station, opened in 1875, was closed to passenger traffic in 1963 and goods in 1964. The booking office was at street level on Derby Road. The by-pass now follows the line of the railway track.

By the mid-1920s a favourite leisure pursuit was a cheap day trip by train. Trips ran each week from Eastwood & Langley Mill Station to Skegness. You could choose either to go in the morning and return early evening, or go in the afternoon returning at night. I think it was a half-crown return for the former, and five shillings for the latter. These trips were always very popular and at least enabled people to travel away from the area to visit new places, thus giving rise to a host of new holiday resorts.

Kenneth Poynter

We went to Skegness by train every year. We stayed for at least a week, always Skegness. In fact my bucket and spade stayed in the cellar of the boarding house we went to for years and years! It was marvellous, donkey rides and all the rest of it. When I was older we often used to go to London for the day from Nottingham Victoria Station for five shillings.

Winifred Stoakes

The railways were used for trips to Skegness, once a year for the choir outing. Every time you turned up for choir duty a star was stamped on a card, and if you had enough stars on your card you could go to Skeg. There were no corridors on the trains then!

*Mavis Williamson
born 1922*

1939 advertisement

Passengers waiting at Nottingham Station on 25 April 1983 to board a centenary special excursion to Skegness. Among them is Marie Smith of Eastwood (4th adult from right, wearing white apron over black dress)

A Century Remembered

Chapter Ten

Radio and Television

Leisure Time

The first radio, or wireless as we called it, that we ever had was a 'cat's whisker.' I remember the first programme I heard in the early 1920s was a piano lesson given by Sir Henry Walford Davies. I thought it was wonderful to be able to hear this because I was learning the piano at the time. You had to listen through headphones attached to the box, and you worked a thin wire (the whisker) over a crystal and adjusted it to get the best signal.

Our first proper radio, in a cabinet, was an EKCO. It was wonderful, but an aunt of my father's who came to stay with us refused to believe that voices could come over the air from London. She said that there must be a gramophone record inside! The first radios were powered by an accumulator which had to be charged at regular intervals. When we lived at the shop on Nottingham Road we took it across to Mr Sleath's shop, and then to Neville's Garage when we moved to Percy Street.

Winifred Stoakes
born 1909

Smaller's Garage,
Radio Stores, Cycle Depot and Electric Petrol Filling Station.

Sole Authorised Agents for Philco and Kolster Brandes Radio.
Cossor, Marconi, Aerodyne, Lissen and Ferranti Sets in Stock from £5 15 9d. or 2s. 6d. weekly.
Sole Agents for Radge Whitworth, Sun, James and Hercules Cycles from £3 19s. 9d. or 2s. weekly
Baby Carriages from 7s. 11d. or 1s. weekly.
We Specialise in Repairs to Cars, Motor Cycles, Cycles and Radio Sets.

Everything on Easy Terms.
All at 151 and 153 Nottingham Road, Eastwood.

1935 advertisement

My husband was quite handy, and when he learned how to wallpaper and paint he would often earn a few shillings. With some of this money we purchased our first radio and a new world opened up for us. I listened to it in the daytime and sang at the top of my voice with *Music While You Work*. I could reach high notes in those days and keep in tune. What a wealth of melody unfolded for us. At this period we had *The Isle Of Capri, It's a Sin To Tell a Lie, Red Sails In the Sunset*, many songs of the '20s and old music hall songs. One morning I saw all my elderly neighbours out in their gardens and went out to apologise for the loud music and my singing, but they were enjoying it. We listened in the evening while my husband pegged a rag rug and I cut bits for him or knitted for our children.

Alice Geeson
born 1912

In the 1920s radio was becoming all the rage and consisted of 'crystal' sets and earphones. A favourite hobby of mine was to build these sets from drawings in the newly founded amateur radio magazines. I think I was probably one of the country's first radio 'hams.'

Kenneth Poynter
born 1904

Bob Smaller at his premises between Eastwood and Hill Top

I remember our very first radio which was powered by batteries. A friend of Dad's made this wireless for him and it was the only one on our street. On one Cup Final day our living room which was about ten feet square was bursting at the seams with neighbours listening to the game. So that you could understand exactly where play was taking place the *Radio Times* used to publish a drawing of the pitch marked out with numbered squares, and the commentator reporting on the game would quote the relevant square number.

Ken Marsland
born 1924

My mother saved hard to buy a Mullard wireless set with a battery and accumulator which had to be recharged frequently. I remember her listening avidly to the news of the death of King George V and the eventual abdication of Edward VIII. She was a staunch royalist and was dreadfully upset. *Monday Night At Eight* was our very favourite radio programme, with Henry Hall's orchestra and Inspector Hornleigh, and my brother and I were allowed to stay up and listen.

Leila Keam
born 1930

I have no first-hand experience of crystal sets but the early radio sets came in when I was a child, and very few homes had one. The first one I heard was when I was standing in our garden at Bridge Terrace and from next door's radio came a sweet voice singing *Over The Rainbow*. It was Judy Garland's record, and I still like to hear it even today.

When our family moved to Mill Road we had our first radio which worked on batteries or an accumulator. In spite of its many squeaks and whistles we learned to use it. We quickly learned to pick and choose from a wide variety of programmes. The BBC Home Service was the main output, so if we 'fiddled' with the set and 'lost it' we were in trouble. One day I was playing in a neighbour's house with their boys when *I.T.M.A.* came on, and we were ejected forcibly by a burly miner so that he could listen to Tommy Handley, Mrs Mopp and the Colonel who would crack jokes about Hitler and the other Nazis. 'Can I do you now, Sir?' was Mrs Mopp's catch phrase; 'I don't mind if I do' was the Colonel's.

Of the many bands and orchestras I liked Geraldo. His signature tune was sung and it has stuck in my memory: 'Hello again — we're on the radio again — and as you recognise the style — we need not tell you — the name Geraldo — because it's just the band you prefer — Yes Sir!' Big Bill Campbell and his Rocky Mountain Rhythm was on at Sunday lunchtime, if I remember correctly, and was like a camp-fire get-together with songs, tales and chat. 'Pass the applejack, Buck' became a catchphrase that we listened for (applejack was scrumpy or whisky). Of the many organists who each had 15-minute slots, I liked Sandy Macpherson. He was a great entertainer. Great memories do live on!

Fred Skillington
born 1931

A Century Remembered

I think we owned the second television set in Eastwood (Jack Hallam had the first one). The screen was only 9 inches wide but very clear. Our son was only young then and he used to go round to the back of the set to see where the picture was coming from!

Winifred Stoakes

When we moved house to Newthorpe and Grandad later came to live with us, my Dad bought a television set so that he could watch cricket. Gramps could not understand how all those people could fit into so small a box. One day football was on; just before Mum switched the set on, the Newthorpe United team who changed in the Miners Rest opposite our house went up to the Dovecote Road recreation ground to start their game. Lo and behold when Mum switched on there was a game taking place and Gramps said, 'By God, they've soon got started; they've just this minute gone by!' He knew the aerial wire had something to do with the pictures on the television, and he used to say, 'I don't know how they get down this wire into the box.'

Ken Marsland

Cricket

Greasley Church Cricket Club, 1921.
Back row (l to r): Mr Saxton(1), Mr Saxton(2), Hector Burrows, Alex Smith, Len Coulton, — , Vic Pilbeam, Ted Pearson, Harry Durose, Mr Meakin, Jack Hallam, Harry Walker, — , Mr Byfield.
Middle row: Jack Donnelly, W Lowe, Miss Galloway, Rev Sydney Galloway, Sam Anthony, W Carlin.
Front row: Herbert Orson, Mr Baker, Randle Burrows, Vic Charles, Jack Garton, Ernest Kirk.

A Century Remembered

Beggarlee Cricket Club, 1921.
Back row (l to r): Charlie Burrows, —, Albert Cutts, Joe Berry, —, Tom Heele, Fred Rowland, Henry Wyld, —, Sam Allsopp, Fred ('Chedda') Wyld.
Middle row: George Fotherby, Bill Burrows, Harry Swain, C Pacey.
Front row: Oliver Kirk, Harry Rowley, Les Beeton.

I think it was in 1936 that holidays with pay were introduced. That year the Australian cricket team were as usual opening the Test series at Nottingham. My husband Jack was passionately fond of cricket, always watching his local team. Now he had a whole week off and chose that week. It is the only thing I ever knew him queue for. He left home at 8 a.m. to get a front place in the queue. The weather was glorious and he saw his beloved Dennis Compton, the Bedser twins, Bill Edrich and the incomparable Donald Bradman. I don't think he ever forgot the joy of those days.

Alice Geeson

Eastwood Town Cricket Club Through the Ages

Cricket, as with the other national game football, has always been a team game to be played by and watched by masses of people for sheer enjoyment particularly during the hot summer months. In the early years of the 20th century when times were not so affluent, it was commonplace for schoolboys to be seen in the fields and meadows playing cricket. The boy who owned the cheap bat or one made by his father would always be welcome; the wickets — a bundle of coats tied up by the sleeves of the outer one — and a tennis ball made up their equipment, but they were happy days.

The records show that in 1856 the local colliery owners, Barber Walker & Co., set aside a plot of land for cricket — the current Eastwood ground — and the team to play on it was the Eastwood Amateurs. A decade later cricket was also being played at Eastwood Hall for in 1868 an Eastwood XVIII (eighteen) captained by Thomas Walker of Eastwood Hall played an All England XI (eleven) in a three day match at the Hall.

I have fond memories of cricket in Eastwood in the late 1920s and '30s leading up to the Second World War. All sorts of local firms had teams; two that I recall were Allcock & Sisson the builders and Skeltons the chemist. In that period and the decade after the war there were seven cricket clubs and grounds within a radius of two miles from the Sun Inn, and the list does not include teams at Kimberley and Underwood: Eastwood Town CC; Eastwood Collieries CC (Eastwood Hall); Eastwood St Mary's CC; Langley Mill Co-op (Dairy) CC; Shipley Boat CC; Digby Colliery CC; and Greasley Church CC, whose ground was the first field after the Horse and Groom.

Eastwood Town Cricket Club, Season 2000. Back row (l to r): Miss A Buckley (scorer), Michael Naylor, Dean Blake, Gary Lycett, Musarritt Hussein, David Richardson, Geoff Stocks. Front row: Gareth Painter, Stuart Hill, Neil Gregory (captain), Nagasir Sookram, Tony Gregory.

Many fine cricketers have graced the cricket grounds of Eastwood this century and a lot have gone on to play for their county. Names like McIntyre, Oates, Burrows, Carlin, Shaw, Webster and Doctors Dixon and Robey from earlier years, and in more recent times the Astles, Bates, Buckleys, Gregorys, Whites and Thompsons have all been a credit to the town and the game. Probably the best known of the lot was Jeff Astle who was not only a very fine all-round cricketer but also scored the winning goal for West Bromwich Albion in a Cup Final at Wembley.

It is sad that now in the current climate of sporting diversity there is only one cricket club left in the town, and it is seriously hoped that in 100 years time it will still remain in being for it has a wonderful history. From 1880 to 1920 Eastwood Amateurs played on the ground and a photograph in the Club's possession dated 1910 shows the team pictured in front of the first wooden pavilion. From 1920 after the First World War Eastwood Collieries were formed and occupied the ground until 1939. In 1922–24 the local miners, who were keen cricketers, built the present pavilion which has tons of character. During that period Nottinghamshire Cricket Club used the ground on a regular basis for fixtures. In those days too Beauvale School and the Eastwood Council Schools used to march the pupils down to the ground for their sports days. During the Second World War, when cricket ceased, there was great deterioration at the ground and for two or three years after the war it was used for football.

It was with great help and foresight from Eastwood Town Council, who purchased the ground, that a number of Eastwood cricket lovers were able to re-form the Club as Eastwood Town CC around 1952, and in the last almost 50 years the Club has gone from strength to strength. The facilities at the Club are continually improving. Nottinghamshire CCC use the ground every season and there are many representative games played on it.

The aim of the Club is to provide entertaining cricket free of charge for the people of Eastwood and more importantly to encourage the youngsters in the district, boys and girls, to play cricket. We have detected an increase in popularity amongst the current generation of young people which can only be good for the game. Now the officials of the Club hope that with its long traditions it will be functioning long into and throughout the new millennium.

Bill Gregory
(President, Eastwood Town Cricket Club)

Adventures in the Countryside

Years ago the village of Underwood where I grew up was surrounded by what I used to think of as Robin Hood land. In the 1930s my friends and I would unlock magic every time we ventured there. We called it 'going down Felley.' School holidays at that time signalled weeks of unfettered play — play that cost nothing. Tree houses were built high in the branches, serviced by crude ladders made from a log and rung with six-inch nails. Another favourite pastime was the Tarzan swing. We hung a rope from a branch which reached over the brook and a piece of wood tied to the end served as a foothold. I remember one day the branch broke and I really did see stars as it hit me over my head.

In 1940 when the German army was rumoured to be preparing to invade Britain, we were playing on the 'common' one day when we spotted a uniformed man wearing jackboots riding fast towards us. Convinced that he was a German officer we quickly hid in a clump of gorse. Later, a little disappointed, we found it was one of the Chaworth-Musters family!

Moorgreen Reservoir, with the boathouse. The road (now the B600) is rather busier today!

Swimming in the reservoir and afterwards basking in the sun like contented seals was as good as a holiday at the seaside. That we were trespassing made it more exhilarating. It took days to build a raft; nails were hard to come by and nobody seemed to have a sharp saw. Mark Twain would have been proud as the young Sawyers and Finns set sail.

Stalking wildlife in Felley was better than visiting any zoo. To sit in a hide of bracken and gorse and wait for the shy roe deer to come walking by was never boring because there were so many other animals and birds around. A fox might slink by or maybe a pheasant. We observed rabbits, hares and squirrels, and linnets, siskins and yellowhammers settled on the gorse. In the cloudless sky a skylark would pour forth cascades of song. A free paradise indeed! Pulses would run high whenever we children were taken to see a badger sett. Fishing was always exciting. Bullheads were easy if you could see them among the mud, but perch were often too fast. Crayfish — and water rats — frightened the girls who preferred minnows, but these invariably died when taken home in a jam jar.

There was a cornucopia of treasure to be found in Felley. Mushrooms, blackberries, wild strawberries, hazel and beech nuts abounded. I remember an old lady who kept a field full of blackberry bushes and charged sixpence a basket. During the war a bomb dropped there and the crater filled up with water making a miniature pond. We made pipes from acorns, and some children even tried to make corn dollies.

Now in the television age unfortunately children are thought not to be safe anymore on their own in what we called Robin Hood land. They really were the 'good old days.' To me places like Felley and Moorgreen Reservoir are little bits of heaven. People tend to be too materialistic today and don't seem to appreciate the natural things of life. I believe it is true that by trying to catch stars people miss the flowers at their feet.

Maurice Holmes
born 1933

I was born on The Breach (now Greenhills Road and Garden Road). One character I strongly remember from my childhood is Jimmy Bonnet who was the 'policeman' for Barber Walker & Co., the colliery owners. Known to everyone as 'Bobby' Bonnet, he lived on Coach Road at the back of Beggarlee Yard near to the private road which led to Lamb Close, the home of the Barber family.

Bobby Bonnet seemed to have the knack of being in two places at once, shouting at the children, 'Don't run, I know all your names' — which he did! I can recall an incident when a gang of us went for a walk round Coney Grey Farm and decided to go into the Spinney, a small wood near the farm. We knew we were trespassing, and we had been there for half an hour when someone shouted, 'There's Bonnet!' We jumped up and ran as fast as we could all the way home. Within half an hour Bonnet arrived, knocking on the door and asking, 'Is your lad in?' My dad asked what I had been up to and Bonnet told him. Dad said, 'Leave it to me, Jim.' Bonnet knew I would be dealt with!

On another walk up Coney Grey Lane we found a pheasant's nest and took some of the eggs. When I got home I put the eggs under my dad's fowls. Twenty minutes later Bonnet was knocking on the door asking about the eggs, so I had to tell the truth. My dad said, 'Right my lad, go and get those eggs and put them back where they belong.' Off I went with Bonnet and returned the eggs. Then with a clout around my ears he sent me home, and when I got there I was given a good hiding with the belt (a pit strap). That taught me a lesson.

On another occasion a dozen of us from The Breach were walking through Beggarlee Yard onto the Coach Road when Bonnet appeared out of the blue. 'Hello Mr. Bonnet,' we called, to which he replied, 'Stop right where you are!' Then he told us to empty our pockets and he confiscated all the 'gadders' (catapults). 'Off you go,' he said, 'and remember I've got my eyes on you,' which is what he also used to say when we tried to get 'back-road' into Beggarlee Baths for a swim.

Bonnet was always there with his cry of 'Don't run, I know all your names!' He never missed anything. We were playing football on the meadows one Sunday afternoon when Bonnet and the sergeant from Eastwood Police Station walked through. The sergeant asked Bonnet what he was going to do about us playing on a Sunday. 'Nothing,' he replied. 'While they're playing here I know where they all are!' Bobby Bonnet was a hard but fair man whom we respected, just as we did our parents and teachers. What we did in our younger days was more for devilment than being destructive. I do not know what became of him, but Bonnet's name will be remembered by many in Eastwood.

James Whitehead
born 1920

My family were always enthusiastic foot sloggers (two of my brothers once walked 150 miles to Bristol in four days and nights to get work on a cattle boat), and twenty miles in a day's family ramble was about our average. Summer picnics to Felley Mill or Bulwell Springs were popular, when in return for a few jobs done by our lads the farmer would give us milk and some delicious ham and eggs to be cooked over a big bonfire. High jinks and childish games followed paddling in some stream, then round the fire's dying embers we sang a few songs before trailing home across the fields carrying our pots and crocks. Sometimes there would be a two-mile gap between the first and last of us, but a roll call taken about midnight saw all of us safely back in the nest.

Some long Sunday walks began at dawn! Our shop shut at ten on Saturday nights, then we had a bread and cheese supper with beer, and after a short nap we would set off for the Hemlock Stone or Crich Stand and Ambergate or Papplewick and Hucknall Aerodrome (where incidentally I saw my very first aeroplane in 1915). Our odds and ends — coats, woollies, umbrellas, food parcels etc. — were pushed along in our old bassinet pram which also came in useful carrying home the odd casualty or 'dropout.' I remember one midnight stroll to Strelley Woods to hear the nightingales and the birds' dawn chorus. We ate breakfast in a graveyard — I wonder what the spirits thought of our intrusion? These outings were not always sweetness and light for sometimes it rained and rained, and that meant we ended the day soaked, bedraggled, weary and bad tempered!

Percy Cross
born 1906

Before the 1939–45 war Moorgreen Reservoir was a playground throughout the seasons for many people from all walks of life. I can remember groups of lads and lasses from Underwood using the reservoir as a holiday resort during the summer holidays. It was special for me as I didn't see the sea until I was 13, and then they told me it wasn't the sea but the Bristol Channel!

We don't seem to have those balmy magic days anymore when the sun shone incessantly and the air was so calm that the sky seemed to be holding its breath. Most of the lads could swim like dolphins and would complete the whole length. Bread and jam would be our caviar, and in those days spring water tasted like wine. I remember one Sahara-hot day when about twenty of us were at the reservoir all day. Unfortunately we didn't have sun cream and everyone returned home sunburnt and blistered except for one lad of Italian origin.

Nature seemed so exciting in those enchanting days. It was a feather in one's cap to catch sight of a kingfisher — like a sliver of rainbow snapped off and skimmed across the water; and to glimpse a sly furtive fox slinking near the bank; or to see a stately heron, silent as a stick, its snaky head sunk deep into its shoulders. Those were the days: no money, no television, but plenty of friends in a natural wonderland. For a time an entrepreneur from South Normanton ran a bus to the reservoir. Parties came from as far away as Nottingham to picnic on its banks. In the end it got so commercialised that Colonel Barber fenced it off and ordered his keeper to keep folks away.

Maurice Holmes

My special area of bygone Eastwood and district was the meadows which lay between Giltbrook and Cotmanhay. The top and bottom meadows were reached via Pit Lane, an access for the miners who daily tramped to Billy Hall's Pit. This quiet traffic-free lane also saw our first attempts at roller skating and bicycle riding. As children we filled the wheat fields, brooks, canal side and clayhole with our laughter and play, ate our picnic bread and jam sandwiches, and drank our bottled water long before reaching the mowing grass meadow.

Jean Duckworth's favourite childhood playground, the meadows at Giltbrook. On the left is the Nottingham canal, and on the right the 'Forty Bridges' railway viaduct which was demolished in 1973.

As the tough ones of the gang climbed and swung from trees, the more gentle gathered violets, gillyvers, buttercups and daisies. The daisies were made into chains which adorned our soiled dresses, and other flowers intended for Mother were discarded well before we reached home. The compacted earth towpath snaked along beside the canal with its swing bridges and the strongly built viaduct known as 'Forty Bridges' in the background.

As a family we journeyed once a year to Ilkeston Wakes and our walk took us past the sewage farm, over the canals and swampy marsh where bluey-green winged dragonflies fluttered from bullrush to marsh marigold. A chuffing steam train broke the silence and we always waved to the guard who happily waved back from his van. When we reached Cotmanhay we caught a waiting bus which took us to our swings of delight. The return journey brought us back the same way.

In later years as I sat in the office of the newly-built Newthorpe Sewage Works, which boasted the latest technology in sewage treatment, I listened to the dynamite blast which failed to blow up the viaduct. They had to replace the shots three times because the bridges had been constructed too well. The two farms had now gone; the sewage works and a housing estate covered the land and a new road took the place of the railway track and canal. No longer would I stroll casually by the allotments where Grandad and Dad grew all our food, or gather blackberries from the hedgerow in the lane. The following generations of children would never clang to and fro on the iron weighbridge at the pit entrance, or shout under the canal bridge and laugh at the echo, nor would they enjoy the meadows I once enjoyed.

Jean Duckworth
born 1941

When I was young we walked because walking did not cost money, but from that early experience I grew to love walking and the countryside. We walked in the Felley area which my mother knew well, having lived there throughout her childhood. From our home in Underwood we would walk down the hill, over the three brooks and sometimes turn left and go over the hills towards Annesley; sometimes over the Misk Hills to Hucknall; and other times we would turn right when we had gone over the brooks and head towards Moorgreen Reservoir.

When my mother was a child the woods were open and she could wander wild and free, but in my day they were fenced off and there was just one public track through. The notice said 'Trespassers Will Be

Prosecuted,' but we often found a gap in the hedge and went through because we were told Robin Hood had lived there and somewhere in those woods was Robin Hood's larder. However, we never found it and of course we always had to keep a wary eye open for the gamekeeper although we could escape before he got to us!

I could go to Felley without being accompanied by my parents so we were able to spend long summer days down there. A whole lot of children would come down from Underwood and the Alfreton Road area where I lived, setting out in the morning with bread and jam sandwiches and a bottle of cold tea. We stayed there all day, particularly in August when we had a whole month's holiday, paddling, fishing, gathering wild flowers and doing all the things you do in the countryside.

Our other walks were in the Erewash Valley area. This was the part that Dad knew best, having spent his childhood in Brinsley. As we walked down and reached what my father called 'The Meadows' we could see cattle grazing and children playing or bathing. We crossed the bridges over the River Erewash and the canal to get to Stoneyford, a little hamlet which at that time had its own tin church. We used to walk along from Stoneyford beside the main railway line; thirty years later my nephew, doing his trainspotting, would run down from Brinsley School to watch the Thames-Clyde express going through at about 4.15. From the Boat Inn we walked across the fields to the Monkey Bridge, occasionally extending the route to Ironville and Codnor Castle before returning to the Boat. Sometimes we would turn left and walk along the towpath past Wharf Row, up Stoney Lane and back into Brinsley.

Vera Musgrove
born 1918

We always seemed to have lovely summers and so picnics and paddling were popular. With a parcel of bread and dripping or lard, a piece of lardy cake and bottle of water we were off to the meadows. En route we would purchase for twopence a bag of fallen apples or pears from a cottage garden. The meadows through which the Coach Road ran was our favourite place. We played tiggy in the grass, made daisy chains, climbed trees — not me! — paddled in the brook, and only trespassed when we disturbed the haycocks left to dry. I must have been alone one day because I was missing for several hours. I was found asleep in one of the piles of hay, but no-one was unduly worried. Cases of child molestation were extremely rare; I suppose it happened but I do not recollect any in my neighbourhood.

Alice Geeson
born 1912

Childhood Games

I loved all the games but my favourite was skipping. We girls generally used an old clothes line or a piece of thick rope from an old orange box given to us by the greengrocer. There was very little traffic in our side street so we played on the road. Two girls would choose the name of a girl or perhaps of a flower. The rest of us would skip once, calling out a name. If it coincided with the chosen one we had to take an end of the rope. Sometimes two ropes were turned together. I think this was called French skipping, and keeping your feet disentangled called for speed and agility. We played 'pe-pi-po pepper,' each syllable speeding up the rope until with 'pepper' it was going like an express train! I was not very good at running in, i.e. jumping in while the rope was turning, so the day when I mastered the trick was a truly red-letter one. Some of us were given manufactured ropes complete with handles and bells, but generally our makeshift substitutes sufficed.

(L to r) Les Whitehead, Charlie Rowley and Mo Bailey enjoying a game of cricket in 1950.

I loved my whip and top, and I covered the top with coloured chalk and paper. I also played marbles with the boys but was not very clever. Some children had the same marbles for years and added to their total with skill. Luckily someone in my family could usually find a penny for me to buy fifty coloured clay marbles. I think perhaps battledore and shuttlecock was top of the pops with the girls. We used solid wooden racquets or the tennis type depending no doubt on the economic climate at home. It did not matter. We were all friends. We sat on the steps of the house across the street and played snobs. We joined the boys in the skills of 'duck stone' and 'tin-a-lurkey.' And always there was wonderful skipping.

They were such simple pleasures; there was no radio or television to distract us, and the toys we owned were, like us, very unsophisticated. The summer passed and back to school we went with the dark to look forward to. Then we played 'chink, chink, shine a light,' and in winter made slides and snowballed one another.

Alice Geeson

Brittains

FOR

SPRING GAMES

Battledores, Shuttlecocks, Marbles, Whips and Tops, Toy Footballs, Etc.

1924 advertisement

We spent hours fashioning bows and arrows from willow and hazel so that the outlaws of Sherwood could march again. But nobody wanted to be Friar Tuck! Once I was in serious trouble when I cut a piece off my mother's clothes prop to make a sword like Robin Hood's. Cowboys and Indians would appear, bringing the Wild West into Felley. Pea-shooters made out of the stalks of hogweed or cow-parsley took the place of guns, and pheasant feathers made a good Indian head-dress.

Maurice Holmes

Our playground games at Beauvale ranged from singing *On The Mountains Stands A Lady*, *Blue Bird* and *The Big Ship Sails* to skipping with a rope, couples who skitter-scattered, and the 'gang' members who paraded in long lines shouting, 'Anybody on our gang!' By the time the bell went no-one could remember what pursuit the gang was forming for! The boys skimmed cigarette cards and cardboard milk bottle tops against the wall. Whips and tops, balls, handbags and jewellery were all forbidden.

Jean Duckworth

Does anyone remember the game called trap bat — an oblong wooden box with one end missing and a swivelled piece of timber on which a ball was placed? The ball was struck with a small bat and as it rose into the air the striker would attempt to hit it and run. The rules were similar to cricket; you could be caught or run out, and if the striker failed to hit the ball three times in succession he was out.

Girls and boys usually played different games. Girls played hopscotch, battledore and shuttlecock, hoopla and skipping. They also played snobs which were five cubed stones, coloured if bought from a shop, or else small matched stones or flints found in the road. Boys played football, cricket, cowboys and indians, stick and peggy (similar to trap bat), and 'rustica bomm stick' or as we called it 'rusty bum finger or thumb.' Another boys' game was marbles, variously called prits, blood alleys, pops, taws and stealies. Both sexes played leapfrog, often on the way home from school when we also played marbles in the gutter.

Cigarette or 'bacca' cards were a favourite occupation. Inserted in each packet by the manufacturers, they were collected into sets of various subjects. We swapped cards with our friends to make up sets. With any surplus cards we played skimming games such as 'knocks down'— having stood four cards against the wall we skimmed other cards towards them and the player who knocked down the last card standing would win all the cards on the floor. In 'skims on' we skimmed cards until one player succeeded in placing a card onto another; the winner would then collect all the cards.

Ticka was a game in which the player who was 'on' would place a tin can in the middle of the street. The other children would hide, and if the player on saw another one peeping both would rush towards the can. If the hidden player reached it first he would kick it away and go and hide again. If the player who was on got there first the hidden player took his or her turn at being on. On winter nights we used to punch two holes in a large empty tomato tin and attach a piece of wire. We filled the can with live coals from the fire at home, then we would twirl it around our heads to get the coals really hot. We called it a 'winter warmer.'

Ken Marsland

We played lots of lovely games in the playground at Bagthorpe; games of chase, making long trains one joined on behind the other, chain tag or just racing around. Our playground had a good slope so in the wintertime it was lovely to slide from top to bottom.

Vera Musgrove

When I was a kid at New Eastwood, along with the other 'brats,'
We played at cricket on the 'rec' with planks of wood for bats.

If and when we lost the ball, over some garden fence,
We threw the bats at a conker tree; we then had no more sense.

Sometimes the fruit came tumbling down, in thick green spiky shells.
Then conkers were collected, in numbers no-one tells.

The game of conkers was a must, a regular autumn scene.
The competition often rough, always fierce and keen.

With conker one'ers, two'ers, three'ers, my, those kids were mean.
To get a higher score than six, they would brag sixteen!

No Strings Attached

Conkers were hung on strings at home to harden in the sun.
Some were buried in cowpats; even that was done!

A few were baked upon the hob, as hard as any stone,
So if they broke upon first hit, there wasn't half a moan.

That conker tree's still standing there, although it's now much bigger,
And still the kids throw sticks at it; I bet it has a snigger.

It's seen us kids all squaring up, then going home for dinner.
But it will see us all out, the conquering cobbler winner!

Fred Skillington

Children could 'play out' then. We played whip and top, having coloured the tops with chalk so that when they whizzed round they made a pattern. If you had a leather lace in your whip you were very posh! We played on the Dovecote Road 'rec' enjoying the Bobby's Hat and the Big Swing. One day I was hit on the head by a swing and had to go home. As I passed Renshaw's bike shop, opposite Newthorpe Baptist Church, I caught sight of myself in a large mirror in the shop window. I was shocked to see a 'duck egg' sticking out from my forehead. Until then it hadn't seemed to hurt! On the way to Beauvale School we would gather cobwebs on a bent stick. On damp autumn mornings you could see them clearly. If you gathered enough, one on top of the other, you ended up with a thick mat. We were convinced we had made real rubber!

Pat Potter
born 1942

I remember once 'scooting' down Gilthill in an old pram. We cut a hole in the hood so we could see where we were going!

Florence Smith
born 1918

Being twins, my brother Ian and I were expected to be together, play with and share the same friends, look after and generally never lose sight of one another. Consequently, being a girl I tagged along with Ian and his mates. Reluctantly they allowed me to join them but insisted I remain silent, do as I was told and keep well in the background! My choice would have been to play at home with dolls and prams with my friends who were nice little girls, instead of with bullying boisterous boys. We certainly were 'street children,' enjoying games of hopscotch, snobs, marbles, whips and tops, skipping, 'tin-a-lurkey,' 'hot cockles' and 'British bulldog', with the occasional 'rusty bum' and 'odds and eve's.' All these activities took place in the street, rain or shine, in the obvious absence of motor vehicles.

Jean Duckworth

I was born on Bishop Street. Most of the children used to congregate and play at the junction with Ratcliffe Street because of the gas lamp situated there. There was no need to worry about traffic then, and even now I can see my sister in the centre of the road playing with her diabolo (a two-headed top tossed and caught on a string attached to two sticks, held one in each hand). We used to race round Queen's Square with hoops, or 'bowlers' as we called them. The girls had wooden ones (the bigger the better), and the boys iron ones complete with iron handle. 'Tin-a-lurkey' was the 'in' thing on dark nights, scampering over back gardens. Another popular game was rounders, but we were careful not to hit the ball into Maggie Pounder's garden as she would keep it. The plot of land making the corner of Church Walk and Queen's Square was vacant for years and the boys made great use of it for football! and cricket, although we girls were never allowed to play.

Lily Whittamore
born 1915

A Century Remembered

Football

Football was played at the back of Lynncroft on 'Cow Closes' or on the Breach (Garden Road). The players would rub their legs with 'hoss oils,' the stuff which the colliers used on the pit ponies. In those days there were few rules and certainly no protection for the goalkeeper. He was a breed apart, the bravest of the brave. A goalie with the ball in his possession was fair game for a good kicking!

Palmerston Arms Football Club, 1949. Back row (l to r): Albert Holmes, Les Harvey, Albert Noble, Walter Berry, Ken Harvey, Harry Ward, Doug Griffiths. Front row: Eddie Worrall, Jack Lowe (the landlord), Arthur Rowley, Fred Lambert.

Mavis Williamson born 1922

Eastwood Town Football Club 1953 - 2000

Although an Eastwood Town FC team competed for two seasons between 1920 and 1922 in the Notts Alliance, the current Club dates back only to 1953 when founder members like Jack Grainger, Les George, Ted Sanby and today's Chairman George Belshaw were leading lights in its formation. The original team seems to have been drawn mainly from two sources, the recently folded Eastwood Collieries side and a local engineering firm G.R. Turner.

Between 1953 and 1961 Eastwood Town competed very successfully in the Notts Alliance, the highlights being a Senior Division title in 1956–57 and an Alliance Senior Cup victory in 1955–56. In those eight seasons their overall League record reads: P216 W162 D27 L27 F904 A305 Pts351. The reserve side was equally successful with Division One honours in 1957–58 and 1959–60.

Page 177

A Century Remembered

'Town' entered the Central Alliance in 1961–62 and in the following season moved from their old ground, where the bowling green is now, to their present home. In 1963–64, inspired by 70 league goals from Brian Richardson, Eastwood Town won the Premier Division title by six points from Alfreton Town. Of the 181 goals scored in that campaign (4.3 per game average) almost 100 were contributed by 'Richo' and his partner Alan Boardman.

Another move in 1967–68 took Eastwood Town into the East Midlands Regional League and in 1971–72 they renounced their amateur status to obtain access to the famous Midland Counties League. Forced to have at least three semi-professional players, Eastwood Town signed a striker called Bill Jeffrey who was destined to make quite a name for himself. In 17 seasons as player and manager Bill's honours list includes a Midland League title, two League Cup wins and no less than seven County Senior Cup successes. A striker himself, Bill had a remarkable ability to sign goal scorers — from the incomparable Martin Wright through Geoff Kemm to Mark Richardson, the elder son of Brian.

When the Midland and Yorkshire Leagues amalgamated in the early eighties to form the N.C.E.L., Eastwood notched up runners-up spot twice in the new set-up before becoming founder members of the Northern Premier League (now Unibond) Division One in 1987-88. Since then honours have been limited to a couple of Senior Cup wins.

The present manager, Bryan Chambers, has kept Eastwood Town at the forefront of national non-league football by finding and selling on a succession of young players. Fees received for players like Richard Liburd, Martin Bullock, Neil Illman, Lee Marshall, Andy Todd and Glenn Kirkwood have allowed Eastwood Town to build up the reserves now being used to supplement a Football Trust grant in the latest development of their ground. Appropriately, the company granted the contract for the new stand and

Eastwood Town Football Club, 1999–2000. Back row (l to r): Richard King, Jamie Eaton, Freddy Morgan, Scott Bonsall, Andy Todd, Gavin Worboys, Gary Breach. Front row: Gary Castledine, Paul Gould (captain), Paul Tomlinson, Richard Parkin, Jay Bonser, Richard Smith, Martyn Chadbourne.

A Century Remembered

Breach United Football Club, 1932–33, photographed behind the old Palmerston Arms on Greenhills Road.
Back row (l to r): Jimmy Phillis, Fred Farnsworth (the landlord), Ernest 'Egge' Preston, George Ward, Arthur 'Tart' Kirk, Tommy 'Fob' Fotherby, George Darkins, Cyril Cope, Jim Wyld, Joe Eyre, Bill Burrows, Jim Tomlinson.
Middle row: Fred Hallam, Jack Wilbur, Jack Jefferies, Gersh Hallam, Keith Towle, Joe Fletcher.
Front row: George Worthington, Harold Perkin, George Martin, George Pykett, Walter Rowley, Sam 'Snebbie' Wardle, Boyd Syson, Harry Ward, George Mayfield, Bill 'Dodger' Wright.

dressing rooms complex (first used on 5th February 2000) is headed by Ian 'Arthur' Rowley who in a marvellous Eastwood career played over 800 First Team games and was never even cautioned by a referee.

No history of Eastwood Town FC would be complete without mention of their FA Amateur Cup exploits, particularly in the 1963–68 seasons. In that short period Eastwood three times reached the third round of that famous competition and captured some illustrious scalps including Woking (attendance at Coronation Park 1760), Whitby Town (2643), Bishop Auckland and Whitley Bay. The record home attendance, set on February 13th 1965, for the visit of Enfield who won 3 – 2 still stands at 2723.

The County Senior Cup had been Eastwood's 'holy grail' for nearly a quarter of a century until Bill Jeffrey worked the oracle in April 1976 at Priestsic Road, Sutton (do you remember Martin Smith's stunning header?), and went on to run up seven successes in all. Only sporadic good years since then leaves the overall total at nine but Bryan Chambers is keen to mark the new millennium by not only reaching double figures but also by making a long overdue impact in one of the top national trophies. The seeds for this were sown on Saturday October 30th 1999 when Eastwood Town FC made history as they competed for the first time ever in the first round proper of the FA Cup, losing 2 – 1 to Exeter City in a hard-fought game.

Paddy Farrell
(Secretary, Eastwood Town Football Club)

Guides and Brownies

The 1st Eastwood Guide Company has its certificate of registration dated April 20th 1927 and the signature on it is Robert Baden-Powell. We like to think that this is an authentic signature because we know he was still alive at that date and fully involved in the Guide movement when our 1st Eastwood Company was registered. The Guide movement then was just sweet seventeen. Today Guiding, of which 1st Eastwood Guide Company is part, is still alive and well and moving strongly into the 21st century.

It is the only uniformed youth organisation in Eastwood with an unbroken record of more than 70 years' continuity. The unit was formed by Miss Kathrine Ives, the daughter of the then Rector of Eastwood, together with Miss Ivy Jordan and Miss Connie Wheeler as Lieutenants, and meetings for girls were started in a barn in the Rectory grounds. Those were the days of black stockings, bloomers, felt hats and lots of drill — but lots of fun too. Miss Ives later became Lady Sherwood. Miss Wheeler is now Mrs Butterworth and still lives in Eastwood.

1st Eastwood Guides setting off for camp, c.1927 ...

It was about 1930 that Mrs Ada Birkin took over as Captain. She was warranted as Guider until 1954 and those 24 years saw very many changes in Guiding. I became a Brownie in the 1st Eastwood Brownies in 1952 and remember meetings in the old Girls' School with Miss Elsie Cary as Brown Owl and Miss Peggy Bowmer as Tawny Owl. They are both still interested supporters of Guiding in Eastwood today.

In 1954 Mrs Trudy Fogg became the warranted Guider and the Company was now meeting at the Community Centre on Church Street. We used to go past the fire engines and the dust carts and up some dreary concrete stairs to a strange room with windows so high that we could never see out. The place was pretty grim but the Guiding was great!

... and their successors enjoying camp in 1995.

Those were the days of the beginnings of 1st Eastwood's camping traditions. The Guiders gained their Campers' Licence and the Company began to acquire a wonderful collection of camping equipment. 'Don't throw that away, we can use it at camp!' was a phrase often heard in some households. But it was not all second-hand, and today the girls are well equipped for their camping expeditions thanks to regular replenishment of that early stock. 1957 was the date of the first Queen's Guides in Eastwood. They were June Clifton and Sylvia Crampton. In 1960 I received my Queen's Guide award, and the County Commissioner, Mrs Dulcie Hanson, came to present the badge and certificate.

1962 saw the fulfilment of something which 1st Eastwood Guides had talked and dreamed of for many years — our own Girls' Centre. We had held garden parties on Dr Gladstone's lawn ever since some of us could remember. Miles of pennies had been laid along Nottingham Road. Jumble sales, coffee mornings and all the rest were held for many years to raise money. Now, thanks to a lot of hard work on the part of the Committee led by my own father Horace Webster, and with the help of the parents of the children and the Guides and Brownies themselves, it really happened. The Dora Phillips Hall was opened in September 1962 by Mrs Hazel Robertson, the daughter of Dora Phillips and herself a member of 1st Eastwood Guides when she was a child in Eastwood. The Hall was unique in being built for the use of girls' uniformed organisations in the town and it is still a cherished home for Guiding.

In 1962 as the Guides moved into the Girls' Centre, Sylvia Crampton (now Mrs Lambert) became the Guider in Charge and Mrs Fogg moved to the Ranger unit. Camping continued as Sylvia gained her Licence. Sylvia's 21st birthday party was shared with the Guides at one of their meetings. In 1965 I took over as the Guide Guider and Sylvia moved into the Brownie pack. Our Queen's Guide tradition continued as

Marion Martin gained the award in 1966, Helen Keam in 1968, Jean Bailey and Kathryn Peck in 1972. In 1977 Sheena MacCulloch received her award and in 1981 Janet Hallam was the last Eastwood girl to reach this standard before the programme and age for this award changed completely.

We camped at least once every year in rain and sun. There were some tough times but we always went again! I have many fond memories of those camps and remember some silly things that happened too. The lions at Stapleford Park — we heard them roar as we lay in our tent at night and they sounded very close! The thunderstorm at Lamb Close, when we were taken into the house by Lady Barber and played tiddlywinks on the drawing room floor. The Guide who got her foot stuck in a cattle grid on a moonlight hike. The day the policeman brought back one Patrol after they missed the bus, and many more! We made heart-warming visits to old people's homes and children's homes with gifts at Easter and Christmas. We spent wonderful warm summer evenings at Lamb Close watching the sun go down as we sang 'taps' after a supper hike.

The Company celebrated its Golden Jubilee in 1977, the year of the Queen's Silver Jubilee. Our 60th birthday celebrations included a boat trip and a memorable camp at Waddow, the Guide Association Training Centre in Lancashire. Guides and Guiders from 1st Eastwood have represented their country in Japan, Iceland, Switzerland, Mexico and India as delegates of the Guide Association, and they have entertained Guides from many corners of the world in their homes after international camps in this country. I now meet women who were girls in the unit years ago and many are still involved, with their children and grandchildren being part of the Guiding family.

I continued as Guider of 1st Eastwood Guides until 1995 when I became Guider of 1st Eastwood Rainbow unit. During those years of leadership I also had opportunities in the county. I was Training Advisor for eight years and then Assistant County Commissioner for five years. I remember taking Guides on the train to London to sing carols under the Christmas tree in

Trafalgar Square, and ushering them into the Ladies Room at the Ritz to use the facilities! Brownies, Guides and Rangers came with me to present a cheque towards the building of the fourth World Guide House in Hampstead and we shared a taxi with the Chief Commissioner. Now our Guides stay at this house called Pax Lodge when they go to London.

1st Eastwood Guide unit has been part of the worldwide family of Guiding for most of the life of the Association, and girls and women of this town have enjoyed the privileges and opportunities which belonging to the largest female organisation in the world can bring. They are still doing that — every Thursday night and many other times too. Long may it continue!

Eileen Harvey (née Webster)

My daughter Sharon was in the 3rd Eastwood St Mary's Guides and so I joined the supporters' association committee, and because I had access to and could use a typewriter I became the Secretary! Marion Wilson the Guide Captain was Chairman, and Mrs C Stevenson Treasurer. A fund-raising programme was drawn up and one of the ideas put forward for 1972 was a pantomime *Cinderella*.

A script was obtained locally, and after some lines had been adapted to suit an Eastwood audience I set about typing scripts for all the major parts — quite a task! When we began rehearsals I was given the job of 'Prompt.' We also had to consider the costumes required and I made my daughter's Town Crier outfit. The shirt was an old school blouse, with lace jabot and cuff added. The black knee breeches were an old pair of black trousers cut off just under the knee with elastic threaded through. The top coat was an old red dressing gown with the bottom cut off which was used to make deep cuffs. Copious gold buttons were added and a black tricorn hat, again edged with lace, made from cardboard and black tissue paper. A gold waistcoat was also made for the grand finale.

I also supplied the costume for the two sisters in the grand finale — two of my old ballroom dresses. My daughter wore her outfit again as a highwayman when riding in an Eastwood Carnival procession, this time complete with black mask. The tricorn hat and the mask did not survive the damp on the day of the Carnival but I still have the rest of the costume — and the script!

Jean Brinsley

Although there was a flourishing Guide company, formed in 1927, there was no Brownie pack in Eastwood for younger girls. However, in 1935 two of the older Guides, Kathy Wardle and Elsie Cary who were also Sunday School teachers at St Mary's Parish Church, decided they would remedy this and so with six recruits from Sunday School they started the 1st Eastwood Brownie pack. Kathy being the older was Brown Owl, Elsie became Tawny Owl and the pack was registered at Guide Headquarters in 1936. Meetings were then held in the old St Mary's parish room, which was later demolished and Plumptre Hall built on the site. The pack quickly grew and thrived, and thus over the years countless little girls started learning knots, flags, shoe cleaning, sewing on buttons, plaiting, badge polishing and darning.

1st Eastwood Brownies in 1938 ...

I became a Brownie in July 1937 and because I lived opposite Brown Owl Kathy Wardle on Nottingham Road she would take me along with her. Brownie meetings quickly became the highlight of my week and I have very fond memories of Brown Owl, Tawny Owl, all my Brownie friends and all the activities. Learning to darn is something that I particularly remember. No-one taught how to darn by Miss Cary

... and their successors in 1964, with leaders (l to r) Peggy Bowmer, Mary Britain and Elsie Cary.

has ever lost the skill; although she was a gentle taskmaster, a second-rate darn was just not acceptable! Marching and drill for parades were an important feature in the early days but we also had a lot of games, singing, nature walks and tracking, picnics and swimming at Beggarlee pool.

Meetings were held throughout the war. Miss Cary became Brown Owl in 1943 with Miss Peggy Bowmer as Tawny Owl and both continued until 1966. They are still held in great affection by generations of Brownies, including my own daughters, and they continue to maintain a close interest in the pack. I was very happy to take over as Brown Owl from Miss Cary who had taught me so much nearly thirty years earlier, and I continued until 1987. Throughout the 65 years of its existence the pack has been led by only four Brown Owls, the present leader being Mrs Nova Scrimshaw.

Since 1962 meetings have been held in the Dora Phillips Hall, the Eastwood Girls' Centre, for which the Brownies helped to raise the money. Inevitably over the years changes have taken place to both the programme and the uniform, but enthusiastic little girls still keep their promise and law, do good turns and most importantly — have fun!

Leila Keam

Theatres

The first show I ever went to was in the Tent Theatre at the Croft (just below the Sun Inn). It was known as the 'Blood Tub' and was owned by Mr Teddy Raynor. I loved all the plays and revues, especially *Maria Marten and the Murder in the Red Barn*.

Lily Rose
born 1902

A yearly treat was the visit to the pantomime at the Nottingham Theatre Royal. Along with my mother's friend and daughter we travelled the eight miles by tramcar and were first in the queue for the upper circle. Taking it in turn we visited the Empire Café round the corner for hot Bovril and the time soon passed. We chose the middle of the front row where we ate our sandwiches, and then the curtain went up on three hours of magic. We saw the villain get his just deserts, heard the lovely singing of the principal boy (sometimes Dorothy Ward) and his sweetheart. We joined in the songs which were printed on a screen. *Yes, We Have No Bananas*, *I'm an Airman and I Fly, Fly Right Up In the Sky* and *Home In Pasadena* were three I remember. Perhaps the Clothing Club and the insurance hadn't been paid that week but my mother had filled a little girl's heart with tenderness and magic.

Alice Geeson
born 1912

Birnam Products Ltd Concert Party in 1948. Back row (l to r): Vic Hart, Arthur Poxon, Sheila Davies(?), Cyril Bye, Doreen Wilmot, John Sisson, John Leivers. Front row: Jim Menzies, Iris Cooper, Lucy Meakin, Stella Meakin, Joyce Smith, Duggie Dickman.

A Century Remembered

The bus company used to have a 'worker's ticket,' ninepence return to Nottingham, so when I was earning a bit more money I used to go with my friend to the Empire Theatre. We thought it was lovely, a seat up in the 'gods' for about a shilling, and I remember seeing Joseph Locke and Sandy Powell.

Mary Bend
born 1918

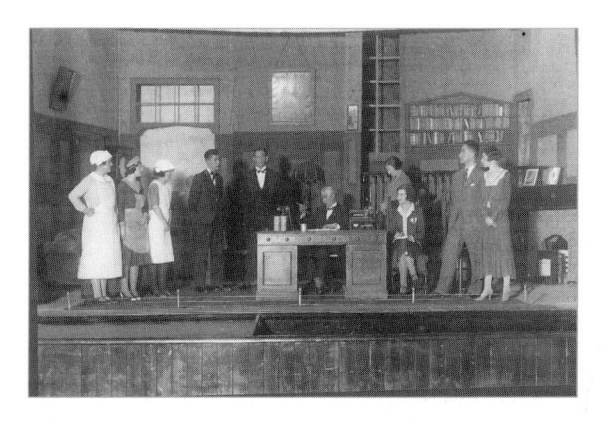

The Eastwood Players in The Sport of Kings on the stage of the Empire Cinema, c.1930.
(L to r): Edith Butler, Phyllis Wigley, — , Fred Wigley, — , William Bentley, Winifred Brittain, Ellen Slater, Eric Williamson, Ivy Jordan.

I used to do amateur dramatics in the winter. We called ourselves the Eastwood Players, a group which had been started by the Revd Shave, a minister at the Congregational Church. When he moved to a church in Liverpool, Mr Whitelock who was the Surveyor for Barber Walker & Co., took over as producer. I think the first play we did was *Tilly of Bloomsbury*. We put on one play a year right up to 1939 — I remember we were starting a play when the war broke out and we had to stop.

We started rehearsals in the winter as the nights got darker. They were great times because we rehearsed in the big rooms of the Whitelock's house, The Hollies, on Nottingham Road where the market is now held. I think Mrs Whitelock had been a famous cook in her day, and I remember she gave us some lovely refreshments. At first we performed the plays at the Mechanics Institute (Miners Welfare) on Mansfield Road, but when they got so popular and there was not enough room for the audience we took over the Empire Cinema. I think we hired it for three nights, Thursday to Saturday (the film programme was changed mid-week in those days). We were a happy little band of people and really enjoyed doing the plays.

Winifred Stoakes
born 1909

A Century Remembered

I have always been a keen theatregoer, with frequent visits to the Theatre Royal, the Nottingham Playhouse and many theatres throughout the country. However, my earliest recollection of the stage was when my mother took me in 1937 to the Sunday School room in Beauvale Methodist Church. This was for a performance of the famous scene from Charles Dickens' *Great Expectations*, where a bitter and scheming Miss Havisham sits in her fading wedding weeds beside her decaying wedding cake, complete with cobwebs and mice on the table. I suppose it could have been rather frightening for me as a child, and it has always been etched so vividly in my memory. The 'strolling players' were a husband and wife team who acted excerpts from the classics.

Patricia Purdy
born 1927

I remember George Stubbs building his Empire Theatre (now Woolworths) in 1913. My brother George started work there operating the stage limelights. They engaged some good talent there in those early days, including a young Gracie Fields, Harry Tate, Archie Pitt and Florrie Forde.

Later it changed to a cinema of silent film delights. For a penny we kids could see the Saturday matinée and get a free ticket for the Tuesday evening show! Those penny seats were just wooden forms — 'Bring your own flea powder.' For twopence you had posh tip-up seats and access to one of the new wonders of the age — real chain-pulling, water-gushing water closets! I still remember the almost unbearable excitements of those Pearl White and Eddie Polo serial films. Charlie Chaplin, Tom Mix and Rudolph Valentino were other unforgettable stars.

Next to the Sun Inn was a field in which stood Parker's Picture Pavilion, a wooden shack which pre-dated the Empire for films, probably 1912, and

Cinemas

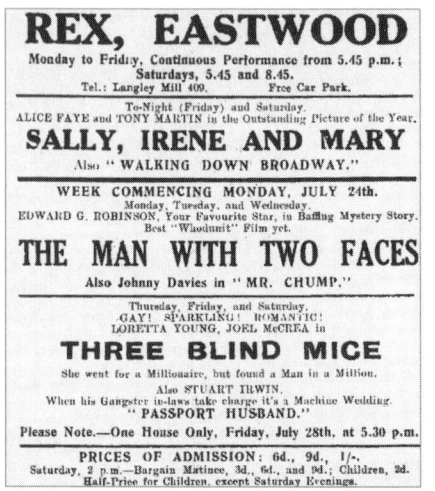

Eastwood cinema programmes for July 1939

The Eastwood Empire, c.1920

Eastwood Empire Cinema programme

survived until about 1919. That same field was the venue for the Michaelmas Statutes Fair and for big shows like Lord John Sanger's Circus and Bostock & Wombwell's Wild West Show, all exciting stuff!

Percy Cross

Living at Brinsley we had two choices of cinema, the Eastwood Empire and Jacksdale Picture Palace. A little bus run by Walters used to run on Friday and Saturday nights from Brinsley taking people to the 'pictures' in Eastwood. We preferred Friday nights because we also went to the market. On one occasion my brother and I, along with a lot of our friends, decided to walk over the fields to Jacksdale Picture Palace but coming back we got caught in a storm and had to shelter in a barn. That experiment was not repeated!

Vera Musgrove

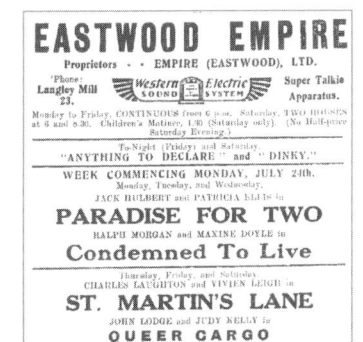

The pictures were a must on Saturday afternoons. At first they were silent films, with Jimmy Webster playing suitable accompaniment on the piano — and he was good. Admission cost a penny in the 'chicken run' and twopence at the back. An old lady known to everyone as Aunt Polly kept us in good order. Occasionally we were treated to a live show which we called 'talent.' Some of the performers were local girls, others came from afar and they always lodged with Mrs Welch on Queen's Square.

Lily Whittamore

My mother and father were friends of Mr Stubbs who built and owned the Empire Cinema, and I was friendly with his daughter — we were nearly the same age. There was a special matinée for children on Saturdays from 1 o'clock to 3.30 or 4. Of course the children were only allowed to sit downstairs, but Mr Stubbs insisted that his daughter sat in the balcony and I was allowed to go with Eileen, along with the Clements girls. We felt very superior sitting up there! The films always included a serial which ended with the heroine trapped in a pit and surrounded by snakes, or something like that, so you had to go the following week to find out what happened. It was very exciting.

Winifred Stoakes

Of the two cinemas my favourite was the Empire because after the film we visited Hawksworth's restaurant for the finest chips, meat pie and gravy. There were often queues for the Saturday night performances, the longest I remember being for *The Jolson Story*. I often visited the Rex after school on my own. If taken in by an adult the admission price was only sevenpence; otherwise it was a shilling. We never considered this practice to be a risk — an age of innocence!

David Richmond
born 1938

In 1951 I started work as a projectionist at the Rex Cinema, just below the Sun Inn on Derby Road. The manager was Mr Jimmy Leyland who had previously worked at the Elite in Nottingham. The owner of the Rex was Mr Fulwood, a plumber by trade, who with a business partner had built the cinema as an investment in 1938. I was employed full-time, but there was also a part-time projectionist, Eric Derbyshire, who taught me the whole system. He had a full-time job at Ormonde Colliery, but came to the cinema in the evenings and we ran the show together.

The original machinery had been replaced in 1950 with Gaumont Kalee 20 projectors, but the original sound system — British Acoustic — was retained. For an 850-seat cinema the amplifier's maximum 12 watts output was not very powerful, but it was adequate except on Saturday nights when the place was getting quite full, and then we definitely had to turn the fader

400 local people were recruited as extras for the filming of Sons and Lovers on location in Eastwood and Brinsley in 1959. Five - year old Elizabeth Naylor (right) waits to take part in a scene being shot on Princes Street. The film, starring Trevor Howard, Wendy Hiller, Dean Stockwell, Heather Sears and Mary Ure, had its first showing in Eastwood at a special charity performance at the Rex Cinema on Sunday 27 November 1960.

up a long way. Saturday was always the best night of the week. From the projection room I could see the people queueing all the way past the Sun Inn and around the corner down Mansfield Road. At the front of the Rex on the right-hand side was Mrs Fulwood's sweet shop, useful for patrons as they queued. (On the other side was an office used by Councillor Long, whose son was the pianist for the singer Frankie Vaughan.)

The films were always hired by the manager. As a little independent local cinema we did show a lot of rubbish. We usually got the better films for the Thursday to Saturday run than at the beginning of the week. The majority were black and white, colour films being still quite rare then. When we got the 20th Century Fox features with Betty Grable and similar stars the cinema used to be full.

We could never get a licence to show films in Eastwood on Sundays. From Monday to Saturday we opened at 5 p.m., showing the second feature, adverts, news and main feature. This took us up to 8 o'clock when we ran the whole programme again. It was a continuous showing, so the patrons if they wished could go in at 5 and not come out again until 10.30 or even 11 o'clock. (Eventually the independent cinemas would show the main feature first, the second feature just once, and finally the main feature again). Saturday was the only night when the show was not continuous but two separate performances. The audience had to leave at half-time, and the usherettes cleaned the cinema ready for the second showing.

The only matinée was for children on Saturday afternoons from 1 o'clock until just after 3. I think it cost threepence to get in, and if it was a good film the children were usually quite well behaved. Sometimes they were so noisy that we had to run the film with the house lights on so that the usherettes could keep an eye on them, and for obvious reasons no children were allowed in the balcony.

A Century Remembered

Breakdowns were few and far between, but a lot depended on the quality of the prints. They did not come on spools but as a flat film in a box. An oldish film would come in 1000 feet reels, and two of those joined together would go onto one spool. I had to join all those reels together and make up the whole programme. On Wednesday nights I had to break them all down again, and then prepare to make up a programme on Thursday mornings for the Thursday to Saturday show.

There were two projectors in use. A feature film would probably consist of six or seven reels, each running for 20 minutes, so I was switching from one projector to the other throughout the show. If the projectionist forgot to run the leader down the film, the audience saw the '5, 4, 3 …' on the screen. The projectionist's worst nightmare was a 'run-off,' where the film ran out of the projector before the reel had been changed over.

For every reel of the film I had to put fresh carbon in the lamp house at the back of each projector. If I forgot, and the carbon burnt away before the end of the reel, I had to change over before time and miss out a bit of the film! If anyone was off, Mrs Fulwood, the owner's wife, used to help in the projection box, mostly with re-winding the films for us. The re-winders were in a separate room.

At the Rex we had a spotlight which we shone on the ice-cream girl. We made sure that she wore a diamanté necklace which always sparkled in the light. There were no facilities for playing music, but many years ago they had pantomimes on the stage and there were some very primitive dressing rooms underneath.

Apart from the projecting I had to do other jobs such as repairing seats and putting up posters, not only on the front of the cinema but also on notice boards throughout the area. There was one at the top of Maws Lane, Kimberley and every month I had to go out on my bike and pin up the programme posters. In the winter I had to keep the coal fire going in the boiler, which was right at the other end of the cinema. The heating was not very effective. The big problem in winter was in deciding whether to leave the huge fan running which extracted the cigarette smoke but let cold air in, or to keep the patrons warm but sitting in their smoke! Some nights, with everyone smoking, I couldn't even see the vital cue marks on the film which warned me when to change reels.

I was friendly with the projectionists at the other Eastwood cinema, the Empire. My working day was a split shift from 10 a.m. to 1 p.m. and then from 5 p.m. until the end of the show. In the afternoons I used to meet George Plowright and Roger (whose surname I have forgotten) at Fletcher's Milk Bar, on the opposite corner to the police station. We would argue about which cinema was showing the best films and how many patrons we were attracting. The Empire did not have a spotlight, and its projection box was much smaller than at the Rex. The projectors were older Gaumont Kalee 12s, but the Western sound system was very good. It had a newer and more powerful amplifier than the Rex although it was an older cinema, seating probably 500.

In the 1950s and '60s the owners could not afford to spend money on the cinemas, and the Empire closed in November 1956 to be refurbished as Woolworth's store. The Rex ceased to show films in June 1966. It was used as a bingo hall until 1987 and the building was demolished in 1992. I later worked at the Gaumont and the Odeon in Nottingham, and at the Regent in Kimberley. The projection room there was at street level, and I could talk to people on the pavement!

Noel Pratt
born 1936

Between the wars we had carnival bands — the Eastwood Arcadians, the Kimberley Diamonds and the Newthorpe Crusaders. Some collieries had brass bands and choirs; the Eastwood Collieries and Pye Hill Male Voice Choirs are still flourishing.

Ken Marsland

Music

> **REX CINEMA**
> **Piano Accordion Competition**
> For REX DISCOVERIES' PROGRAMME.
> CONDITIONS.
> Dress and Selection played Own Choice.
> Judges' Decision will be Final.
> 1st PRIZE—SILVER CHALLENGE CUP AND A PLACE IN
> THE REX DISCOVERIES' PROGRAMME.
> Entries to be made at Rex, Eastwood   CLOSING DATE, AUG. 5th.

1939 advertisement

The Crusaders (later the Greasley New Crusaders) Carnival Band was founded in 1935 by local people in Newthorpe. The uniform was a red jacket with brass buttons in the shape of a cross, and white trousers or skirt for the women. My father was the founding Secretary, and his minute books for the first few years show a busy programme of parades, competitions and other events, including appearances at the Eastwood Carnivals and the 1937 Coronation Day festivities. However, not everyone appreciated the band's efforts as the minutes for April 1937 record that 'the Secretary should write to Mr Cliff of Hill Top, apologising for the Band playing while he was ill!'

The Crusaders Carnival Band performing at Ilkeston, c.1937

Pat Potter

The present Eastwood Arcadians Band was formed in 1976 and by 1980 were the Carnival Band Association Champions. Although it now has fewer members, the band still competes in carnival band contests and gives displays.

Derek Hickinbotham

Much of our leisure time was spent in home entertainment. At some point my Grandma acquired a splendid new gramophone and

GRAND CONCERT

will be held in the

Rex Cinema,   Eastwood,

Sunday, 15th January, 1950,

at 7.30 p.m.

As a mark of appreciation to
Mr. Elijah Smith

Artistes:

ORMONDE COLLIERY BAND

Miss C. GRATTON	Soprano
Mr. R. COOKE	Bass
Mr. G. PRESTON	Tenor
Mr. A. SINGLETON	Monologues

EASTWOOD & DISTRICT MIXED CHOIR
(Conductor : Mr. G. H. MBE)

Accompanist — Mr. A. TAYLOR

Chairman — Mr. G. LONG

Programme — Threepence

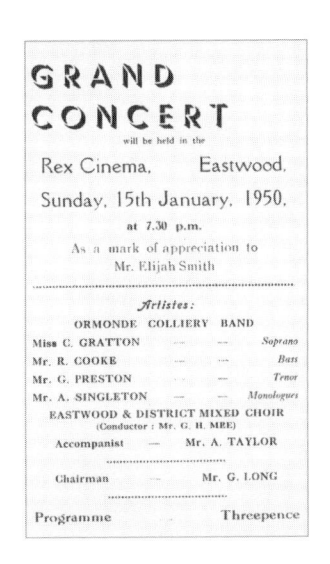

we would sit in her living room with a coal fire blazing. I sat on the sofa at my mother's side and I can remember listening to the boy soprano Ernest Lush singing *Oh For The Wings Of A Dove*. I also remember Grieg's *Morning* and Ketelby's *In A Monastery Garden*, my father's favourite. I think that is where an appreciation of music began which has stayed with me all my life. There were also records of comedians like Sandy Powell whose catchphrase was 'Can you hear me Mother?' And I remember sitting in delicious terror by my mother's side listening to a record of the melodrama *Maria Marten and the Murder in the Red Barn*.

Vera Musgrove

The Co-op Girls Choir at Neath Eisteddfod in the 1920s. The back row includes Miss Linwood (2nd from right) and Agnes Eyre (4th from right). George Teather, the choir's conductor, is on the far right.

In 1939 I decided to have piano lessons. My tutor was Miss Gwendoline Gibson who lived with her mother on Barber Street. She invited me to join the Co-op Girls' Choir for which she was the pianist. The rehearsal room was above the Co-op store at 28-30 Nottingham Road (later to be Machin & Hartwell's shop). The room was reached by some rickety wooden stairs at the side of the store and was the same room that saw the beginning of the Co-op Women's Guild which played a very important part in the local community. The choir's conductor was Mr George Teather from Langley Mill, and we were entered for a number of contests including Selston Music Festival. I cannot remember if we gained any prizes but we thought that we were quite grown-up, travelling all the way to Selston, and it became one of the highlights of our year.

Patricia Purdy

A Century Remembered

One of the several bands taking part in the 1935 Eastwood Carnival pass the Empire Cinema and the Wellington Inn.

1935 advertisement for one of the most popular shops in Eastwood at 95 Nottingham Road

I can remember Moorgreen Reservoir being frozen. One Sunday afternoon we walked down and it was one mass of ice. On it people were standing in groups talking to each other; there were children sliding and others skating, but I felt a very deep sense of unease thinking of all that deep water beneath me and I was pretty thankful when we came off the ice!

Vera Musgrove
born 1918

Skating

A Century Remembered

Skating on the Cromford Canal at Langley Mill, c.1960

In the winter — and we had severe ones when I was young — Moorgreen Reservoir often froze. Skaters would come from all around to use this natural ice-rink, and it is said that about 500 skaters have been seen on the reservoir at one time. To test the ice a heavy horse and cart were used. I often wondered what would have happened if the poor horse went through the ice. I suppose they backed the cart on first. One skater saw a big trout frozen in the ice. He tried to chip it out with his skates. After half an hour he had no success, but he had to be carried home because he could not walk, having used muscles he didn't normally use!

I remember getting my first second-hand ice skates when I was 16. At that time they were steel blades set in wooden blocks. My older cousin took me to the Nottingham Ice Rink where I learnt to skate. One day I skated alone on the frozen reservoir near the Felley end. It all seemed so unreal — the vast expanse of snow-covered ice, here and there bristling with reeds, and the odd twisted tree branch thrusting out of the ice like a prehistoric reptile. There was an uncanny, portentous feeling in the air, all so quiet; just the sound of blades cutting the ice, and my breath visible in the frosty air.

Maurice Holmes
born 1933

The canals froze over nearly every winter. My father was a good skater, and I remember running along beside him while he skated. You could have skated all the way to Riddings on the canal. Moorgreen Reservoir too regularly froze over and Mr Greenhalgh, who kept a cycle shop in Eastwood and was a wonderful figure skater, was always the first to test the ice. Once he'd been across we knew it was safe to skate, and it was lovely.

Winifred Stoakes

Tennis and Hockey

My mother and father were founder members of the Eastwood Tennis Club. Mr Sheldon lived at the top of Alexandra Street but his garden was separate, lower down on Church Walk, with a croquet lawn and a grass tennis court, and that is where the Club started and is still there today. When I first went there as a child I remember having a great time with Mr Sheldon's daughter, sliding on cushions down the slope leading to the croquet lawn. At Heanor Grammar School we played a lot of sport and I was keen on tennis all my life. I played in the Notts. League. Later the Club bought some allotments adjoining the church to make a second court, and the croquet lawn was then filled in to become the third tennis court. My late husband Ian and I worked hard all our lives for the Tennis Club — various dances, whist drives and other events — and it is still going strong.

In the 1930s Eastwood had a very good hockey team which played in a county league on Saturdays. The pitch was on Coach Drive at the Grange.

Winifred Stoakes

Members of the Eastwood Tennis Club, c.1912

'The Monkey Run'

In the early 1930s when I was in my teens our favourite activity on Friday, Saturday and Sunday evenings was the 'Monkey Run.' From the Market Place at the Sun Inn to the Empire Cinema at the corner of King Street the young men and women would promenade along, showing off to one another. It was all very good-natured, but PC Hammond would not allow any congregating in shop doorways and moved us on with a quick flick of his gloves around our ears!

Mary Bend

Dancing

As a young girl I went to a dancing class at what is now Durban House, then the offices of Barber Walker & Co. In a big room upstairs Miss Poyser taught the tradesmen's daughters and sons to dance. We girls, wearing flat pumps with elastic round them, had to sit with our mothers, and the boys, who sat with their mothers, would cross the room and very properly ask us for the dance and return us to mother afterwards. Even when we later went to dances in town the boys came and politely asked for a dance and returned you to your seat. The girls always wore long gloves; the boys also wore gloves — I suppose so that their sweaty hands did not dirty the backs of the dresses! There were dances at the Mechanics Institute (the Miners Welfare) on Mansfield Road, and the Eastwood Tennis Club held one every year. When Ian and I were engaged we went regularly to the Palais de Danse in Nottingham, including Saturday afternoons, and also to dances at Ilkeston, Codnor and Morley's rooms at Heanor.

Winifred Stoakes

Eastwood Tennis Club dance, c.1950.
Standing (l to r): Fred Farnsworth, —, Win Farnsworth, Dorothy Smaller, Louis Rowley, Bob Smaller, Jack Hallam, Michael Clifford, Granville Gregory, —, Ian Stoakes, Eric Pearce, Bernard Roome, Brian Sanders, Reg Purdy, —, Irene Sanders, Tony Hallam, Jean Hudson, Alec Hudson, Ruth Hallam, Jill Hallam, Cyril Williams, Edna Williams, —, Esther Menzies, Jim Menzies, —.
Sitting: Mary Mather, Phyl Clough, Christine Archbold, Winifred Stoakes, Lucy Purdy, Elsie Cary, Jessie Chambers, Mabel Rowley.

Eastwood Miners Welfare was a popular venue for dancing. (The annual Coal Queen competition, open to wives or daughters of Moorgreen miners, was also held there.) During the early 1950s jiving and rock 'n' roll were beginning to take over but were not popular at first at the Saturday evening ballroom dance, and the 'threepenny hop' was set up on Wednesday evenings. Alf Savage and his trio played dixieland jazz and popular music enjoyed by the younger scene. Birnams Products put on Saturday dances in their canteen during the '50s, and the Victory Club also introduced dancing as part of its entertainment programme in the '60s.

Hilda Hill
born 1937

I went to Betty Rose's dancing classes which were then held in her mother's front room of a terraced house on Nottingham Road on the way to Hill Top. Betty was very young at this time, only in her teens, but very competent. I remember taking part in a display held at the Miners Welfare, dancing to the *Skaters Waltz* in a 'winter' sequence of the four seasons. I was dressed in a red and white tutu, with bandages on both knees!

Leila Keam
born 1930

1939 advertisement

I did not take up dancing until I was in my 60s when I learnt sequence dancing. However, when I was working at Bairnswear in the 1930s there was going to be a tea dance at the Nottingham Palais. I remember one of the factory girls, also called Mary, saying,'Come down to the toilets at quarter to eleven and I'll show you how to do some steps,' and we shuffled around!

Mary Bend

During the mid-1950s the newly developing rock 'n' roll music gained a huge foothold in Eastwood with regular Wednesday night sessions at the Miners Welfare. These dances (admission sixpence — or was it one and sixpence?) were always packed with older teenagers many of whom dressed in the high fashion style of the day, Edwardian! Immaculate Teddy boys and girls graced the floor of the Welfare 'dressed to the nines' in drainpipe trousers and drape coats. Much of this clothing was obtained from the Teddy boys' Mecca, Hickingbottom's shop situated just up the road from the Welfare. The resident live band at the time was Alf Savage and the Stardusters. Alf, who worked at the nearby Beggarlee Yard, was often described as the finest trumpeter in the Midlands.

Mick Brown
born 1941

Playing for dancing at the Victory Club in 1949 is entertainments secretary Herbert Skillington (right) on the trumpet. He played several instruments, and was a member of the Brinsley Brass Band.

A Century Remembered

Dances — the 'threepenny hops' — were held at the Eastwood and Greasley Miners Welfares. The men would usually stay in the bar drinking until the last waltz, and then it was a free-for-all to the tune of *Who's Taking You Home Tonight!*

Mavis Williamson
born 1922

Swimming

Living in Underwood all my life I have always had a close affinity with Moorgreen Reservoir. When I was young, I along with many of the village children used it as a swimming pool during the school holidays. I always kept to the shallow end near Felley Mill, but some of the better swimmers swam the whole length. We didn't realise how dangerous the reservoir was, especially where Felley Brook carved out a deep channel as it entered the deeper water. One day a Mr Purdy, who could not swim very well, got into serious trouble where the channel was. Fortunately Mr Smithurst swam from the other side and pulled him out.

Another time Frank Clifford dived in at the deep end and lost his false teeth. A posse of divers was immediately assembled but although they searched the muddy depths for hours the teeth were never found. Most of the older lads, some already working in the pits, would have the audacity to change on the 'basin' which took the overflow, near the main road. 'Bobby' Bonnet, Barber Walker & Co.'s policeman, was always a thorn in the side of young trespassers on colliery property. But when he came to remove these bigger lads from the basin one of them would say, 'Whe'er shud weh chuck 'im in, lads?' — and tactfully Bonnet would beat a hasty retreat!

The Beggarlee Baths were opened in 1913.

Maurice Holmes
born 1933

Page 201

A Century Remembered

An extension to the Eastwood Lads Club was the Beggarlee Swimming Baths built just off Engine Lane by members and miners in 1912 during the strike. Water from the nearby brook which flowed at the side of the baths was run into the pool. The changing rooms were old railway carriages — excellent facilities for those days in spite of unheated and untreated water.

David Machin
born 1929

The diving board at Beggarlee Baths, 1948

We went from school to learn to swim at the Beggarlee Baths and I could have lived there. The bridge over the brook and the green banks with flower beds were beautiful.

Lily Rose

The noise emanating from the baths on a fine weekend could be heard right round the district! To provide changing rooms two railway carriages had been hauled to the site and set up on brick bases. Later, more facilities included a diving board and seating around the pool. There was a wooden office with a ticket window where Mr Pitts ruled supreme. There he sold 'pop,' snacks and ice-cream, and the trade was brisk.

Fred Skillington

The grounds were nicely landscaped. We used to go down for picnics and take lunch and tea. I was quite envious as I watched the boys jump off the diving board.

Winifred Stoakes

A Century Remembered

At present Eastwood does not have any public swimming facilities. This is a retrograde step as in the 1920s, '30s and '40s there was a choice of 'pools.' The heating and filtration system at the Beggarlee Baths may not have been up to today's standard but thousands of Eastwood folk regularly enjoyed their time at the baths. It was 'first in, clear the frogs out!' and at the end of the day free use of the big mangle to wring your trunks out. Alternatively on fine summer days dozens of families could be found picnicking on the banks of the canal at the Gudgeon Hole, where hundreds of lads learned to dive — off the lock gates. It was not unheard of for bets to be made in the Stars, Raglan and Vaults on races between Gudgeon Hole and Langley Mill locks.

Mick Parkes
born 1939

The Lads' Club

At the highest point of Church Street stood a large three-storey house of very imposing character; large bay windows to the front; an entrance with steps and stained-glass doors; walls of red brick; and many chimneys in a 'Welsh slate roof' setting. It stood slightly angled to the street, with a tall red brick wall enclosing a green lawn to the front door. An archway in the wall had a painted sign overhead which very simply said 'Eastwood Lads Club.'

The ground fell away sharply at the side and rear, so the front garden was terraced by a retaining wall built up in Derbyshire rockery stone that sparkled with crystals. Below this was a large square with disused stables, and in the square were two ex-Army type barrack huts which were used as drill halls and games rooms. It was in those huts and in the Club that I spent my early growing years.

Fred Skillington

Did you Know that Eastwood can boast of the Finest Youths' Headquarters in England Outside the Large Cities?

THE

Eastwood Training Corps and Lads' Club

Has been carrying on for many years work which the Board of Education is now proposing for all youths.

At the Eastwood Lads' Club there are Three Departments:—
Life Boys and Cubs, 9-12 years. Subscription, 1d. weekly.
Boys' Brigade and Scouts, 12-16 years. Subscription, 1½d. weekly.
Ambulance, Army and Air Cadets, 15-20 years. Subscription, 2d. weekly.

There are Physical Training, Educational, and Christian Instruction Classes, Gymnastics, Cricket, Football, Swimming, Games, Billiards, Library, Canteen, Games Close, Swimming Pool, and Camping Holidays at a nominal charge.

The aim of the Eastwood Training Corps and Lads' Club has always been to train Eastwood youths to become gentlemen.

Apply to the Warden for full particulars.

1944 advertisement

A Century Remembered

At some time in 1900 the late Captain Chambers formed the Eastwood Lads Club which met at several places in the town including the British School on Albert Street, until it got its own permanent premises in a large old house at the top of Church Street. This house had been the home of a doctor and used as a hospital in the First World War. The outbuildings had been stables and store places for carriages, hay and horses, and there was a large underground water storage tank built in brick with a vaulted roof.

David Machin

Governors and members of the Eastwood Lads Club in 1918, including (2nd row, 2nd from left) William Bentley, and his son Alfred (standing far left).

Over many years Eastwood Lads Club saw thousands of Eastwood and district lads pass through its doors, each benefitting from the physical, moral and spiritual training given. There was always friendly rivalry between the various organisations — Cadet Corps to Scouts, Cubs, Boys Brigade, Life Boys, Air Training Corps — in sports, swimming, annual displays etc., but they all joined together to form one of the finest bands in the district.

Mick Parkes

I became a member of the Boys Brigade in 1910. The headquarters then was in the old Mission Hall on the Breach (now Garden Road). It was there that I had my first lesson in the art of boxing from Captain Dawson Chambers, and I remember that he didn't half give you a belting at times! You could hit him as hard as you liked but at the same time he did not always pull his punches.

Eastwood Scouts at the Lads Club, 11 November 1922. Captain Dawson Chambers is on the far right.

After the Brigade finished on the Breach they transferred to the top rooms over Naylor's toffee shop (now the NatWest Bank) at the corner of Victoria Street. This was certainly an improvement as there were now facilities for a games room including a billiard table. Here on Sunday evenings the Captain would give us readings from *The Green Eye of the Little*

Yellow God or *The Monkey's Paw,* and distribute among us the usual bag of sweets which he had always brought with him. The Brigade eventually moved into new premises yet again, this time Dr Forbes' old house on Church Street, along with the other uniformed organisations.

Kenneth Poynter

The club building had a full size billiard table in the large room on the ground floor, and a chapel in the room above that. On the landing at the side of the chapel stood an old German machine gun and a large shell from the First World War. The lower-level rooms were used to serve refreshments.

David Machin

Mr and Mrs Hemingway lived in the top-floor flat at the club which was a no-go area to us. 'Skip' Hemingway was a larger than life character who was in charge of everything. He was a pipe smoker, and his Bruno smoke pervaded every nook and cranny. He was the only man I ever knew (apart from the Co-op barbers) who shaved with a cut-throat open razor.

Fred Skillington

People who remember the Lads Club will have fond memories of Mrs H's pea soup after meetings; meetings in the 'dens' (upstairs of the old stables in the yard); Mr Poyser's non-stop whistling while guarding his beloved billiard room to make sure no under-14s entered; and the highlight of the year — the annual display on prizegiving night.

Mick Parkes

Annexed to, but over a mile away, was the summer meeting place of the Club, the Beggarlee Baths. In the grounds of the baths, over the brook, was a large sports field where we held our meetings and learned outdoor activities. Camping

— and camp-fire singing — was one of the more enjoyable of these, and prepared us for the real annual camps in August at Wirksworth. We will always be indebted to men of insight like Captain Chambers who funded most of the activities and who, incidentally, told us ghost stories when we camped at Wirksworth!

Fred Skillington

The Club was fortunate that it had its own camp site (by kind permission of its benefactor Dawson Chambers) at Hob Farm, Gorsey Bank, Wirksworth. What a fine sight it was to see all the lads on the back of Grainger's haulier's lorry being waved off by crowds of parents on Church Street. As I recall, my first week in 1948 cost 12 shillings. Needless to say, there was no sleep on the first night at camp and about 3 a.m. 'Skip' would get everybody out in the field to tell them that bags would be packed at 7 o'clock and we were all going home. Apart from the inevitable rumblings of 'He can't send us back – we've paid for the week,' or 'He can't get the lorry to come until next Saturday,' not another word was heard!

Mick Parkes

The Cadets' Cross memorial at Edward Road was always the place where we marched from or to on our monthly parade services. We visited all the local churches in turn, and so became familiar with interiors which we would never normally have seen.

Fred Skillington

Until 1950 the 1st Eastwood Scouts wore plain green neckerchiefs. The number of shades of green depended on how many lads attended the meeting! It was in 1950 that King's Scout Ron Smith went to an international jamboree at Blair Atholl and brought back with him a Royal Stewart tartan neckerchief which, to the envy of all other local troops, was adopted by Eastwood. At least they were now all the same colour. Until about 1970 they were a thick

A Century Remembered

Scouting as it used to be! Gordon Leverton (brother of Jean Duckworth) at camp in Wirksworth in the 1940s. He was made a King's Scout in 1949.

woollen weave — very hot in summer but very smart.

Mick Parkes

Scouting For Boys was a book written by Robert Baden-Powell to help young men into a better understanding of the outdoor life. From it sprang a great worldwide movement which is still relevant today. I joined the Scouts in the early 1940s and it had a great influence on my life from then on. The war took away men who normally would have carried on the movement to even greater heights, and restrictions were placed on the work from which it never really recovered. But we were still served by dedicated men who had the foresight to provide an outlet for our energies and turn us into useful citizens.

The Scout Shop on Shakespeare Street, Nottingham was the 'in' place at that time. Books, uniforms, badges, woggles, whistles, lanyards, neckerchiefs, belts, scout staffs, camping gear and a great deal more of what was needed then. A cornucopia, a veritable fantasy world to us who had so little to spend, and there was so much that we needed. Apart from our annual camp at Wirksworth, on special occasions we camped at the very large purpose-built camp at Walesby Forest. One week I remember camping there was for a special rally to meet the Chief Scout, Baden-Powell, who was to speak to us en bloc.

By this time I was a Senior Scout and had to show an example to the younger ones. Uniforms got tatty and Scout hats had floppy brims which needed steam ironing to stiffen them up to smartness. I was busy doing this task on a table when the *Post* photographer came along. He grouped us round the table, with a primus stove for a heater, me holding the iron, and a Scout hat getting the treatment. The picture was in the evening paper with the caption 'Preparing for the Chief's Visit.' A week later I went back to work at British Celanese Ltd at Spondon, and there was the picture on the works notice board. I was a celebrity for a day!

I returned to Walesby on another occasion to train as an Akela (wolf-cub leader). There we became children again and 'dibbed and dobbed' to get the feel of the object of the course. I was able to help with a cub pack until it was time to move along to other things. Scouting too has moved on now, but the nostalgia of the camp-fire songs and the *gin-gan-gully* that became such a joke later is still vivid.

Fred Skillington

The Club house on Church Street belonged to British Coal who charged the Club one shilling a year rent. Income was generated by Friends of the Club, Eastwood Trades Guild, Eastwood Rotary Club, Eastwood Town Council and the Coal Industry Welfare Association. There was also income from the rent charged for letting the old stable and carriage areas as warehouses.

When work started on the widening of Church Street the building had to be demolished, and the Club moved to Sunny Croft on Derby Road but the break-ins there caused so much cost and disruption that the Club closed. Before the demolition in May 1974, the machine gun and the shell which had stood on the landing were removed but then it was found that the shell was still live and the Bomb Disposal Squad had to be involved!

The £1000 received from British Coal as compensation after the road widening plus £2100 invested in War Loans were used to form a charity named the Eastwood Training Corps Trust. Its objective is to help with finance for young people under 25 living in an area within two miles from Eastwood Church (excluding Derbyshire) for corporate youth projects and/or training for youth development.

David Machin

To me, the day that the Lads Club closed was a very sorry one for the youth of Eastwood.

Kenneth Poynter

Chapter Eleven

New Year's Eve

High Days and Holidays

The beginning of another year had a very special magic when I was little, with all the hopes and dreams we cherished and the resolutions we made but seldom kept. Looking back now, I realise that those homely rituals have gone forever. One special memory concerns New Year's Eve when we went to Grandma's home, long after my usual bedtime — a thrill in itself.

At Grandma's there was always a blazing coal fire to gather round. The table was set with cake and biscuits plus a bottle of wine. Wine glasses twinkled in the firelight, ready for our New Year greetings and a sip of wine for me. This was my big treat of the year, but the rest of the time I was considered much too young for anything alcoholic. However, the arrival of the New Year was so special and 'seeing it in,' as we called it, was a really great event. Conversation flowed whilst I listened. In those far-off days children were seen but not heard.

I remember waiting for the magic midnight hour and the booming of Big Ben on the wireless. Then our glasses were filled and we all drank to the New Year. For me it was awe-inspiring, to be up so late and sipping sherry! Afterwards I remember so clearly scampering up the street to our house, leaving Grandma and Grandad to their own memories. Always, in my memory, on our way home the air was crisp and cold, the sky twinkled with stars and a bright moon bathed everything in its silvery light. In the distance we could hear the church bells pealing joyfully to welcome the infant year. Magic moments indeed!

Doris Reeve
born 1921

On New Year's Eve it was the custom for anyone with a dark complexion or black hair to go from house to house to let the new year in for the occupants. A piece of coal was placed on the fire and in return you received a half-crown, a glass of wine, sherry or whisky and a mince pie. A child was given a mince pie and a glass of lemonade.

Ken Marsland
born 1924

Shrove Tuesday was a special day. It was a school holiday and there were pancakes. It was also the start of our outdoor activities which seemed to last until the leaves had fallen.

Alice Geeson
born 1912

Shrove Tuesday

A lively and joyous annual celebration was our Pancake Day. We raced home from Beauvale School with a half-day holiday, collected our free orange from the Co-op fruit store and then gorged ourselves on a dinner of tasty tossed pancakes. Every family made pancakes of course — the ingredients were cheap. Egyptian eggs cost a shilling for up to sixty, although at least ten and often twenty would be rank bad and the rest decidedly 'squiffy' in those pre-refrigeration days. Milk cost a penny a pint and sugar twopence ha'penny for two pounds. Flour was bought by the stone (14 pounds) and sold in four grades: best, seconds, thirds and fourths. This last grade was very cheap and very dirty, really intended for animals, but many households — ours included — used it for family needs.

After the feast came the emergence from winter hibernation of whips and tops, bowling hoops, marbles, skipping ropes, scooters and dolls prams with dolls in new dresses. The pavements were thronged with noisy juvenile activity — spring had arrived! This festive mood spread to the grown-ups, and it was their turn after tea. Sixty-foot washing lines became skipping ropes turned by two men at each end, and thirty or forty girls and women would jump in together. Hill Top had three or four ropes twirling at the same time, each with its complement of skippers. There were skips for 'men only,' a few turns for 'grannies only,' and 'sweethearts only' for embracing couples! This last turn was always the most popular and had to have several encores. Youngsters enjoying their first courtship would shyly just hold hands, but many couples with years of fair and stormy married life behind them would for a moment or two forget their nagging and tiffs, heartily embracing and hugging each other as they skipped in a revival of love and affection. A most happy end to the day.

Percy Cross
born 1906

St George's Day

At Beauvale School on St. George's Day (23rd April) we would gather in the hall and sing our heads off to *I Vow To Thee My Country*, *Land Of Hope And Glory*, and *Jerusalem*. The flags would fly on the churches. We were proud to be British!

Enid Goodband
born 1924

May Day

Malcolm Caporn crowns Enid Gibbs as May Queen at Devonshire Drive Junior School in 1956. The attendants (l to r) are Joan Gregory, Jennifer Watson, Terri Leivers, Diane Mottershaw, Barbara Beacon, — , Dawn Adams, — . Sitting on the footstool is Alan Sleath.

In the playground at Bagthorpe we danced around the maypole, boys in one direction, girls in the other, making pretty patterns at the top of the pole, while we sang *Come Lasses and Lads*.

Vera Musgrove
born 1918

At Devonshire Drive Infant School's May Day celebrations in 1956 I was chosen to be one of the flower girls and we had to scatter petals on the floor before the May Queen entered. At the Junior School we held May Day celebrations on the Rectory field with maypole dancing. The girls wore long skirts with net underskirts, velvet waistcoats, and flowers in our hair.

Karen Clarke
born 1950

At Beauvale School we always celebrated Empire Day (24th May). We wore red, white and blue bonnets and ribbons.

Florence Smith
born 1918

Empire Day

When I was at Beauvale School the girls were invited to wear their Guide or Brownie uniform on Empire Day.

Hilda Hill
born 1937

We seemed to have lovely summers in my childhood and a favourite spot on Whit Sunday was Moorgreen Reservoir. Outside the gate was a stall which provided sweets, minerals and hand-churned ice cream. We opened the gate by the lodge and were immediately engulfed in that

Whit Sunday

natural beauty described so vividly by D H Lawrence.

Alice Geeson

The Summer Festival

One of the big days I remember from about 1915 to 1920 was the annual summer children's festival organised by the Langley Mill & Aldercar Co-operative Society. We were conveyed on farm carts and waggonettes a few miles to Laceyfields to enjoy a great afternoon of fun, sports and competitions. There was a big tea in marquees followed by a prizegiving and fireworks. Then, satiated with Co-op buns and Co-op tea and with our pockets filled with more Co-op cake and buns, the leftovers, we sang our way home. It was a great afternoon.

Percy Cross

The Sunday School Treat

Each year at St Mary's Church we had the Sunday School treat in the Rectory grounds. I once lost an expensive silver snake bracelet there. I also used to sneak in at Wellington Street Primitive Methodist Chapel's field when they had their treat, which was held down Queen Street, where William and Pickering Avenues now are.

Lily Rose
born 1902

Rectory Fields, the scene of many Sunday School 'treats' and sports.

Bull's-eye

Excitedly the primary children of the Newthorpe Common Methodist Chapel Sunday School gathered on the church steps for their annual picnic outing one Saturday. The venue was a chosen grassy field in the local meadows, half an hour's walk away. The 25 children chattered as they crocodiled towards the farm gate, entrance to picnic paradise. Every year something unusual happened, and this year was to be no exception. Each child was carefully helped over the narrow stile by three teenage teachers and instructions were given to place carrier bags, rucksacks and quickly-shed duffel coats in a heap in the centre of the field. Playing games and singing songs was extremely hot and thirsty work, but the children interspersed their energetic activities with short breaks to eat and drink from their pre-packed teas.

Nobody noticed how the brown and white young bullocks which grazed quietly at one corner of the large field had stealthily crept closer as the play proceeded. Suddenly these docile creatures charged, their hooves thundering menacingly, scattering 25 frightened screaming children in many directions. The bewildered leader shouted instructions to steer the children to the single stile and each child was hauled over as quickly as possible. The happy bullocks seized their chance to trample on the discarded coats and half-opened food parcels and began to munch their food bonanza.

Bulls-eye! The children of Newthorpe Common Methodist Church Sunday School on their ill-fated picnic in 1965.

Finally the children calmed down and began to sing again in their new field but eyed the 'cows' rather dubiously. Andrew, a smart four-year old, said, 'They'll jump over the hedge and get me.' 'No, no,' assured teacher, trying to comfort him, 'they can't jump over the hedge.' 'Well,' replied Andrew, 'the cow jumped over the moon!' The next important job to be done was for the 'not so brave' leader to retrieve the pile of coats and food. This was tackled by choosing a long stick and charging with a loud 'Tally Ho!' into the centre of the melée. The bullocks looked up momentarily then carried on eating the children's picnic. One instant dive to gather the booty from the hot panting jaws was achieved with gyrating magnificence, then short white legs ran as fast as they could towards the single stile! 'I'm not eating those sandwiches,' exclaimed Annie, 'the cows have had them.'

The little party walked home chatting about their adventure, and the teachers were apprehensive about the parents' reaction and whether the children would ever appear at Sunday School again. However 25 smiling children appeared the next morning, none the worse for their adventure.

Jean Duckworth
born 1941

The highlight of our summers was the Sunday School treat. There were sports and tea in the superintendent's field, and on one magical day we were transported on a flat-top dray to Felley Mill.

Alice Geeson

The Wakes

The origins of Hill Top Wakes are a survival of the ancient revels and feastings associated with the dedication festival of St Mary's Parish Church at Greasley. These were held at the beginning of September.

Showmen in Victorian times brought their amusements to a field on Walker Street and the annual event was always eagerly anticipated by the local folk. In his novel *Sons and Lovers* D H Lawrence mentions the steam horses, coconut shies and peep show in the latter years of the 19th century. In the early 20th century fields on either side of Walker Street were occupied by showmen for the annual Wakes. Hollands' rides and stalls were set up where the Victory Club now stands, whilst Proctors occupied the field opposite which was known as Three Tuns Croft. A painting by the late Walter Reeve shows Proctors' traction engines, a Dragons and Peacocks ride and other amusements in 1930. A report in the *Eastwood & Kimberley Advertiser* for 1932 describes how in spite of poor weather conditions the celebrations were as successful as ever and were visited by large numbers of people. The two distinct sites introduced the very latest amusements and made a wonderful spectacle when brilliantly illuminated after dark.

Pete Birkin, Albert Holmes, Les Hodgkinson, Joe Hall, Howard Rowley, Ken Powdrill and Roy Leary on the steps of a ride at the Eastwood Wakes in the 1930s.

Each year on Wakes Sunday a memorial service for some local young men who died in the First World War was held in the afternoon at the Cadets' Cross at the corner of Edward Road. In the evening a united religious service was held by courtesy of Messrs Hollands on the Wakes ground. This evening event had been started in 1890 by Mr T Ball, JP and a group of local Methodists. It included communal hymn singing and was always very well supported. Collections were made for local charities.

In 1932 Proctors occupied their usual site but Hollands had to find a new ground because their site of many years' standing was required for the erection of a new school. This new site which was further along Walker Street presented numerous difficulties by reason of its uneven land. It was ingeniously overcome by the application of tons of ashes.

In 1933 Proctors too had to find a new pitch because their site was also claimed by the builder. They moved across the main road to the Basford Council ground behind Boundary Cottage and brought all their usual modern amusements including the Ghost Train. Although there was some distance to walk between the two sites, nothing could kill the Wakes spirit nor daunt the enterprising showmen.

My own recollections of the Wakes are based on visits in the 1930s, in the years before the Second World War. The traction engines would struggle up into Eastwood with their wagons and living vans in tow. We did our shopping early on Friday evening and then visited the

Wakes. We always made the Hollands' site our first call. Two traction engines which belched out dirty black smoke from their tall chimneys provided power for the rides and stalls. The music, the lights and the smells created a never-to-be-forgotten atmosphere. Mr Holland himself could often be seen, looking dignified and complete with bowler hat. He had a distinctly ornate living van. Rides often had to be built up on wooden blocks to counter the sloping land. The gallopers, Noah's Ark, cakewalk and dodgems were great favourites, along with the helter skelter, children's rides and an assortment of stalls and sideshows. The Moon Rocket was introduced on one occasion and proved to be very popular. There were the usual 'fairings' — coconuts, candy, flying-birds and silver balls on elastic etc. We would then cross the main road to visit Proctors' showground. Often we would visit the Wakes again on the following Monday evening.

Margaret Braithwaite, aged 9, and her sister Joan, 13, 'rolling the penny' at the Wakes held in front of the Three Tuns on 7 July 1943.

On Saturday night September 2nd 1939 the lights were dimmed — it was amazingly quiet. The following day the Second World War began at 11 a.m. The Wakes Sunday service at the Cadets' Cross continued during the war, and an occasional Wakes was held in front of the Three Tuns Inn. In 1943 Rosaire's Royal Command Circus visited Eastwood on September 1st and 2nd. After the war the Wakes resumed for some years. On one occasion a group of friends visited the Hollands' site and enjoyed a ride on the Noah's Ark. One member sat astride a pig and had difficulty in dismounting when the ride stopped and was in fact still astride the pig when the ride restarted. The ride had to be stopped again and the lady assisted, much to the amusement of her friends. Hollands had to abandon this site when the school was further extended in the 1950s.

In 1953 contrary to tradition the Wakes enjoyed glorious weather, and the site on a portion of the Coronation Park estate was thronged with people. The showmen brought along the old favourites. The traditional service was held at Cadets' Cross in the afternoon and on the Wakes ground in the evening. The evening concert on the floodlit site was voted the most successful to date. In 1954 the evening concert was held at the Rex Cinema and in 1955 at the Eastwood Miners' Welfare. The service at the Cadets' Cross continued for some years on Wakes Sunday, but after the resiting of the town war memorial in 1978 it was incorporated in the annual Remembrance Sunday observance in November. Occasional Wakes were held on land fronting the Three Tuns public house, but the Wellington Place car-park became the new site for several years. Proctors held a four-day Wakes there in September 1970. Several weeks after the new library opened in 1975 there were showmen's amusements to the rear of it. In 1981 several local residents organised a petition when they learnt that the Wakes was planned again on the 'Canyons' near Lynncroft. This offered a very uneven site with the added problem of difficult entry. Unaware of the petition, but fully aware of the nature of the site, Mr Albert Proctor said there could be no Wakes that year — or the next if things didn't improve. Chatting with members of the Holland family some years ago I learnt that they always enjoyed their annual visit to Hill Top Wakes. Along with Proctors they still take their amusements to Nottingham's famous Goose Fair.

In his short story *Tickets Please* D H Lawrence describes a visit during the First World War to the Eastwood Statutes Fair which was held at the Sun Inn Croft annually in November. This is not to be confused with the Hill Top Wakes. The origin of the Statutes was for the hiring of labourers for the coming year. I have no personal recollection of this event. Interestingly however, Hollands held a fair in November 1978 and brought along quite a number of both traditional and more modern rides including the Cyclone and Chaser. In September 1985 as part of the D H Lawrence Centenary Festival an 'Eastwood Wakes Fair' was held at the old Brinsley Colliery site. Stallholders and some visitors were dressed in period costume.

Those magical weekends at the beginning of September are all now part of local history. The memories linger on and may be prompted by the Wakes memorabilia, including a galloper and parts of a stall and sideshow, at the Durban House Heritage Centre.

A Century Remembered

I am indebted to several local residents and reports in the Eastwood & Kimberley Advertiser for much of this information.

Don Chambers
born 1930

Big crowds used to gather for the Wakes Sunday service, and people who had moved away to find work elsewhere came back for it, some from as far as Doncaster. Sometimes the band of the Salvation Army accompanied the singing.

Mary Bend
born 1918

Showmen's wagons at the 1921 Wakes

As a child I lived at Brinsley and Underwood. From July to October there were various local fairs, most of them known as Wakes, leading up to Goose Fair. The first was at Selston near the Bull and Butcher pub and was always in July. I can remember the vicar preaching from the tower of St. Helen's Church. I have a glass dish which my father won at Selston Wakes over 75 years ago. Then came Brinsley Wakes, held in a field behind the Wagon and Horses, and at Michaelmas the Underwood Wakes (Underwood Church is St Michael's).

All these local Wakes culminated in Goose Fair in Nottingham. I have only a vague memory of the Fair being in the Market Square before it moved to the Forest in 1928, but I can clearly remember walking up Gregory Boulevard on an autumn morning. The trees were lovely and golden in the sunshine, and as we walked up we would hear the sound of the organ music on the merry-go-rounds. That set the scene; it created an atmosphere of fun which we were all going to enjoy.

I remember being fascinated by the dragons. I would look at their heads, their wild eyes and open mouths with huge teeth — I expected smoke and fire to come out at any moment. The dragons seated about ten people and used to go up and down as well as round. I also remember the big and little horses, the helter skelter, the swing boats, the coconut shies and the cakewalk. I always looked at Tiny Tim who must have been about two feet high. He seemed to be there every year. I couldn't believe he was alive; I would stand and look and wait for his eyes to blink and then I knew he was alive. We used to come away from the Goose Fair with a coconut or a toffee cock-on-a-stick which were the mementos of the fair in our day.

When I think of the Wakes I always think of my great aunt Edith, a very large elderly lady. She arrived at Underwood Wakes dressed in a fur fabric coat and she looked enormous. She was an adventurous spirit and she decided that she was going to have a ride on the cakewalk. However, because of her size she could not negotiate the moving platform. She was absolutely immobilised. There she stood, the queue behind her growing and the people getting more and more impatient. On the other side a crowd gathered to see what all the fuss was about. A poor slim Wakes man did his best to try and remove her but he couldn't manage it. He went away and eventually came back with what seemed an army of strong men. After a great deal of pushing and shoving she was finally frogmarched out of the nearest exit. This incident was our family joke for years!

Vera Musgrove

For me the best Wakes time was when it was set up in Newthorpe. I think this was about 1950. At the top of Stamford Street where I lived there was a piece of waste ground called the 'old yard.' This was on the opposite corner to the Foresters pub, before the bungalows were built. Having the Wakes on the doorstep was great. It was safe to go alone, and when the pennies had been spent you could go home and pester for a few more. The Wakes only came that once to Newthorpe but the wonder and delight stick in the memory!

Pat Potter
born 1942

The first week in November used to be the 'Status,' or November Fair, which was held in the Sun Inn field. It was usually typical November weather, damp and foggy, but that did not stop the crowds who patronised all the roundabouts and stalls which were on both sides of the road, as far as, and part way down, Alexandra Street. They were lit with paraffin or naphthalene flares which gave the street a peculiar odour all of its own.

Kenneth Poynter
born 1904

Christmas

When we lived on Alexandra Street Joe Birkin, a miners' union representative, used to come and play his violin for us early on Christmas morning. Later, when we lived at the shop, I remember Mr Harwood, who was manager of the Co-op shoe shop, and Mr Goddard coming to our dining room and playing the harmonium while we were having Christmas breakfast. It was such a lovely atmosphere.

Constance Barrett
born 1924

On Christmas morning Jack Hallam, who lived at the corner of Edward Road and Nottingham Road (at what is now Edward House), used to have a couple of cornet players come and play carols such as *Christians Awake*. They could be heard at a distance.

Mary Bend

Page 221

Schooldays at Beauvale were good and Christmas time very special. The Christmas play was a wonderful event and I was thrilled to be chosen as an angel, little realising that those who did not have a special part were added to the angelic host. Angels did not wear glasses, so mine were removed and I had great difficulty in seeing! However the applause from the OAPs who came to see the play was compensation enough.

The Christmas party was always an exciting time. We walked the usual two miles to school on party day clutching one plate, cup and saucer, fruit dish and spoon (all name tagged), hoping we did not slip on the icy road and break the pottery. The party hat, previously made in class, was donned with pride but afterwards stuffed behind the huge hot water pipes to avoid the payment of twopence, as funds did not allow purchase. The school post box was opened and I was thrilled to receive a tiny bottle of scent given by the teacher. All the girls received scent, and the boys sweets. The realisation that our teacher loved us enough to give us a Christmas present was a lovely thought to end the year!

Jean Duckworth

Beauvale School nativity play, c.1950. Standing (l to r): Jean Leverton, Rachael East, Pat Oates, June Clifton, Pauline Rockley, Dorothy —, Pat James, Hazel Williams. Sitting: Meryl Wardle.

We always went to Nottingham before Christmas as my parents had some contact with a warehouse. We were allowed to choose a book and one large toy. I remember once choosing a doll's pram and a cradle. My brother chose a bright red engine which he could sit in, and later a blue car which he pedalled along.

Vera Musgrove

The children were asked to bring things for the school Christmas party in 1949. Most of us took things like home-made cakes, cheese, spam or a packet of marge, but Alan Middleton who lived at the shop at the corner of Albert Street and Scargill Street took a tin of salmon. Now this was unusual because most of us had only heard of salmon, and Tom Middleton was not known for giving much away. After the party Alan's mum asked if the children had enjoyed the salmon. None had even seen it, but the teachers had beaming smiles on their faces!

Mick Parkes
born 1939

As a little boy I remember going up the stairs, holding the shiny blue hand-rail, right to the top of the Co-op to see Father Christmas. When I was taken up there the following summer, to my Dad's embarrassment I sobbed my heart out on finding all the gardening things on display and no Santa. I thought that Santa lived up there all year!

David Price
born 1963

When I was a child one of my father's fellow shopkeepers, Mr Cullen, used to buy me wonderful Christmas presents from Pearsons in Nottingham. One year it was a little cooker on which you could really cook things. Of course my mother had to light the burners which ran on methylated spirits, and I remember cooking some apples which I took to Mr Cullen to eat. Another year his present was a beautiful real china dinner service, with two tureens, oval dishes, plates in two sizes and a basket containing all the cutlery. I set it all out on a white enamelled table which had been an earlier present, and the dolls sat on stools. I played for hours with my dolls, putting them to bed then getting them up and dressing them again.

Winifred Stoakes

Halfway between Hill Top and Ilkeston in Johnny Daw's fields stood an isolated old caravan half hidden in nettles and undergrowth. A pathetic trail of smoke from the tin chimney was its only sign of life. We children were warned to keep well away from that van, for in it lived a father and daughter aged about 60 and 30, both dying from advanced consumption (tuberculosis). One night at Christmas time a long trail of songsters from Hill Top chapels, about 40 of them, carrying lamps and candle lanterns, crossed the fields and sang Christmas carols followed, inevitably, by *Abide With Me*. How beautiful and sad it must have sounded across those gloomy Erewash meadows. After a short prayer was spoken the van was left to its silent solitude — and hovering death. I never knew the names of that doomed couple.

Percy Cross

Silent Night
Holy Night

Chapter Twelve — A Miscellany of Memories

Memories

When you are feeling lonely and think nobody cares,
Think only of the good times, the fun you once did share:
When you were young and frisky, boys and girls you used to meet;
Games you played that were risky, but really were quite sweet;
Evenings at the pictures — never mind what film was on!
Dancing at the Welfare while Alf blew on his trumpet
And the rock 'n' roll played on.
The lovely long hot summer days that seemed to last forever;
The walks and picnics down Cutside, memories we must treasure.
The changing days when autumn came, when the leaves began to fall;
The nature walks along New England Lane;
Bluebells the girls gathered were like a carpet in the woods,
While the boys the conkers gathered.
After autumn winter came, and always brought the snow.
All around were snowdrifts, they made a lovely scene.
I hope you feel much better now, having strolled down memory lane.
Oh! just a little postscript, we must not forget the spring,
With all the pretty flowers that only spring can bring.

Christine Cook (née Moore)
born 1939

A Royal Visit

I remember seeing King George V and Queen Mary when they came through Eastwood in 1914, probably on their way to stay with the Duke of Portland at Welbeck. I stood on a chair at the edge of the pavement outside our shop on Nottingham Road. I waved my little Union Jack for all I was worth and the King waved to me; he was sitting in the carriage on my side of the road, the Queen on the other.

Winifred Stoakes
born 1909

A Century Remembered

When King George V and Queen Mary came through Eastwood in 1914 a large stand was erected on Nottingham Road, and the Chairman of the Council received the royal couple. We had a free show at the Empire cinema in the morning, and a film was taken of us filing down the steps. (A lot of us were caught with our curling rags in our hair!) This film was shown regularly on Good Friday each year and brought more laughter than Charlie Chaplin. I heard later it was burned in a fire at the Empire after the war.

Crowds waiting outside Beauvale School to see King George V and Queen Mary pass by in 1914.

Lily Rose

Many of the side streets were unlit but the main road had gas lamps which were lit every night by a man who went round carrying a long pole with a hook on the end. Using this he would pull on a metal ring to ignite the gas, and in the morning he had to turn all the lamps off again. This time the pole served a second, unofficial, purpose because many people asked him to knock on their bedroom window to wake them up.

The Lamplighter

Winifred Stoakes

In my youth 'bare fists' were the arbiter in settling many adult quarrels, soon over and argument settled. My mother was gentle but strong, and made no adverse criticism of these incidents. 'What's a bloody nose among friends?' was her verdict. Much more secret, however, because they were illegal, were the bare-knuckle contests arranged to find a local champion.

Bare-Knuckle Contests

The first matches were fought out in Ball's fields between Dovecote Lane and Newthorpe where a crowd of several hundred miners and a few very interested sporting gentry gathered. One of my

A Century Remembered

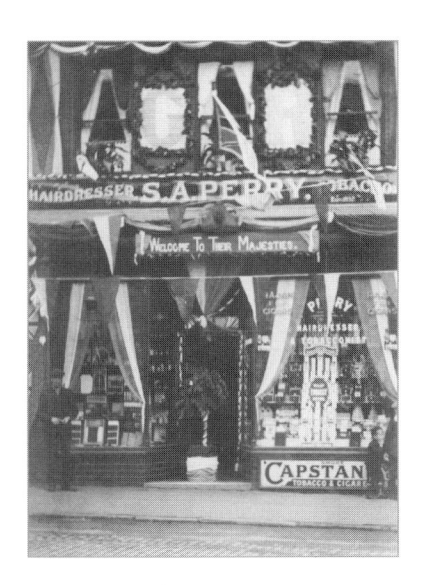

Perry's shop at 87 Nottingham Road decorated for the royal visit.

brothers had a go and defeated two opponents before taking terrible bashings from Alf Watson, the burly publican at the Coach and Horses, and 'Mad Jack' Kinton from Castle Street. No money was involved in these contests, just courage and personal pride.

Increasing crowd interest combined with opposition from some local people necessitated a change of arena to the Erewash meadows. One of the most notorious contests was, I believe, between Snowy Baker, a white-haired young man from Cotmanhay, and Stingo Miller who was a ploughman employed by Lord Rolleston. Stingo lost the battle, and his job. The story goes that his lordship lost a hundred sovereigns in a private bet, and 'took it out' on the ploughman. The local championship was never decided as the outbreak of the First World War gave the coup-de-grace to the whole show. Bare fists were reinforced with rifles and bayonets for a much more deadly contest.

Percy Cross

Carnival Queen 1939

In July 1939 at the age of 18 I was crowned as the fifth Carnival Queen of Eastwood and district at the Welfare Hall. My entrance was heralded by a fanfare of trumpets from the Arcadians Band. I wore a beautiful period dress of ivory Chantilly lace over crepe-de-chine (later that was to be my wedding dress), and a coronation robe of scarlet velvet edged with ermine. I had six attendants — Gladys Gilbourne, Joyce Rowley, Joan Wakefield, Olive Wakefield, Maisie Durose and Iris Cooper.

It had all started three months earlier when in a hall full of people I was chosen by Mrs A E Allen, wife of the managing director of Aristoc, to be the Queen after doing tests in deportment and speech. It certainly brought me 'out of my shell' because I had been very reluctant to enter the competition. I remember my Dad had bought me a pink taffeta long dress with blue velvet flowers and green embroidered leaves down one side. I kept that dress for years and years. The next three months were very busy as all the robes and dresses were made to measure.

That year the crowning ceremony took place a week before the start of the actual carnival. This opened on Wednesday with a Pageant of Queens (the carnival queens from surrounding towns) contest at the open-air theatre set up in the grounds of the Sun Inn, followed by the first of several parades I was to make around the district over the next few days in the 'royal coach.' The climax of the first evening was a Royal Ball in the Welfare Hall, attended by over 100 people who danced to Fred Carlisle's band.

The Grand Parade took place on Saturday afternoon, and starting from South Street the procession made its way via Hill Top and the Breach to Hall Park where among other attractions a carnival band contest was held. With air raid precautions so much in the public's mind at that time, it was significant that at the forefront of the procession were air raid wardens and other defence workers dressed in protective clothing and steel helmets. Five weeks later the happiness that I felt as Carnival Queen and was shared by thousands of people during Eastwood's main social occasion of the year was overshadowed by the announcement of the declaration of war against Germany. The programme of events that had been arranged for my 'reign' was cancelled, but I had the satisfaction of knowing that I was the longest-serving Carnival Queen as we did not have another carnival until after the war.

Ivy Attenborough
born 1921

1939 Carnival Queen Ivy Williamson.

The annual Carnival was revived after the war. (L to r) Sylvia, Betty and Esther Gibbs and Joan Webster take part in the procession on Nottingham Road, c.1951. (The houses on the left have now been replaced by Wellington Court, next to the Library.)

A Century Remembered

The R.101 Airship over Eastwood

I remember one day in 1930 all the pupils of Beauvale School were taken to the recreation ground to see the R.101 airship pass over Eastwood — just a few weeks before it crashed in France.

Mary Bend
born 1918

News of the Titanic Sinking

April 15th 1912 is a date that I never forget, the sinking of the *Titanic*. Although to my knowledge nobody in Hill Top and Eastwood had a personal connection with the tragedy, its impact on local folks was extraordinary. The news filtered through from Nottingham two days after the sinking and quite a hush descended on our village. Some shops closed and many blinds were drawn. An open-air religious service was spontaneously arranged in the square at Hill Top and at the singing of *For Those In Peril* many wept and some fell to their knees. My Mam sobbed openly. I was only six, but I remember that day vividly.

Percy Cross

A Meeting with D H Lawrence

As a lad my father worked at the pit with D H Lawrence's father, and he spoke of him as a kindly man who regularly gave him little treats from his snap tin! My father's family of brothers and sisters, the Gregory Simpsons (always known as the Gregorys) were contemporaries of the Lawrence family. Mother and Dad were in the front garden of our house at 145 Nottingham Road one day when Willie Hopkin, Lawrence's friend and mentor, walked by with Bert (as D H was known) who was introduced to my mother. This was during Lawrence's last visit to Eastwood in 1926.

Leila Keam
born 1930

Are you down on your uppers ?

Go Straight to

W. E. HOPKIN

Who will raise your outlook on life by giving you a New Sole.

HOPKIN & SON,

Next door to Post Office.

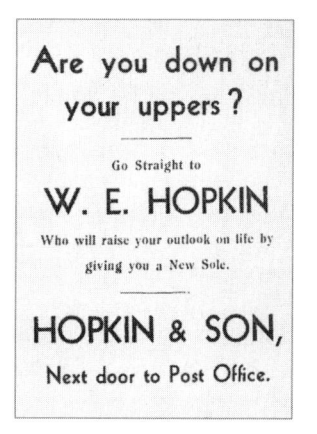

1935 advertisement

A Century Remembered

William Edward Hopkin (1866–1951) outside his home at 166 Nottingham Road. A friend and mentor of D H Lawrence, he was himself a writer whose weekly humorous contributions to the Eastwood & Kimberley Advertiser were enjoyed by readers for nearly half a century. Hopkin's shop was at 24 Nottingham Road.

The Day Red Rum came to Eastwood

One day in February 1979 my wife and I went to see the racehorse Red Rum, winner of the Grand National three times in 1973, 1974 and 1977. He was appearing in Nottingham at the opening of a jeweller's shop. We were so impressed by the event and the crowd the horse attracted that I suggested to the Eastwood Arcadians Band committee, of which I was a member, that we should book Red Rum for our Gala in August and that I would be the sponsor. The committee agreed, and so I went to Southport and booked the horse to lead our 'Gala Spectacular' parade to be held on Sunday August 17th 1979.

The day dawned dry and sunny. People still could not believe that such a famous racehorse was coming to Eastwood, and that morning my 'phone never stopped ringing with people asking for details of the event. Towards 1 p.m. the eight invited bands formed up at the bottom of Plumptre Way ready to march up Queens Road, into Midland Road and Church Street and at the traffic lights to turn into Nottingham Road. They would then go along the main road to Chewton Street before turning into Coronation Park and Eastwood Town's football ground.

Derek Hickinbotham walking next to Red Rum in the 1979 gala parade.

Page 230

Red Rum and his party were a little late in arriving for the 1 o'clock starting time agreed with the police. However, after a slight delay the famous racehorse took up his position at the head of the parade, and with everyone else in place the procession set off. We had gone only a few yards when the Arcadians began to play and the sound took Red Rum completely by surprise. As a result he whirled round to see what was happening and in doing so loosened a shoe. The parade was stopped whilst his boy pulled off the loose shoe and threw it into the crowd. There was an almighty scramble to get the lucky horseshoe, and to this day I do not know who got it!

The parade continued without further incident and was a resounding success, with crowds all along the route taking photographs and stroking the horse when he stopped for a breather. More than 8,000 people turned out, enabling us to raise a lot of money on that momentous day when Red Rum came to Eastwood.

Derek Hickinbotham

Medical Matters

I recall Nurse Wright, a district nurse who not only delivered babies but also 'laid out' corpses. I remember too that Dr Dixon, as well as administering to the sick, extracted teeth — without using anaesthetic!

Sybil Griffin
born 1905

The wife of one of my uncles used to go around as a 'collector' for Dr Robey — this of course was long before the days of the National Health Service. I think the sixpence a week we paid entitled us to home visits. I remember Dr Robey's surgery on Church Street being bitterly cold. We used to joke that if you didn't have the 'flu when you went in, you would when you came out! Dr Gladstone was the 'parish' doctor — he always came to my Grandma who was on public assistance and had cancer of the throat and we did not have to pay.

Mary Bend

One of my earliest memories is of developing pneumonia at the age of four. In those days before penicillin and other antibiotics pneumonia victims reached a crisis after a few days, at which stage either recovery or the sad alternative followed. At this critical point in my illness the Carnival procession was due to come past our house on Nottingham Road, and on the advice of the excellent Dr Fletcher, who was a great favourite with my family, my father went out to stop the band playing. Because I was so ill I was in the front 'best' bedroom, and it was thought that the noise would be too disturbing for me.

Leila Keam

I was still at school during the war and I joined the St John Ambulance nursing cadets. We met at the home of a nurse on Dovecote Road. At the end of training we had to take an examination, and local GP Dr Black came and tested our knowledge of bandages and tourniquets. I was proud to receive my First Aid certificate. Dr Black was a very popular doctor and when he first came to Eastwood he did his rounds in a pony and trap. He cut a fine figure and I remember he had a ginger moustache.

Patricia Purdy
born 1927

It was shortly after the Wakes had visited Eastwood in September 1949 that my sister Mary, who was then fifteen months old, was diagnosed as having scarlet fever. As this was a 'notifiable' disease I had to stay away from school to see whether I too had the illness. The family was kept in a kind of isolation, with Grandma and Grandad doing the shopping for us. My Dad and I did not mix with anyone else, and my mother and sister lived in my bedroom. Mary was quite poorly. She had only just begun to walk when she was taken ill and she became so weak that she had to learn to walk again when she eventually recovered. All the time that she

1947 advertisement

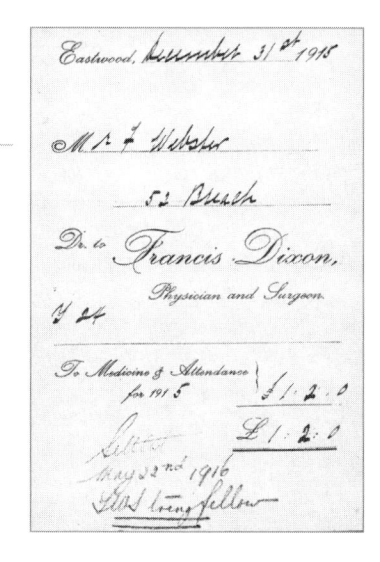

ELECTRIC POWDER
(Trade Mark)
For 'Flu, Colds, Headache, Neuralgia, Rheumatism and Nerve Pains.
J. CHAMBERS (EASTWOOD) LTD., NOTTINGHAM

Chambers chemist shop at 100 Nottingham Road was the first port of call for cures for minor ailments

was ill and confined to the bedroom a blanket was hung over the door, and no-one except my mother went into that room.

The one good thing for me was that I was off school for two weeks. I remember Grandma dabbing Dettol onto the collar of my dress to kill the germs! As Mary improved we would stand on the back yard and she would wave to us through the window. After the six weeks' quarantine we had a visit from Basford Council's Sanitary Inspector who 'stoved' the room where Mary had been, and it was then safe for me to go back. A few days later Dad developed a rash — scarlet fever — but the rest of us were now considered to be immune, so we were not so restricted and I did not get another two weeks off school!

Pat Lord (née Tomlinson)
born 1939

For a temperature Fennings Fever Cure from Chambers was a must, but I remember it having the most obnoxious taste. After taking one dose the threat of having another would send any temperature right down!

Leila Keam

Looking across from Ratcliffe Street to Church Street there is a small building with opaque glass windows which was Dr Dixon's surgery. I well remember entering the small room, with leather seating around two sides, a fire burning brightly in the grate, and a big wall desk where red-faced, blunt but kindly Dr Dixon took a look at his patients. The only other room was a tiny dispensary where the medicines were mixed.

Lily Whittamore
born 1915

Beaty's Place

In the first decades of the century Hill Top's more serious medical needs were served by three doctors of good repute and two ladies of worth, Mrs Charlesworth the midwife and Emily Potter, a trained nurse. Below that aura of respectability, but perhaps of equal value in necessity to our community, were Hubert and Beatrice Poxon — 'Yubert and Beaty' — who lived and worked in one of the better houses down Raglan Street. The place was always known as Beaty's but her husband was far from being a nonentity.

Yubert was our amateur bone setter, fracture mender and sprain manipulator who had learned his skills in a life on ocean-going sailing ships. He could perform miracles in persuading tired worn-out muscles to tick over and slog on for yet more daily drudgeries. He was the man in a crisis, whether it was responding to shouts of 'House on fire!' 'Mad dog!' 'Horse dead in the shafts!' or calming a drunk with an axe. His capabilities were many, including being an excellent self-taught vet. However, when he advertised himself as a 'tooth puller' (high seas fashion) with his only weapons a pair of pincers and a bottle of whisky as anaesthetic, it is said that he had only one customer, a man from Newthorpe. When this sufferer recovered a few days later he called back at Beaty's to pay for the treatment. He did, by giving Yubert a good bashing — the ingratitude of some people!

Yubert was also our 'poor man's barber,' applying a none too clean brush to a piece of soap stuck on a nail in the wall, and bloodily hacking away at the beards of trembling victims with his fearsome cut-throat razor. A breezy sailor-song sung while he worked did little to soothe their miseries. For payment you dropped a coin in a tin. His 'saloon' and surgery was the front parlour, at night a bright haven of light in dreary Raglan Street for the big street window was never curtained and Beaty's was one of the few gas-lit homes in Hill Top. Except on Fridays, because that was Yubert's night out. He shut the shop early, spruced himself up, and took his concertina to the Coach and Horses where he re-lived his life on the ocean waves with sea shanties that could be heard half-way to Nottingham.

Percy Cross

A (Tongue-in-Cheek) Pub Crawl of Local Hostelries Past and Present

A team of *Cricket Players* was invited to take part in a *Stag* hunt, and to reach the venue had to catch a train from the Kimberley *Railway* station. The fare for each of the *Cricketers* was a *Golden Guinea*. They were to meet other members of the hunt who happened to be of royal and noble blood, including *Queen Adelaide, Lord Raglan, Lord Clyde, Lord Nelson* and *Wellington*, along with two *Queens – Head* of their own area, one from Watnall and one from Kimberley.

They tossed a coin to see who was to ride to hounds and who had to walk as they had only one *Horse and Groom* from Kimberley between them at this time. The master of the hunt was a *Highland Laddie*. Now the guard of the train was a very careless fellow as he had lost his two flags and most of the luggage, and all he had was a *Pig and Whistle*.

Main Street, Newthorpe now has only one pub, The Foresters. In the first half of the century there were at least four, including the Old Spot (above) near Bartons Close and the Black Bull opposite Stamford Street. Both are now private houses.

When they alighted from the train at the *Northern* station they entered a field through a *Gate* where they all met for their stirrup cup beneath the branches of a *Royal Oak*. Their quarry suddenly emerged from a nearby *Log Cabin* and nearly trod on a *Lark's Nest*. The huntsmen gave chase through the fields and into the water of *The Three Ponds*, but to their horror their quarry turned upon them. It transpired that it was a *White Lion* who was soon joined by three bulls weighing between them *Three Tuns*, namely *The New White Bull, The Old White Bull*, and *The Black Bull*. A tupp from any of them would have put a *Man In Space*. The huntsmen had a ferocious dog by the name of *Old Spot*.

At this point they were joined by two more huntsmen, a *Horse and Jockey* and *General Havelock* who resided at *Greasley Castle*. Passing by was a group of men who happened to be *The Foresters*. They soon retrieved the situation and decided to *Ram Inn* bullets into *The Miners Arms* which they had borrowed in case they

A Century Remembered

had to open fire on the charging animals, whilst the unfortunate hunters went into hiding in *The Hayloft*.

They were now joined by two more sporting fellows, a *Horse and Groom* from Moorgreen and a *Horse and Groom* from Nuthall who borrowed the *Mason's Arms* to help round up the aforementioned animals along with another *Black Bull* from Awsworth. As they passed through a *Gate* they met two rather *Hardy* fellows by the name of *Robin Hood* and Mr *Hanson* who resided at *The Broxtowe Inn* at Nuthall. They paid a *Crown* to some *Jolly Colliers* and *Gardeners* resting after their labours to help round up the beasts and drive them into the *Noah's Ark* floating on the nearby canal, from which a *Pelican* flew. However, before they could do so they had to remove the ballast from the hold which was a *Shipstone*.

The Black Bull on Main Street

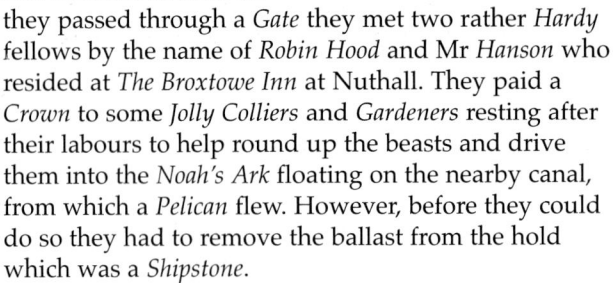

Lord Nelson decided to reinforce their artillery and borrow the *Palmerston Arms* from some *Miners Rest*-ing after a heavy day's work. Afterwards they all took refreshment at a *New Inn* and partook of a feast of goat's meat and *Hog's Head*. The only thing left after the feast was the *Goat's Head*. They then continued on their journey along the canal in a *Shipley Boat*, but with the *Sun Inn* their eyes they soon lost sight of their quarry.

At this point they decided to give up the chase and take further refreshment at the *Bridge Inn* which was built into the Giltbrook Viaduct (better known as 'Forty Bridges'). They then decided to take *Home Ales* for their wives who were waiting for them with their dinner. To have had a bad day's hunting was a *Bitter* pill to swallow but they took it very *Mildly*!

Ken Marsland

I remember seeing an old lady who called regularly for her morning tipple at the old Ram Inn at Beauvale (across the road from the present one). She rode in a bath chair pulled by a cantankerous white goat which also enjoyed a pint!

Percy Cross

The Winter of 1947

The harshest winter that I remember is 1947. I came back on leave from abroad and when I arrived home it was bitterly cold. I put this down to the fact that I was not acclimatised, but next day I opened the door to find a wall of snow blocking my path. That year we had snow until the beginning of July. Many places had floods afterwards. At the Trent end of Nottingham Forest football ground you could see only the top of the goal post, while at the other end the water was a foot deep!

Ken Marsland

In the severe winter of 1947 we were living in a 'prefab' on Newthorpe Common and the snow got so deep, right up to the window ledges, that we couldn't get out. Some Italian prisoners of war were brought in to dig us out.

Mary Bend

The Great Storm of 1987

During the night of October 14th–15th 1987 hurricane-force winds devastated the south coast of England, killing and injuring many people and causing millions of pounds worth of damage. Incredible as it seems now, the effects of that storm were felt as far away as Eastwood and I still vividly remember that night.

On that day I had decided to visit the shops in Nottingham, and there was a real sense of expectancy in the air — something was on its way. I arrived home to hear the police on the radio advising motorists to postpone unnecessary travel because storm-force winds were expected (despite the now infamous Michael Fish TV weather forecast).

In the evening I was completing some artwork in my bedroom/studio when the first gust hit my window square-on with a thud. The force was enormous, literally bending the glass inwards while the frame rattled and banged. As a 'storm enthusiast' I decided that this night was too exciting to remain indoors and so I fetched my coat and shoes.

My first stop was the back garden where the TV aerials were screaming and trees hissed, shaking in the tremendous winds; the noise was immense. The shed roof was being lifted and then dropping with a crash. Fortunately it was holding on. Stepping out onto Dovecote Road I was almost knocked off my feet and I had to turn my head away simply to breathe — like a goldfish out of water! Small branches and twigs from a number of trees were arcing into the road.

As I turned into Barber Street roof tiles swished over my head and exploded in the roadway. A couple of large wheelie-bins rumbled by and some fence panels scraped out onto the pavement, along with a gate. Walking required a lot of effort and I was forced to bend almost double to make progress. I had the most remarkable experience of being physically propped up by the wind. After circling the block I ventured out towards Moorgreen, where I witnessed more of the same, only with greater intensity due to its exposed position.

Throughout this time only one car passed me — it was like a ghost town. Now I was being buffeted from side to side and I stumbled several times. Entering the fields it was nearly impossible to stand. The howl of the wind was deafening and I can still hear the scream of telephone lines as they bucked and tossed.

Feeling a bit battered I returned home in time to go to bed. However I was unable to get to sleep for some time as the whooshing, banging and crashing

In June 1977 street parties were held throughout the area to celebrate the Queen's Silver Jubilee. Here the children of Lynncroft enjoy their party on The Crescent. Those attending were: Cheryl and Steven Air, Dale and Scott Anthony, Carl Cheetham, Lee Davies, Matthew and Robert Flinders, Jean and John Flint, Zoe Foster, Mark Harvey, Arron and Dean Hopcroft, Carolyn and Stephen Ivanowski, Paul Kershaw, Sandra and Alan Leivers, Melanie Longhorn, Jonathan and Shelley Manchester, Alice and Stephen Naylor, Emma Naylor, Teresa and Miguel Perkins, Joanne and David Potter, Dean Purdy, Carl Reeve, Carl Reeves, Maria, Ian and Gary Shillingford, David Simpson, Paul Storey, Andrew Tatham, Lee Walker, Debbie Willetts, and Kellie, Graham and Guy Wright. Each child received a souvenir Jubilee dish.

A Century Remembered

continued for another few hours. The next day, as I walked around the streets to view the aftermath, it was obvious that the storm had been severe: torn branches, shattered roof tiles and upturned bins lay everywhere. It was almost like a war zone!

Carl Richards
born 1968

Coronation Day Celebrations 1953

We bought our first television set so that we could watch the Coronation. About 30 people crowded into our house — we borrowed chairs from Newthorpe Common Methodist Church, an urn from the Mission Church and everybody brought their own food.

Mary Bend

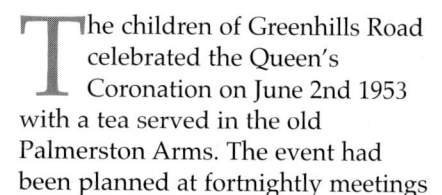

The children of Queens Road South enjoying their 1953 Coronation Day party held at the Community Centre in the council offices on Church Street. They include Brian and David Dodsley, Molly and Mick Gibson, Bernard Kirk, Elsie, Pauline, Brian, David and Peter Martin, Mick Peace, Pat Purbel, Hilary and Valerie Singleton, Barry Starbuck, Leonard Stubley, Daphne Watson and Joe Weirer.

The children of Greenhills Road celebrated the Queen's Coronation on June 2nd 1953 with a tea served in the old Palmerston Arms. The event had been planned at fortnightly meetings in the homes of local ladies. Food rationing was still in force but everyone contributed and pride of place was given to a three-tiered iced cake. Each child was also given a Coronation mug. Mrs Moina Brown played a leading part in these preparations; she loved parties, especially children's, and Greenhills Road was a great place for them!

Rose Keech
born 1919

Our Coronation Day party was held in the upstairs room at the Foresters public house in Newthorpe. I was dressed as Britannia. At Beauvale School we were all asked to bring red, white and blue flowers to make a display in the three tall windows which face onto Dovecote Road.

Pat Potter

Page 239

A Century Remembered

Memories of Eastwood

I recall Eastwood town of long ago.
The scenes of olden times bring back to me
The happy years that now are history
But live in chronicles.
Our family
Of four lived on the main street, and the glow
From the electric lights shone brightly then
Into the bedrooms on the 'Walker's Row.'
The trolley buses sang; they filled the air
In early mornings and on evenings when
The Arcadians passed by. Then the fair
Or 'Hill Top Wakes' came in September.
Yes, they were happy days; I remember
Mervill's fish saloon, and the old Empire;
Lindley's, the Co-op, the church and the spire
Of the Congregational. Daykin's Row
And the 'new school,' the open fields beyond,
The tip, old workings, and the little pond
Near to the house where D H Lawrence lived
In his early years. Looking back, I loved
My childhood days in dear old Eastwood town;
A small place then, but now of some renown.

John Gregory Simpson
born 1928

Organisers of the children's party held at the Palmerston Arms, including Moina Brown on the far left.

The Coronation party cake